ALSO BY JAMES R. GAINES

For Liberty and Glory: Washington, Lafayette, and Their Revolutions

*Evening in the Palace of Reason: Bach Meets Frederick the Great
in the Age of Enlightenment*

Wit's End: Days and Nights of the Algonquin Round Table

THE
FIFTIES

AN UNDERGROUND HISTORY

—

JAMES R. GAINES

SIMON & SCHUSTER
New York London Toronto Sydney New Delhi

Simon & Schuster
1230 Avenue of the Americas
New York, NY 10020

First Simon & Schuster hardcover edition January 2022

SIMON & SCHUSTER and colophon are
registered trademarks of Simon & Schuster, Inc.

For information about special discounts for bulk purchases,
please contact Simon & Schuster Special Sales at 1-866-506-1949
or business@simonandschuster.com.

The Simon & Schuster Speakers Bureau can bring authors to
your live event. For more information or to book an event,
contact the Simon & Schuster Speakers Bureau at 1-866-248-3049
or visit our website at www.simonspeakers.com.

Interior design by Kyle Kabel

Manufactured in the United States of America

1   3   5   7   9   10   8   6   4   2

Library of Congress Cataloging-in-Publication Data
Names: Gaines, James R., author.
Title: The fifties : an underground history / James R. Gaines.
Other titles: 1950s, an underground history
Description: New York : Simon & Schuster, [2022] |
Includes bibliographical references and index.
Identifiers: LCCN 2021042303 | ISBN 9781439101636 (hardcover) |
ISBN 9781439109915 (ebook)
Subjects: LCSH: Gay rights—History. | Gay liberation movement—
History. | Feminism—History. | History—20th century.
Classification: LCC HQ76.5 .G35 2022 | DDC 306.0973/0904—dc23/eng/20211108
LC record available at https://lccn.loc.gov/2021042303

ISBN 978-1-4391-0163-6
ISBN 978-1-4391-0991-5 (ebook)

*For Miles and Hannah Pell
and grandchildren yet to be born*

Contents

You have to be loyal to a dream country rather than to the one to which you wake up every morning. Unless such loyalty exists, the ideal has no chance of becoming actual.

—Richard Rorty,
Achieving Our Country, 1998

Seeing in the Dark

On April 16, 1945, four days after President Franklin Delano Roosevelt's sudden death, Allen Ginsberg and his friend Joan Vollmer, along with millions of other Americans, turned on the radio to hear President Harry Truman's first speech to the nation. Coverage in the next day's newspapers, though darkened by FDR's death, gave Truman credit for clearheaded resolve as the nation faced the last acts of World War II. Outside Washington, D.C., and Missouri, however, most people had never heard Truman speak, and his midwestern twang could not have been less like FDR's familiar, mid-Atlantic lilt. At some point during the speech, Vollmer said their new president sounded like a provincial salesman. "What kind of president is that?" Years later, Ginsberg remembered how surprised he was by that remark, by the idea that anyone would denigrate the president of the United States, someone he had always thought to be the noblest and best of Americans. That the future poet laureate of the Beat Generation could have this reaction is a measure of just how long ago this was, how young the 19-year-old Allen Ginsberg was, before the end of the world came in sight.

Three months later, at the White Sands Proving Ground in south-central New Mexico, the first test of the atomic bomb ignited a light "with the intensity many times that of the midday sun." It "lighted every peak, crevasse, and ridge of the nearby mountain range with a clarity and beauty that cannot be described." The energy of the blast melted the desert floor and left a light-green crater of radioactive glass ten feet deep and a thousand feet across.

By the time President Truman heard that the test had been successful, he was in Potsdam with Stalin and Churchill at the war's last Big Three Conference. Three weeks later, when the atomic bomb was dropped on Hiroshima, he was on the way home, aboard the USS *Augusta*. Three days after that, as Japan's prime minister, Kantarō Suzuki, was discussing the terms of surrender with his cabinet, the second bomb hit Nagasaki.

No precise reckoning of those killed by the two bombs was ever possible, but in the era of "total war," the line between soldiers and civilians was erased, and numbers lost their meaning: Were 6 million Jews murdered in Germany's concentration camps, or was it 6,100,000? Did the Soviet Union lose 26.6 million people, or was it 100,000 more than that, or fewer? Estimates of fatalities from the two atomic bombs ranged between 100,000 and 200,000, but the campaign of firebombing that led up to Hiroshima killed far more people than that. The atomic bomb presented the greater threat because it was a new order of violence, a weapon of instantaneous mass murder that could come without warning and permit no escape. It was also an epic feat of physics and engineering. The wizards of Los Alamos had managed to conjure from the smallest particles of matter the greatest power ever devised, a product of human genius whose gift to humanity was a weapon of global suicide. As such, it threatened long-held verities: that human progress was inexorable, that peace would be peaceful, even that reason, humanity's great gift, could any longer be trusted.

As NBC's radio commentator H. V. Kaltenborn said just hours after news of Hiroshima and the atomic bomb were announced: "For all we know, we have created a Frankenstein. We must assume that with the passage of only a little time, an improved form of the new weapon we use today can be turned against us." When Japan surrendered, CBS's Edward R. Murrow said much the same: "[S]eldom, if ever, has a war ended leaving the victors with such a sense of uncertainty and fear, with such a realization that the future is obscure and that survival is not assured." Even such a reliable wartime supporter as Henry Luce's *Time* magazine reacted to Japan's surrender with solemnity and caution, describing the Allied victory in World War II as "grimly Pyrrhic . . . as charged with sorrow and doubt as with joy and gratitude." The anonymous staff writer of that article was James Agee, coauthor with the photographer Walker Evans of the luminous portrait of Depression-era America, *Let Us Now Praise Famous Men*. By splitting the atom, Agee wrote, the scientists of the Manhattan Project "had put into the hands of common man the fire and force of the sun itself," introducing the "already profoundly perplexed and disunified human race" to "a new age in which all thoughts and things were split."

The atomic bomb was as clear a chronological marker as there has ever been, as fitting for journalists at the time as for historians decades later, to mark the boundary between an end and a beginning.

*   *   *

Something very much like this had happened before, another explosion of trust in reason just when it seemed the indispensable power. The philosophes of the eighteenth-century Enlightenment were filled with confidence that they could finally rid the world of myth, religion, and all such superstitious nonsense and follow the path of reason alone to ultimate omniscience. Sooner or later, the philosophes were certain, human intelligence would discover the truth of all things, cure every disease, and explain the greatest mysteries of life and the universe.

That confidence was shattered by a massive earthquake and tidal wave that destroyed Lisbon, Portugal, in 1755. Tens of thousands of people were killed instantly. The earthquake and its aftershocks spread from northern Europe to northern Africa, and the Enlightenment itself was among the casualties. There had been other earthquakes in the not-so-distant past, some just as devastating, but they had not occurred at a time of such confident assurance that there was an underlying order to the world, an order that reason would ultimately disclose. As the Enlightenment philosopher Gottfried Wilhelm Leibniz put it, this was "the best of all possible worlds."

After Lisbon, Voltaire drew a savage caricature of Leibniz as the ever-sanguine Dr. Pangloss, whose dear friend Candide asked as he watched Pangloss/Leibniz being hanged: "If this is the best of all possible worlds, what are the others like?" Amusing line, very Voltaire, but not funny. Reason had lost pride of place. It was a figment, a mental construction, not a faithful rendering of the world. In this more subjective, re-enchanted world, each individual was their own Adam, Eve, and Creator, and their best guides were not ideas and deductions but emotions, intuitions, and inspirations from the wellsprings of consciousness. Such deeply rooted motives encouraged various forms of individual initiative.

As the Enlightenment gave way to Romanticism, monarchies gave way to popular revolts, and the sonata gave way to the impromptu. "Bliss it was in that dawn to be alive / but to be young was very heaven," Wordsworth wrote about the early days of the French Revolution. The same would be said about the 1960s, with roughly the same proportion of truth and error, hope and disillusionment.

Two centuries after Lisbon, history did not repeat itself exactly, but it rhymed, as Mark Twain is said to have said. Like the Lisbon earthquake, the horror of World War II and its apotheosis in Hiroshima inspired a social, cultural, and political uprising that grew steadily stronger between 1946 and 1963. That period, which came to be known as the "long Fifties," brought film's New Wave, the theater of the absurd, and rebellions in all the arts. Jackson Pollock made the floor his easel and let the paint fly. The avant-garde composer John Cage left music to chance, and the arranged music of big bands at the Waldorf gave way to the dance-defying complexity of Charlie Parker's bebop, the hard bop of John Coltrane and Miles Davis, the "free jazz" of Ornette Coleman, and other musical declarations of independence. Novelists championed disruptive heroes—Salinger's anti-phony Holden Caulfield (1951); Ralph Ellison's nameless, race-beaten *Invisible Man* (1952); Saul Bellow's "free-style" Augie March (1953); and Jack Kerouac's id-driven Dean Moriarty (1957). In 1950, as Ginsberg was giving his ecstatic-apocalyptic voice to poetry, Kerouac wrote his "Essentials of Spontaneous Prose," and the poet Charles Olson issued his manifesto, "Projective Verse": Writers must stop searching for "le mot juste" in favor of whatever bubbled up spontaneously from the creative unconscious, Olson wrote, and time was of the essence; the poet must "get on with it, keep moving, keep in speed, the nerves, their speed, the perceptions . . . the split second acts, the whole business, keep it moving as fast as you can, citizen." Ginsberg called this approach "first thought best thought."

The impulse for spontaneity in the arts was not joined by a drive for social and political change. In a time infamous for rewarding conformity and suppressing dissent, the price paid for that kind of insurgency was widely broadcast and forbiddingly high. Yet even then, there were some who could not or would not tolerate the injustices imposed on themselves and their fellow citizens. To say that the 1950s have not been known for pioneers of progressive change is to state the obvious. At such a time, the remarkable fact is not that there were so few of them but that there were so many.

The Romantic poet John Keats famously coined the phrase "negative capability" to describe the compulsion of great artists to follow their aesthetic vision wherever it led them: people driven to stumble blindly forward, against all reason and doubt, toward the light of some undiscovered or unacknowledged truth. In the postwar period, a time when more than a decade of Depression and war had just given way to a time of precious but precarious stability, the drive for change emerged not so much from theory or principle but from people in a daily struggle with themselves.

*   *   *

This book has its source in a moment years ago when my then young children said they wished their own time was as exciting as the 1960s.

They got that idea not from me but at school and from the music. For me, those years were exciting but also deeply fraught. Decades after I enrolled at the University of Michigan, Class of '69, their comment led me to wonder just what the "dark ages" of the "Eisenhower siesta" could have contributed to the multiple rebellions of the 1960s. In all my reading, I found no better answer than an essay Norman Mailer published in 1957, in which he called the 1950s "years of conformity and depression."

> A stench of fear has come out of every pore of American life, and
> we suffer from a collective failure of nerve. The only courage, with
> rare exceptions, that we have been witness to has been the courage
> of isolated people.

In a time like the 1950s, the courage to raise questions was itself isolating, and worse. Perseverance required some to live with terrifying dreams, some to protect themselves and their families with guns, and others to be imprisoned, beaten, and killed for trying to do what they believed to be right.

Most were over 30, the people my generation told itself were not to be trusted. They were Black veterans of World War II and Korea who had fought for freedoms abroad that they were denied at home. They were champions for LGBTQ rights at a time when each of those initials stood for moral corruption and political subversion. They were feminist activists of the left wing, some in the U.S. Communist Party, who confronted sexism, racism, and class prejudice as inseparable wrongs and barriers to solidarity, which prepared the way for a feminism beyond the Second Wave. And there were scientists prepared to denounce their colleagues' ingenious new biological, chemical, and military technologies as potential threats to the natural world, including humanity itself.

There is a theory that change happens not by winning hearts and minds but by changing the law, after which hearts and minds will follow. Among the "isolated people" of the 1950s, however, there is evidence of an earlier stage in the process of change: the moment when a singular woman or man sets out to confront rather than evade some intimately personal conflict, which inspires them and others to change the hearts and minds of those who make the laws. Though isolated by their personal histories, idiosyncrasies, flaws, and gifts, they have in common the courage, the vision, and a profoundly motivating need to fight for change in their time and the future. This book is about some of the best of them.

"To Be Nobody but Yourself"

The path to progress in a hopeless cause

———

Being in a minority, even a minority of one, did not make you mad. There was truth and there was untruth, and if you clung to the truth even against the whole world, you were not mad.

—George Orwell,
1984, 1949

Picture of an unhappy man: Harry Hay in the late 1930s, when he was living a double life in his marriage and in the Communist Party.

A t the worst possible moment for an unpopular idea and at the worst time of his life, Harry Hay dedicated himself to an idea that everyone told him was impossible, even dangerous. It came to him during what he later called his "period of terror," when he had never felt so alone. He was a gay man in the closet, living with a wife he considered his best friend and two young daughters he adored. He was also a member of the U.S. Communist Party, which cast out gays as "deviates" and "perverts." During his last days at home with his family, he was tortured by nightmares about falling down mountain-sides, crashing in his car, losing his children in the wild, even hurting them and his wife.

He was far from alone in such torment. Like other gay men he knew and millions of others across the country, he was passing for straight at a time when to be gay was beyond shameful: It was criminal. Even the combatant nations of World War II were as one in harshly condemning this "crime against nature." When the Allies liberated the concentration camps, they did not set free all the men with pink triangles on their shirts. Those with previous convictions in Nazi courts for so much as flirting with another man were forced to serve out their harsh prison sentences, with no credit for time served in the camps. During and after World War II, being gay was an especially odious kind of treason.

It was then that Harry Hay had the idea that being "homosexual" should not be an object of shame but was an aspect of human identity worthy of respect and recognition—a notion that was then unthink-able, even among those who had most reason to think it. Failing to find anyone willing to support him in the idea, Harry Hay stood alone with it for what must have seemed to him a very long time.

3

McCarthyism was not a word yet, but it was a fact. The charge of Communist subversion had been a useful political tool ever since the Bolshevik Revolution of 1917. From the 1930s to the 1950s, it was used most often in the effort to discredit FDR's New Deal progressivism and to elect conservative Republicans. The tactic often worked, even when the U.S. and the Soviet Union were allies during the war, but it gained enormously greater firepower within weeks of V-J Day, when the first undercover Soviet agent and the first American traitor came forward to give headline writers and conservative candidates a great gift: news that the U.S. had been riddled with Communist spies and that some were still hiding in their midst. There had been and were still some Soviet spies in the U.S. then, but eventually the hunt for subversives would ensnare an untold number of innocent Americans, who were driven out of jobs, families, and friendships, sometimes to prison, sometimes to suicide. More than any other single group, the "security risks" of the Red Scare were gay or accused of being gay by some chatty neighbor, competitor, or holder of a grudge.

Thanks to Harry Hay's familiarity with the secrecy of Communist cells, the FBI did not discover he was gay even as he articulated, recruited, and organized the Mattachine Foundation, better known as the Mattachine Society, the first sustained advocacy group for gay rights in American history. Eventually, he, other Party members, and "fellow travelers" in the leadership were purged in fear that their toxic politics would taint the cause and its membership.

After Harry Hay lost control of it, the Mattachine Society became rigorously conventional, insisting that its members adopt the appearance and manner of "proper citizens." It also traded the secrecy of cells and anonymity of leadership for alliances with psychologists and psychiatrists who diagnosed gays as "psychopaths." Through a press and a book service co-owned by its new leader, Hal Call, it published and distributed books relevant to the gay community, books that could rarely find a conventional publisher. Its other activities narrowed until financial problems finally led the new Society to break off from all the local chapters.

In the late 1950s, however, thanks to Harry Hay's activist descendants—especially Frank Kameny, a man just as stubbornly principled as Harry—the Mattachine Society recaptured the defiant spirit of its first years, without which there might or might not have been a rebellion at the Stonewall Inn, a gay liberation movement, the freedom to marry the person you love, or the ability of millions of Americans simply to live openly as the people they were born to be.

Harry Hay's story was far from unsung. He sang it himself on every occasion. "Harry snuggles up to interviewers like a cat to a fire," his friend and ally Jeff Winters said. He was also a diligent amateur historian, and thanks to his and others' voluminous records and memories, the birth of the Mattachine Society is richly detailed. Less clear is why Harry Hay, Frank Kameny, and others like them stayed the course, why it was they who did it, what it takes.

*   *   *

A striking clue appears in a story his mother told about Harry as a toddler. He was standing at the top of the stairs in their family home on the southern coast of England. Born into an upper-middle-class Edwardian household, he was dressed all in white—twill jacket, matching trousers, linen hat—in preparation for a walk with his nurse and his baby sister. But there he stood, refusing to come downstairs without his gloves, or, as he put it, his "gubs." His sister was already in the pram, the nanny told him, and his mother, more forcefully, pointed out that the day was warm and sunny, there was no need for gloves. Harry would not budge, however, until his pair of buttoned, gray suede gloves was found and installed. Harry was "born a sissy," as his friend and biographer Stuart Timmons put it, but he was also the product of a strictly formal family with deep roots in the Scottish Highlands, where devotion to clan was mixed with a fierce individualism and resistance to authority. As a preteenager, Harry Jr. once told Harry Sr. at the dinner table that something he had just said about ancient Egypt was "wrong." There was a stunned silence while the family waited for him to apologize. When he did not, his father dragged him outside and beat him bloody with a leather shaving strop. He did not cry. When it was over, he checked his source, saw that he was right, and never said he was sorry.

By that time, the family had moved to Los Angeles, his father's birthplace. Big Harry, as he was known, had been a student of mine engineering at the University of California at Berkeley. He graduated at the peak of Africa's colonization and made his fortune in Johannesburg working for Cecil Rhodes (as in Rhodesia). Rhodes was a lifelong bachelor who was known to surround himself with buff, good-looking male employees, including Harry's father, who eventually became manager of the world's largest gold mine, the South Deep in South Africa's Witwatersrand Basin. Harry finally told his mother he was gay only after his father died, explaining that he had waited because he knew how much his father would have despised him for that. His mother had only one comment, he remembered: "Your father knew Cecil Rhodes." She never elaborated, and they never spoke of it again, so her meaning was never quite clear: Was his father bisexual, or had he pretended to be?

By every account, his father never showed much affection for any of his children. A relative said years later that she thought the family seemed somehow "wounded . . . rigid, cold, unable to express simple love and affection." Harry remembered that when he was 8 or 9, his father—who was "beginning to know what it is he has spawned and is worried about it"—came home with a pair of boxing gloves. He told his son to hit him, but "I just couldn't. I tried to explain to him. . . . He just thought I was wishy-washy, but I just couldn't do it."

When he was 13, his father began sending him to work summers on a relative's farm in Nevada, to make his own spending money, to learn the value of hard work, and to adopt other manly virtues. In the summers that followed, Harry came to like working on the farm, in part because it exposed him to ideas, values, and experiences that would guide the rest of his life. In that first summer, Native Americans among his fellow workers introduced him to tribal culture and rituals that would later inspire him to study sexuality in indigenous cultures, especially the tribes of the Southwest. During the summer after his freshman year at Stanford, he received his first lessons in radical politics from field hands who were members of the Industrial Workers of the World, better known as the Wobblies. After that summer of 1931, he had hoped to continue his studies in theater at Stanford, but by then his father had lost his fortune to the Depression. On the other hand, the theater of the moment made his academic studies pale. Playwrights such as Clifford Odets and plays like his *Waiting for Lefty* were turning the stage into a platform for radical protest, and there was no greater drama than what was happening in the streets.

Less for politics than for love, perhaps, Harry came under the spell of actor Will Geer, later known to TV audiences as Grandpa Walton. He followed Geer to some of the great demonstrations of the period, including San Francisco's 82-day general strike in 1934. There, he was in a crowd of demonstrators when the National Guard opened fire on them. "You couldn't have been part of that and not have your life completely changed," he said later. He also followed Geer into the Communist Party and began serious classroom study of Marxism. His progress in theory was slow at first, but in time he became adept at Party ideology and practice. He stuffed envelopes for the Hollywood Anti-Nazi League, marched for the Loyalists in the Spanish Civil War, protested Jim Crow laws, and advocated for the Party's position that Black Americans, as a distinct cultural minority, should have a separate nation.

He joined the Party despite knowing its hostility toward gays. The Wobblies on the farm and his early comrades made that plain with pointed, offhand slurs. In 1933, Stalin declared acts of male homosexuality to be punishable by five years at hard labor, and in the same year Hitler's Germany criminalized it as part of the campaign against libertinism in the Weimar Republic. Also in 1933, and to the same end, storm troopers confiscated Magnus Hirschfeld's library at Berlin's Institute for Sexual Science and consigned it to a book-burning. Much worse was to come in law-enforcement sweeps and increasingly harsh punishments under the infamous Paragraph 175 of the German criminal code, which consigned gays to prison and concentration camps by the tens of thousands. In the U.S., the legal status of gays was disturbingly similar. By the late 1930s, sodomy was a felony in all but one of the states (New York) and punishable elsewhere by three years to life in prison. Those who submitted themselves to "treatment" faced everything from electroshock to lobotomy to castration.

Given such brutal consequences, many gay men, including two of Harry's closest friends, decided to marry women. Thinking about the decision they made and the prospect of unending conflict between his public and private lives, Harry wondered if perhaps they had made the right choice. To explore his options, he sought out a psychiatrist, who suggested, "Maybe instead of a girlish boy, you're looking for a boyish girl. Do you know one?"

A fellow Party member named Anita Platky came immediately to mind. They were already good friends, and during a long courtship before they married in 1938, he had been open with her about the fact that he was "very actively gay," as he put it. At a time when there was very little reliable literature on the subject of homosexuality, they trusted what the psychiatrist had told him: "All you do is simply make up your mind to close one book and open another." Years later, he said they had had "a wonderful relationship . . . and she never had any problems with me. I never looked at another woman. But the men—oh, the men. . . ."

After the wedding, they plunged into Party work together. They investigated root causes and cures for the slums of L.A. and built an elaborate statistical case for government housing subsidies. They held frequent discussion groups at their home and often went to more than a half-dozen Party meetings a week. In 1943, after five years of marriage, Harry and Anita adopted their first daughter, Hannah, which bonded them even more closely, and Harry supported the three of them with his job in an aircraft factory.

That defense work won him a special deferment from the World War II draft, saving him from what he feared most about life in the military, "falling uncontrollably back into homosexuality." He was right to be concerned about that, wrong to think his deferment could save him from it. Though some draft boards, military psychiatrists, and recruiters tried to weed out gays, others tacitly conspired with gay draftees' wish to serve. Of the 18 million men who eventually served in World War II, only about 5,000 were exempted because they were gay. Chuck Rowland, a draftee who became a founding member of the Mattachine Society, remembered knowing "nobody, with one exception, [who] ever considered not serving. We were not about to be deprived of the privilege of serving our country in a time of great national emergency by virtue of some stupid regulation about being gay." In fact, he joined a familiar gay cohort at Minnesota's Fort Snelling, his induction station. "I found that all of the people I had known in the gay bars in Minneapolis–St. Paul were all officers who were running this 'seduction station.' " For bringing gay men together as nothing had ever done before, World War II actually served as an accelerant of gay liberation.

Harry Hay didn't need to enlist to join in: Gay soldiers found him in Los Angeles, as they found the gay scene in every port of call in the U.S., even though they knew that their uniforms would not protect them from the military police or local law enforcement. The LAPD was infamous for raiding gay bars (and for extorting "gayola" from their owners), as well as spying on public toilets and recruiting hunky Hollywood actors-in-waiting as entrapment bait. In the military, getting caught led to a "blue discharge," a permanent and costly mark of disgrace. On the other hand, drag shows were officially encouraged as entertainment for the homesick, lovelorn troops. Gays were among their top stars, and they were popular with gay and straight soldiers alike, which reflected their service together in combat. As an Army medic who served from the Normandy invasion to the Battle of the Bulge put it: "No one asked me if I was gay when they called out 'medic!'"

Harry tried to resist the waves of men in uniform that regularly flooded the parks and gay bars of L.A., but without success. It did not help that the family home was in Silver Lake, a district of left-wing activists, avant-garde artists, writers, and movie people known as the "Swish Alps," which had some of the best cruising spots in the city. As Harry felt himself increasingly drawn to them, his sleep was visited by dreams of danger. Anita told Hannah about one such dream: "He was holding onto the edge of a cliff, and knew he was going to fall a long, long way. He was just holding on by his finger-nails. It would be painful and very frightening, and he would wake up feeling terrible."

Harry said his "period of terror" began in 1946, around the time they adopted a second daughter, Kate. Friends from that time noticed his increasing anxiety, and pictures of him in the family photo album showed the strain. "Other married men I knew were looking forward to their retirement, to time with their wives," he said. "I didn't have those dreams. I had made a dreadful mistake, and I felt I must simply play it out, getting through every day." He found his refuge in research, teaching, and activism. When he had mastered Marxist theory, the Party asked him to start giving classes in it, and in 1946 he threw him-self into People's Songs, a group cofounded by Pete Seeger to distribute and perform folk music as a way of inspiring labor activism and other progressive causes. Harry's passion for music and politics had already led him to join an early "hootenanny" group that sang at protests and union rallies, and in short order he "became the theoretician of People's Songs," said Earl Robinson, who composed the 1930s anthems "Joe Hill" and "That's America to Me." "Harry took [Marxist doctrine] seriously," Robinson recalled, "so people had to go along with it. And he was able to inspire them. Harry was an enthusiast." He and Anita held monthly People's Songs meetings at their home, and Seeger sometimes stayed at their house when he was in town.

Later that year, Harry began teaching a class in the history of music as a political force at the People's Education Center, an offshoot of People's Songs. His ten-week course gradually expanded to two years, as he covered everything from the "organized shouting" of prehistoric hunters to collective chants, from fertility rituals to rites of magic, from the Middle East in "mumble-mumble B.C.," as his outline put it, to twentieth-century folk music. Its title when he last taught the course in the mid-1950s was Music: Barometer of the Class Struggle.

By 1948, his study of Marxism and the Party's position on Black Americans as an oppressed minority confirmed in him the view that gay Americans fit the same definition. More than being people who happened to be attracted to others of the same sexual orientation, they were *a people,* a distinct identity that brought with it shared burdens, especially the lack of legal protection.

He was still married then and would be for three more years, but he had begun to realize that some reckoning loomed. Anita had not, he said, because she remained "absolutely convinced of the fact that what any homosexual needed was a good woman."

One day at the factory, he shocked a fellow worker with the idea of forming an advocacy group around gay rights. Was he joking? the friend wanted to know. He invited Harry to lunch with a friend at the State Department, who told him just how bad things had become. The Office of Strategic Services, the Office of War Information, and other wartime agencies had by then reassigned thousands of workers to the State Department and elsewhere in government. Some were known or thought to be Communists or fellow travelers, and some were suspected of being spies. After the Cold War broke out—one convenient date is Winston Churchill's Iron Curtain speech in March 1946—every civil servant suspected of being gay was also presumed to be disloyal or a blackmail target, in both cases a threat to national security. Dozens of gays had already been fired or resigned to avoid termination, and the search for others was on. The housecleaning was made easier by a "McCarran Rider" to the wartime Alien Registration Act. Named for Republican senator Patrick McCarran of Nevada, it gave the secretary of state "absolute discretion" to fire anyone without evidence or explanation, which meant, in other words, for any reason at all.

The danger of being fired as a security risk soon spread from Washington to businesses, universities, and public institutions nationwide, and the hunt for Communists crossed party lines. A new group of liberal anti-Communists, Americans for Democratic Action, was formed in part to refute Republican charges that Democrats were "pink." Politics devolved to the question of whether you were "hard" or "soft" on Communism, rhetoric suggesting a competitive masculinity, which fed attacks on gay men.

President Harry Truman, soon to face election, tried to neutralize national security as a political issue with an executive order requiring background checks on every federal employee. The State Department trumped his order with a harsher security program of its own, one that made all its 7,000 employees into informants, each of them "links in a chain" of national security whose responsibility was to identify potential weak links. In a press release announcing the program, the Department implicitly criticized Truman's "loyalty order" on the grounds that loyalty alone was no guarantee of security: There were all sorts of personal "peccadilloes"—pointedly including "sexual peculiarities"—that could make for a potential blackmail target and therefore a chink in the nation's security armor.

Thousands of investigations targeting Communist subversives in the public and private sectors were underway by the time of Harry's lunch with the State Department employee. Eventually some one million "sexual psychopaths" were arrested, accused, or otherwise persecuted. They were dangerous not only because they were presumed to be easily blackmailed but also because, like members of the Communist Party, they were familiar with life in hiding. They knew how to lead double lives. They looked like everybody else.

And they were everywhere, as Dr. Alfred Kinsey proved when his data-rich *Sexual Behavior in the Human Male* rang in the new year of 1948. The Kinsey report made for dry reading but packed a statistically significant wallop: A person was not either heterosexual or homosexual, he wrote. Sexuality was a spectrum, and a person's place on it could change in the course of a lifetime. The study, a minutely detailed, 800-page book, was carefully nuanced, but some of its findings made for easy headlines: Almost 10 percent of all men were exclusively homosexual, but more than a third of all men had had at least one homosexual experience.

The book became a national bestseller within two weeks of its publication and spent months at the top of the bestseller lists. There were umpteen major conferences called to discuss its results, making 1948, as John Cheever wrote, "the year everybody in the United States was worried about homosexuality."

They were worried about other things, too, but their other anxieties were published, discussed, and ventilated, while their anxieties about homosexuality remained in the dark: remained unspoken. Is he? Was he? Did they? Am I? Could I? seemed to be at the back of everyone's mind. A great emphasis, by way of defense, was put upon manliness, athletics, hunting, fishing, and conservative clothing, but the lonely wife wondered, glancingly, about her husband at his hunting camp, and the husband himself wondered with whom he shared a rude bed of pines. Was he? Had he? Did he want to? Had he ever?

Though it was far from Kinsey's intention, his study gave the gay witch hunt the cover of science. Like the World War II military, though, his report worked both ways, serving to raise the level of threat and censure from homophobes even as it reassured gays, especially those in small towns and cities with no gay network, that they were not alone. Confident now that the time had come to break free from public disgrace, Harry Hay carried Kinsey's book everywhere in the spring and summer of 1948 as he tried to find a path forward.

Not long after he heard about the purge at State, Harry attended a "beer bust" with gay friends. At the time and in that group, the talk of the moment was the presidential campaign of Henry Wallace, whose Progressive Party and campaign were known to be supported by the U.S. Communist Party. That night, Harry talked up the idea of an organization he thought might be called "Bachelors for Wallace," or "Bachelors Anonymous." Everybody thought that was a wonderful idea, leading Harry to think he had struck gold. After the party, as his wife and daughters slept, he stayed up all night writing his first manifesto, outlining the aims and purposes of the organization in detail. In the morning, he called the party's host to get the phone numbers of everyone he had talked to so he could take his plan to the next step.

One by one, every person he called expressed horror at the idea, saying they must have been drunk at the party, because such a brazen move would be obviously, insanely risky. By then, the Hollywood Ten—writers and directors who had refused to testify before the House Un-American Activities Committee—had been cited for contempt of Congress, for which they would each serve between six and twelve months in prison. Then an editor at *Time* magazine, Whittaker Chambers accused Alger Hiss of being a longtime member of the Communist Party. Chambers had been in the Party during the 1930s, but he testified that Hiss had been faithful to Soviet Communism ever since.

The accusation was stunning. Hiss had for years been a senior State Department official: executive secretary of the Dumbarton Oaks Conference and senior U.S. delegate to the founding conference of the United Nations, for which he served temporarily as the first secretary-general. He was a top aide to FDR at his last Big Three Conference, which took place near the Crimean resort of Yalta, a word that to conservatives now stood for weak-spined, borderline treasonous concessions to Stalin. Even worse, Hiss was an Asia specialist at a time when Mao Tse-tung's Red Army was pushing Chiang Kai-shek's Kuomintang ever closer to their final retreat to Taiwan. State Department leaders soon became infamous as answers to the question of the moment: "Who lost China?"

For Yalta, for losing China, and with the support of Kinsey's data, Truman's State Department came to be known by the right-wing press and conservatives in Congress as a "garden of pansies" where "10,000 faggots" lay hidden, all of them potential blackmail targets and sleeper agents for the Soviet cause. As his trials unfolded over the next two years, Hiss became the anti-Communists' poster boy. Even decades later, when Hiss's most avid prosecutor had made it to the Oval Office, Richard Nixon was known to call State Department diplomats "cookie pushers and faggots in striped pants."

*   *   *

For all that, the "Lavender Scare" did not begin in earnest until February 9, 1950. On that date, McCarthy invented McCarthyism with his infamous "Enemies from Within" speech to the Republican Women's Club in Wheeling, West Virginia. There, he brandished what he said was a list of 205 State Department employees who were members of the Communist Party. (The number changed frequently after that. At various times the numbers were 81, 62, 57, and 10, none of which turned out to have a basis in fact.) On February 20, when McCarthy repeated his charges in a six-hour rant on the Senate floor, he added some spicy detail: Case No. 14 was a "flagrantly homosexual" translator who had been dismissed as a "bad security risk" and then rehired, and he had "extremely close connections with other individuals with the same tendencies." Case No. 62 also had "unusual mental twists" and hung out with other such suspects.

Despite the lack of supporting evidence, no senator or representative, in this election year, could fail to recognize that McCarthy had handed them a high-caliber political weapon. Two days after his speech to the Senate, a subcommittee was formed to investigate and publicize his charges. Among its choicest targets was Secretary of State Dean Acheson. After Hiss was convicted of perjury in court, Acheson made the mistake of saying to the press that he would never "turn my back" on his colleague Alger Hiss, given his long and distinguished service and the demands of Christian charity. Now, just days after McCarthy's speech, Acheson and Undersecretary John Peurifoy, who led the department's security program, were called before the new subcommittee to repeat testimony they had already given during a closed session. The press turned out in force.

Acheson and Peurifoy had to be pushed to say the word "homosexual," first by New Hampshire senator Styles Bridges, who habitually used State's budget as a club to encourage more investigations and firings of suspected gays. Under questioning, Acheson admitted that in the past year he had fired only one employee under the McCarran Rider. Bridges then asked how many had resigned who were under investigation. At that point, Peurifoy stepped in.

"In this shady class that you referred to earlier, there are ninety-one cases, sir."

"What do you mean by 'shady category'?" Bridges asked, knowing the answer very well.

"We are talking about people of moral weakness and so forth," Peurifoy dodged.

Done with this dance, Senator McCarran, who chaired the committee, told Peurifoy to "make your answer a little clearer please."

"Most of these were homosexuals, Mr. Chairman."

In fact, 90 of the 91 either were or were so charged. Peurifoy also testified that there were no Communists at all in the State Department, but no matter: The tabloid headlines wrote themselves. The *New York Post*'s was PANSY PANIC ON THE POTOMAC.

The next day's story in the *New York Times* focused on how the committee used Acheson's sympathy for Hiss to impugn his loyalty, but "All the News That's Fit to Print" did not include the word homosexuality. Soon, however, the *Times* got hold of a talking-points memo from the chairman of the Republican National Committee that put the issue of gays in the State Department squarely on the campaign agenda. The *Times'* headline read "PERVERTS CALLED GOVERNMENT PERIL: GOP CHIEF SAYS THEY ARE AS DANGEROUS AS REDS." The story included an excerpt from the chairman's letter on what he called "the homosexual angle":

> Perhaps as dangerous as the actual Communists are the sexual perverts who have infiltrated our Government in recent years. The State Department has confessed that it has had to fire ninety-one of these. It is the talk of Washington and of the Washington correspondents corps.

On the floor of the House, Nebraska's Rep. Arthur L. Miller, whose "Sexual Psychopath Act" required commitment to a mental hospital of anyone even suspected of being gay, and he called upon the nation "to strip the fetid, stinking flesh off of this skeleton of homosexuality" and lock up those who "worship at the cesspool and flesh pots of iniquity . . ."

> [In] one of our prominent restaurants, rug parties and sex orgies go on. Some of those people have been in the State Department, and I understand some of them are now in the other departments. The 91 who were permitted to resign have gone some place, and, like birds of a feather, they flock together.

His Republican colleague, Ohio's Rep. Cliff Clevenger, added that the government was still shot through with blackmail targets, thanks to assertions about due process from "the sob sisters and thumb-sucking liberals [who] are crying for proof of disloyalty in the form of overt acts. . . ."

Newspaper accounts quote Senate testimony indicating there are
400 more in the State Department and 4,000 in Government.
Where are they? Who hired them? Do we have a cell of these perverts hiding around Government? Why are they not ferreted out and
dismissed? . . . It is an established fact that Russia makes a practice of
keeping a list of sex perverts in enemy countries and the core of Hitler's
espionage was based on the intimidation of these unfortunate people.

Time would tell that there was no reason for panic over gays in
government, but the postwar years were filled with reasons to suspect treachery or use that suspicion to political advantage. In 1949,
the Soviet Union tested its first nuclear weapon, and Mao's Communist forces prevailed in China. In 1950, supported by both Mao and
Stalin, North Korea invaded the South, which raised the threat of a
"worldwide Communist conspiracy." As the U.S. led the "police action"
in Korea, fear of traitors and spies became epidemic, inspiring the
McCarran Internal Security Act and other oppressive legislation. It
also intensified the homophobic strain in American society, which
infected elections in the 1950 midterms and beyond. As McCarthy
boasted to a gaggle of reporters: "If you want to be against McCarthy,
boys, you've got to be either a Communist or a cocksucker."

*   *   *

It was at this improbable moment that Harry Hay decided the time for a
gay rights movement had arrived. Less than two weeks after the Korean
War broke out, he struck up a conversation at his daughter Hannah's
dance class with a member of Lester Horton's Dance Theatre, Rudi
Gernreich. Soon enough, Harry brought up his idea for a gay organization, and, for the first time, he was rewarded with wholehearted
enthusiasm. They kept talking until the class was over, made a date
for lunch two days later, and Harry spent the time until then rewriting
the manifesto he had written after the "Bachelors for Wallace" party.

Reflecting the still unresolved conflict between his life as a husband, father, and committed Communist and his other life as a gay man, the new draft contained references to homosexuality as a "physiological and psychological handicap" and invoked the self-help model of Alcoholics Anonymous. But even this statement—"Preliminary Concepts: International Bachelors' Fraternal Order for Peace & Social Dignity, Sometimes Referred to as Bachelors Anonymous"—was revolutionary for the summer of 1950, written with all the rhetorical ambition of another declaration of independence.

> With full realization that encroaching American Fascism . . . seeks to bend unorganized unpopular minorities into isolated fragments of social and emotional insecurity;
>
> With full realization that . . . the government indictment against Androgynous Civil Servants . . . [relies on] the legal establishment of a second type of guilt by association . . .
>
> We, the Androgynes of the world, [will] eradicate the vicious myths and taboos . . . fight against, and eliminate, police brutality, political and judicial shakedown, and civil blackmail . . . [and] integrate ourselves into the constructive progress of society. . . .

This draft ran to 2,000 words and called for a service organization that would promote new legislation; provide legal defense and financial help, including bail money, for victims of entrapment; hold self-help discussion groups; and provide round-the-clock volunteers to give counsel and help as needed.

When Gernreich finished reading it, he said that it was "the most dangerous thing I've ever seen" and that he loved it. The question then was what to do next. The plan they settled on, two weeks after the outbreak of the Korean War, was to take a peace petition to the gay beaches around L.A. and ask for signatures. "Because the media were whipping up support for the Korean War and Red Scare hysteria was going full blast," Harry recalled later, "we figured that asking brothers to sign our Stockholm Peace Petition would be so far-out-scary-radical that they'd be more interested in agreeing to come to a 'Kinsey Report' discussion group, right? Wrong."

That reaction should not have been shocking: They were attempting, during wartime, to create an activist group of presumptive security risks, people whose identification with the group might very well bring ruin. Hundreds of men signed their anti-war petition, Harry recalled, but "by the end of the summer, we . . . had found not one person who would dare come to our discussion group, so overpowering was the terror of police reprisal or blackmail."

Finally, in November, Harry decided to try the idea on Bob Hull, a gay man in his music class. Hull brought it home excitedly to his roommate, Chuck Rowland, who had been talking up a similar idea. Two days later, when Anita and their daughters were away from home, Hull and Rowland brought a friend, Dale Jennings, to meet with Harry and Rudi. Thanks to those five men, four of them current or former members of the Communist Party, the Mattachine Society came to life.

Harry found the name in his research, which had led him to male dance troupes of the twelfth and thirteenth centuries known as *les sociétés joyeuses*. As Harry described them, they were "secret fraternities of unmarried townsmen, known as *mattachines*."

> [They] never performed in public unmasked [and] were dedicated to going out into the countryside and conducting dances and rituals during the Feast of Fools at the vernal equinox. Sometimes these dance rituals, or masques, were peasant protests against oppression—with the [*mattachines*], in the people's name, receiving the brunt of a given lord's vicious retaliation.

In other words, they gave voice to unwelcome ideas, spoke truth to power, and took the punishment sometimes exacted from those who would make change.

Dale Jennings, for one, thought the name and the story were dubious, but Harry had a way of talking everyone to the point of surrender. He perfected that practice in Party meetings, whose discussions were sometimes known as "democracy by exhaustion." That came naturally to Harry. As the toddler got his "gubs" and the preteen took a beating for truth, Harry fought with obdurate fidelity for what he believed to be right. In rare moments of self-criticism, he acknowledged paying a price for that trait. Daughter Hannah remembered nights when he carried her to a high point near home and told her "all about the stars and what was going on in the sky—the relations in the universe. He made the moon very special to me, and animals. He could be very spiritual. Any creature that died—bird, rat, cat—we would bury it and sing a special song." Yet in the 1970s she stopped talking to him because of his "tormenting gay chauvinism."

Perhaps that depth of conviction was what empowered him to do what starting the Mattachine Society now required of him: to drop the mask of heterosexuality, to leave home and family, to quit the Party, and to say goodbye to virtually every friend he had, excepting only his fellow founders and a few longtime gay friends. Leaving the Party was also like leaving home, but it was at least less painful and more straightforward: It took a four-hour conversation at the kitchen table of a close comrade, then a yearlong waiting period before the Party decided not to purge him but to release him with thanks for his past work. The pain of divorce and leaving his daughters was lifelong.

Anita was of course shocked when he told her he was leaving her. She fought back, calling him sick, a traitor to her and the Party, just unwilling and too weak to change himself. There was little he could say, but he responded as thoughtfully as he could and stayed at home until Anita had the chance to make the decision to divorce her own. He also met his financial and other responsibilities to the family over the years, which kept his place in their lives. Most of his comrades and Anita's friends, however, never forgave him. They stopped calling him, ignored him at social events, and crossed the street to avoid him.

Offsetting the pain of separation was freedom from the daily trial of trying to be somebody he was not, and the next draft of the Mattachine mission statement made no mention of "handicap." By early 1951, the Mattachine Society's founding members and first recruits were meeting five or six times a week. The task before them—inspiring solidarity in people who had never wished to be known as a group, around questions most had never asked—sometimes seemed overwhelming. "As far as we knew," Harry told one interviewer, "we were the only people who had ever tried this. . . . [T]here were no guideposts to go by. We felt we couldn't make a mistake, because if we did, we might possibly deter the movement from developing for years to come. After all, we were facing McCarthyism. . . . So we operated by unanimity, which meant, among other things, the meetings over weekends would often last sixteen to eighteen hours."

To guarantee anonymity, they settled on a strict vetting process for new members and a Party-like cell structure that would keep connections between groups to an absolute minimum. The founders managed to agree unanimously on a one-page statement of "missions and purposes." The Society would work to free their members from a state it called "bewildered, unhappy, alone, isolated from their own kind and unable to adjust to the dominant culture." It would add to the "woefully meager and utterly inconclusive" literature on homosexuality with research of its own, and it would work to "erase from our law books the discriminatory and oppressive legislation presently directed against the homosexual minority."

At the beginning, the regular group meetings were disguised as quasi-academic discussions of sexuality and the Kinsey report. Some of the gay men brought "wives" to the early discussion groups as cover, and for the same reason the few lesbians who joined the earliest meetings sometimes brought "husbands." But as the organization's true purpose became clear, both heterosexuals and lesbians fell away.

It was then that the Mattachine Society found its footing and the groups began to proliferate, each new one beginning with a quiet side conversation as a meeting broke up. Dorr Legg, who became a mainstay of the homophile movement, remembered Dale Jennings taking him aside after one of his first meetings to say, "You may have noticed that the group is more than it appears to be." When Legg expressed enthusiasm about its actual purpose, Jennings introduced him to the inner circle. "Once you were in, you were given a discussion group," Legg said. "That was your baby. You had to keep that going. . . . That's how they grew."

The most persistent divide in the Mattachine groups, Harry remembered, was between what he called "the conservative element" and the "street queens." Arguments between them erupted periodically. When they did, Harry insisted on tolerance, but the conservatives were never quite comfortable with that, wishing mainly for social acceptance and an end to legal harassment.

For the moment, however, they were not driving the Society's agenda, the radical founders were, and their goal was *self*-acceptance—a sense of pride in themselves, however they appeared to others. "We were talking about the right of self-respect," Harry said later, "and to appreciate that we are strong, not weak people—that a sissy means a stubborn person who's put up with an awful lot of stuff and comes through being exactly what he is," which is a fair description of Harry Hay himself. As they worked together to confront the conflicts within and among themselves, he said, there were moments when it came as a "glorious shock" just to be with other gay men and "suddenly find one another good . . . at home and 'in family,' perhaps for the first time in our lives."

Seven decades later, the idea that self-respect was ever a radical demand would seem tragic, but in 1952, it was indeed a revolutionary assertion and led to the Mattachine Society's first success.

*   *   *

That spring, Dale Jennings called Harry at three a.m. from a local police station. Entrapped and arrested on a charge of "lewd and dissolute conduct," he needed $50 for bail. Harry brought the money and took Jennings to breakfast to talk over what had happened and what to do next. Jennings said it had been an egregious case of police entrapment. He admitted he had been cruising and had used a public restroom, but he said he had resisted the undercover cop, who then followed him home and tried to force him to have sex. When it didn't work, Jennings said, he was handcuffed and arrested anyway.

Once he told Harry what had happened, breakfast changed from a discussion to a disquisition by Harry on why and how Jennings should fight back. He told Jennings he should deny that he had done anything wrong but admit that he was gay. As far as they knew, no one had ever thought to defend himself that way.

At a founders' meeting that night, Jennings tentatively agreed to go forward, and, for a change, there was little debate. Most such cases ended in a guilty plea in exchange for leniency but also a lifelong criminal record—a result that was often obtained at great legal expense, sometimes with judicial bribery, just to avoid a public appearance in court. This time, however, Harry and company formed a new organization, the Citizens' Committee Against Entrapment, to publicize and otherwise support the first defense against entrapment by a man who admitted to being gay.

At trial, the arresting officer was caught in a lie, and the jury deadlocked thanks to one holdout for acquittal. The city prosecutor dismissed the charges so that Jennings's argument could set no legal precedent on appeal, but the case did set off celebration of his principled stand against entrapment. When the press showed no interest in the story, the Citizens' Committee mailed and passed out leaflets titled "VICTORY!" to mark "the first time in California history an admitted homosexual was freed on a vag-lewd [vagrancy-lewdness] charge." With that, the Mattachine Society was on the map.

Jennings himself wrote about the case in the first issue of ONE: The Homosexual Magazine, which was born on the sidelines of a discussion group in the afterglow of his victory in court. In an article headlined "To Be Accused Is to Be Guilty," he gave credit to the Citizens' Committee for raising funds for his defense. Pointedly, however, he added, "I am not abjectly grateful. All of the hundreds who helped push this case . . . were being intelligently practical. . . . Were heterosexuals to realize that these violations of our rights threaten theirs equally, a vast reform might even come within our lifetime. This is no more a dream than trying to win a case after admitting homosexuality."

After the Jennings case, the Mattachine Society's 10 groups became 20, then dozens. As new groups sprang up from Southern California to the Bay Area, the Society decided to test its political power. It sent questionnaires to the candidates in upcoming elections to the Board of Education that asked their position on various gay issues, including the vice squad's practice of entrapment. They received few if any responses, but in the spring of 1953, one of the questionnaires found its way to a columnist at the *Los Angeles Mirror*, who reported that "a strange new pressure group" representing "the homosexual voters of Los Angeles" was "vigorously shopping for campaign promises." The columnist, Paul Coates, said he had tried but failed to find an officer of the Mattachine Foundation, the legal entity behind the society; but he did discover that the lawyer who filed its papers, Fred Snider, had been an unfriendly witness before the House Un-American Activities Committee. To Coates, that raised the possibility for a "well-trained subversive to move in" and turn such a group into a "dangerous political weapon." Still, his column ended on a conciliatory note: "To damn this organization before its aims and directions are more clearly established would be vicious and irresponsible. Maybe the people who founded it are sincere. It will be interesting to see."

"We all thought it was pretty good," Harry remembered, "and so we ran off twenty thousand copies to send out to our mailing list and to be distributed city- and state-wide." That was a mistake, in effect a stick in the eye of every conservative member of the Mattachine Society.

"We'd forgotten what the detail about Fred Snider's being unfriendly to the House Un-American Activities Committee would do to the middle-class gays," Harry said. When the column appeared, "all the status quo types in the discussion groups were up in arms. They had to get control of that damn Mattachine Society, which was tarnishing their image, giving them a bad name."

In May 1953, a month after the Coates article was published, the Mattachine Society was to hold its first convention, whose purpose was to ratify a constitution. The founders had spent weeks drafting a document that was likely to be acceptable to the invited delegates, one from each group. "Five hundred people showed up," Harry said later. That was an exaggeration, but each person in the audience represented at least 10 others—at a time when just being there made them suspected felons. "Can you imagine what that was like? . . . [Y]ou looked up and all of a sudden the room became vast—well, you know, *was there anybody in Los Angeles who wasn't gay?* We'd never seen so many people." Blinded by the inspiring turnout, the founders could not see what was coming.

In his speech, Chuck Rowland, the constitution's principal author, tried to inspire the crowd with the founders' vision of a future "when we will march arm in arm, ten abreast down Hollywood Boulevard proclaiming our pride in our homosexuality." He said later he thought that image would bring the house down. Instead, his speech ended in a disturbing quiet. "People were more in shock than anything else," he said. "One of my friends in Mattachine said he almost had a coronary at such an outrageous thought."

Undaunted, Harry followed Rowland with a speech whose title took off from the witch hunt's infamous question of suspected Communists: "Are you now or have you ever been homosexual?" In a typically passionate appeal, he denounced the Mattachine Society's "status-quo types" for refusing to speak out in support of the gay men who were being forced to testify in Congressional hearings, and he showered praise on witnesses who refused to "name names." After elaborating his larger vision for the future of gay liberation, he closed with one last jab at those who would endanger the "oppressed gay minority" by compromising with Red-baiters, and he left no doubt about the direction he had chosen for the organization he founded.

> It would be pleasant if the social and legal recommendations of the [Mattachine Society] could be found impeccable both to the tastes of the most conservative community as well as to the best interests of the homosexual minority. But since there must be a choice . . . the securities and protections of the homosexual minorities must come first.

Both men had said what they meant to say and what they firmly believed, and their speeches hit the convention like matches on gasoline. The "conservative element" rose in open revolt. By the next day, as the founders gathered to plot next steps, it was clear that their constitution was going nowhere. Word had also reached the convention that a Senate committee planned to hold hearings in L.A. to investigate nonprofit advocates for left-wing causes, and the double trouble of former Communists leading a gay-activist society would make them a very large target. At a somber founders' meeting on the last morning of the convention, they agreed that their Communist Party backgrounds could end up destroying the Mattachine Society. After that, they appeared together on stage and announced their decision to step down. Before the convention broke up, the insurgents called for another convention the following month to install new leadership and ratify a new constitution. When Rowland asked to be recognized as a delegate to that convention, he was told bluntly, "We don't seat Communists."

None of the founders stayed in the new society. Rudi Gernreich put his political ideas into fashion design and left gay activism behind. Bob Hull eventually committed suicide, which in Rowland's opinion was caused indirectly by the Mattachine breakup. Rowland said he felt suicidal himself for a time: "This was my life. I was prepared to quite literally devote my life to the Mattachine, and here this bright glory was all gone. It all turned to shit."

Harry seemed to disappear, Rowland said, becoming "so inaccessible that we thought he hated us." Harry would eventually discover a new role for himself in the movement for gay liberation, but during the intervening years, he said later, he was living in shock, set utterly adrift. He found himself in a parody of a bad straight marriage to one Jørn Kamgren, a handsome but possessive and demanding Danish refugee half his age. While Harry supported him as a designer of handbags, Jørn stood between him and his old Mattachine comrades. "He simply cut them off," Harry said. "He made my life miserable if I had anything to do with them." Even years later, Harry spoke of the Mattachine breakup with uncharacteristic brevity. He shut down Mitch Tuchman, his interviewer from the University of California's Oral History Research Center, this way: "It broke my heart. What do you think?"

These years included, oddly, Harry's time of reckoning with the House Un-American Activities Committee. The FBI had been watching him since February 1943, when "Source A" disclosed that he was a member of the Communist Party's Joe Hill branch. Reports to Hoover suggested fairly close surveillance of him in the years after that, but Harry made his way into the bureau's files labeled COMSAB (Communist saboteur) and DETCOM (detail as Communist in case of national emergency), which suggests they still had not discovered he was gay, nor that he had quit the Party. In any case, when he was called to testify, he went beyond refusing to "name names." He let the committee have it: "I wish to state that I have neither opinions nor recollections to give to stool pigeons and their buddies on this committee." After that, he refused to answer any questions at all.

He could only watch from a painful distance as the new leaders of the Mattachine Society courted psychologists and psychiatrists who said gays had only themselves to blame for their legal troubles and social ostracism. The leader of the new society, Hal Call, seemed to be saying their only goal was to be recognized as responsible citizens. "Discretion here," he wrote, "is certainly the better part of valor." At the next convention, someone who rose to criticize the leadership's new direction was refused recognition. When he persisted, he was threatened with criminal charges.

Harry read about that in the next issue of *ONE*, which stayed in L.A. There, Rowland and Jennings kept alive the spirit of the original Mattachine Society, Jennings for a time as editor and Rowland in a social-services branch that offered counseling and other forms of help to gays. In these and other ways, they worked to protect the spirit of the original society. Its legal battles with the U.S. Post Office, for example, helped to settle the fact that the mere discussion of homosexuality was not pornography, which affirmed *ONE*'s right to use the public mails. Their greatest ambition, however, was to be not a litigant but a voice for the gay community. In 1954, an article by Jeff Winters reminded *ONE*'s readers of all they had lost in losing their founders, who "spoke the truth in the face of brutal authority, no matter what the consequences." If gays were ever to get "that which is their due as citizens," he wrote, "there must be a militant organization. No such organization now exists." The new leaders of the Mattachine Society "must either give over the reins to braver, more capable hands or stand up and fight. There is no other choice."

History proved Winters right. The new organization kept its name alive but not its spirit. Members were exhorted not to try and change society but to demonstrate exemplary dress and behavior, to fit in. Their meetings sometimes featured psychiatrists who spoke of them as patients in need of a cure. Among the least invasive of such cures were massive injections of testosterone and aversion therapy, in which subjects were given high-voltage shocks while watching men having sex. Meanwhile, the FBI found in the new leader of the Mattachine Society a willing intelligence asset. According to his FBI file, Hal Call told local agents that he "would be willing to cooperate . . . in assisting and locating homosexuals whether they are members of the Society or not." By that time, however, members had already begun drifting away from the meetings and financial problems were mounting, so the organization's demise was only a matter of time.

* * *

Enter Frank Kameny, who was no militant in the early '50s but clearly had the makings of one. He was brilliant, a child prodigy who dreamed of becoming an astronomer from the age of 6. Three months before Pearl Harbor, at 16, he enrolled at Queens College as a physics major, and he was almost ready to graduate when, at 18, he joined the Army. Asked at his physical if he had "homosexual tendencies," he lied—"as everyone did on this subject in those days."

PFC Frank Kameny was known in his unit as a "non-conformist," as he put it, but also as a mortar crewman who was determined and reliable under fire. "I dug my way across Germany slit trench by slit

Frank Kameny, who fought in the 58th Armored Infantry
Batallion, 8th Armored Division, 9th Army, was
destined for a lifelong war at home.

trench," he said. "I came within a hair's-breadth of losing my life several times." When he returned home after three years, he was prouder of nothing more than his Combat Infantryman Badge.

He finished his undergraduate degree quickly, then went on to get his PhD in astronomy at Harvard and, in 1956, a teaching fellowship at Georgetown. Just before school started, on a trip to San Francisco for a meeting of the American Astronomical Society, he made the mistake of committing a "lewd and indecent act" with another man in a public bathroom, one that happened to be a regular vice-squad stakeout. Both men were arrested. Like so many men before and after him, Kameny chose to plead guilty in exchange for leniency, which in his case meant a $50 fine, six months' probation by mail, and after that a letter saying he was "not guilty: complaint dismissed."

At the end of his fellowship year at Georgetown, he took a job as an astronomer for the Army Map Service, hoping to make his way into the growing space program and a place among the early astronauts. Five months later, however, just a few days after the Soviets' successful launch of Sputnik encouraged that dream, he was called into a meeting with two civil service investigators. "Information has come to the attention of the U.S. Civil Service Commission that you are a homosexual," one of them said. When he didn't respond, they confronted him again, then again. Kameny finally composed himself sufficiently to respond, "That's none of your business. That question is irrelevant to my job performance." Months of appeals later, he was fired for "immoral conduct."

As of December 20, 1957, at the age of 32, Dr. Frank Kameny was without an income, savings, or his security clearance. He was banned from any work for the federal government or defense contractors, which ruled out teaching at some of the best astronomy departments in the country. He took that as "a declaration of war."

He borrowed $600 against the value of his car to support himself as he appealed to everyone and anyone in the Army, the Civil Service, the Defense Department, Congress, and the White House. In time he was down to a budget of 20 cents a day, which called for a diet of franks and mashed potatoes, no butter. He lived in a single room with a sink, toilet, bathtub, bed, and a table for his old black typewriter, which he used to beat back his landlord's eviction notices and to paper the capital with letters of protest. When all he got were refusals and silence, he found a pro bono lawyer who was willing to wage the legal battle. They spent a year taking his case through the courts and lost every appeal. At that, his lawyer gave up, but Kameny did not. As a parting gift, the attorney left Kameny with a pamphlet on how to file an appeal to the Supreme Court. In that process, Kameny sharpened his argument, discovered his passion, and built the intellectual foundation for a newly activist Mattachine Society.

His 60-page petition in the case of *Franklin Edward Kameny v. Wilber M. Brucker, Secretary of the Army, et al.* never had much chance of success. It was a legal case built on principle and precedent but drafted as if in the heat of passion. There was a "thread of madness" in the Civil Service's "infamous, tyrannical, immoral, and odious" policy, he wrote. The government "would dissolve into chaos" if the gay ban actually succeeded, and such an outcome would be "a stench in the nostrils of decent people . . . an affront to human dignity . . . a disgrace to any civilized society. . . ."

Response to the petition, which he filed just one day after the inauguration of President John F. Kennedy, was among the first duties of the new solicitor general, Archibald Cox, who tried to narrow the question: The Court should deal only with the policy by which an employee was dismissed, not the specific grounds for it. Apart from that, he noted wryly that Kameny's petition violated the Court's "requirement of brevity."

That it did, but it also articulated Harry Hay's original ambition for the Mattachine Society and prefigured the motto Kameny would shortly coin for the cause, "Gay is Good."

Petitioner asserts, flatly, unequivocally, and absolutely uncompromisingly, that homosexuality, whether by mere inclination or by overt act, is not only not immoral, but that for those choosing voluntarily to engage in homosexual acts, such acts are moral in a real and positive sense, and are good, right and desirable, socially and personally.

Markham Ball, then a clerk for Chief Justice Earl Warren, thought Kameny's case had merit. No one, he argued, should be forced "to answer the incredible question, 'What and when was the last [sexual] activity in which you participated.'" He doubted the Court was ready to take on the issue, however, and he was right. On March 20, 1961, the Court denied Kameny's petition without comment.

*   *   *

By then, Hal Call had given up on the Mattachine Society, though he tried to hold on to the name. He told every local chapter in the country to change their names and go their own way. By that time, there were not many lively chapters left, and those few ignored him by keeping the name and renouncing the national leadership.

After eight years, the new Mattachine Society's strategy had done virtually nothing to relieve police pressure or reduce public opprobrium. In the most recent San Francisco mayoral race, the city's growing gay population was portrayed as a "cancerous growth on the body" of the city and became so great an issue that the Society moved that year's convention to Denver. There, police raided the homes of the local chapter's leaders, confiscated the group's mailing lists, made several arrests, and sent members scurrying for cover. The following year, a mere discussion about opening a Mattachine chapter in Philadelphia prompted a police raid that led to more than 80 arrests, and the chair of the Detroit chapter announced he was stepping down and could no longer keep his promise to try to save a dying chapter in Chicago. "Things are too hot right now," he explained, "and I value my new job." The 1960 convention of the Mattachine Society broke out in multidirectional rancor, and that was when the national leadership decided to cut itself off from the local chapters.

By that time, the Mattachine Society of Washington, D.C., was among the moribund. Nowhere did the society's national strategy of accommodation betray its failure more plainly than in the capital of discriminatory agencies, homophobic congressmen, and a D.C. oversight committee that urged ever more forceful measures by the Washington vice squad against "deviates" and "perverts" in the nation's capital. In an occasional newsletter, the D.C. chapter celebrated gay men of singular courage who managed to fight and prevail against entrapment, but it could not help them pay their legal bills or otherwise support them as Dale Jennings had been supported. Discouraged from assertive advocacy, the Washington chapter had been reduced by the end of the decade to a gay bar without the bar. People "didn't stay long after they met somebody," as one member explained. Two by two, the membership drifted away.

Though Frank Kameny knew of the Washington chapter, he had never joined it. He followed what was going on in the more politically active Mattachine Society of New York until he saw that it too was riven by "the turf wars going on inside Mattachine, of which I knew almost nothing and cared less." His focus was on discrimination in hiring throughout the federal workforce, and having lost his case at court and getting nowhere with his many personal appeals, he knew he needed help.

He found it first in Jack Nichols, who introduced himself at an after-hours club when he overheard Kameny talking about the early gay hero Donald Webster Cory. Like an untold number of others, Nichols credited Cory's book of 1951, *The Homosexual in America: A Subjective Approach*, with changing his life. Reading it as a teenager inspired him to come out to his family when he was still in high school. His father, who worked for the FBI, was furious, saying his career could be ruined if word got out that he had a homosexual son.* Nichols's parents then tried psychiatry, military school, even a female prostitute to attempt a "cure," with the predictable result.

By the time he met Kameny, Nichols was not only untroubled about being gay, he was enthusiastic about it, perhaps the first such person Kameny had ever met. For Nichols, his lover, and a few of his friends, the Mattachine Society of Washington became "a rallying point, a cause, around which we centered our lives."

Together, Kameny and Nichols reached out to activists in the New York Mattachine Society, a few of whom came to Washington for a meeting, bringing along a list of their contacts in Washington. By the end of the meeting, Kameny and Nichols had what they needed to start a new group. Kameny did not particularly want to name it Mattachine because of its recent history, but it was a name recognized in the gay community, and given the collapse of the national leadership, it required nothing of them. They were free to find their own way, with no commitment to the direction of its founders or its more recent incarnation. The new group would forsake the "genteel, debating society approach," which "impelled [it] to present impartially both or all sides" of an argument, he told an early meeting. "This is a movement, in many respects, of down-to-earth, grass-roots, sometimes tooth-and-nail politics."

At the first official meeting of the new Mattachine Society of Washington, on November 15, 1961, Kameny was elected president. With the power and stationery of a new organization behind him, he redoubled his letter writing campaign against the U.S. Civil Service's discriminatory policies. He wrote to the president, the vice president, the cabinet,

---

* Nichols's father was later presented with evidence that he had failed to report his son's homosexuality. He offered to cut himself off from his son, but Hoover, despite or perhaps because of his own homosexuality, put him on probation for his "inexcusable" deception and then sent him to Milwaukee, where he ended his career. Father and son never spoke again. Cervini, *Deviant's War*, loc. 3839ff.

agency heads, every member of Congress, every justice of the Supreme Court, and many others; and he wrote to them repeatedly over months and years. A couple of liberal congressmen responded politely, and uncomfortable FBI agents pleaded with him repeatedly to take J. Edgar Hoover off his mailing list. There was also an infuriatingly peremptory brush-off by the head of the Civil Service Commission, John W. Macy. Otherwise, silence.

On the other hand, in the same month Kameny's new Mattachine group came into being, he won a monthslong struggle to get the local ACLU to take on the nation's still draconian sodomy laws and denial of security clearances to gay men. The ACLU's D.C. branch cleared the campaign with the national organization, and Kameny found himself the cofounder of a stand-alone National Capital Area branch of the ACLU. The new Washington branch came with a powerhouse team of civil liberties attorneys committed to Harry Hay's argument of a decade before: that gays were a distinct minority and subject to discrimination as such. Kameny also won—after more than a year of argument with his Mattachine board—agreement on a constitution that called for the group to act "by any lawful means . . . to secure for homosexuals the right to life, liberty, and the pursuit of happiness, as proclaimed for all men by the Declaration of Independence, and to secure for homosexuals the basic rights and liberties established by the word and the spirit of the Constitution of the United States."

Kameny then issued a press release pledging the group to oppose every political, administrative, judicial, and police policy that oppressed gay men and women. Every official on Kameny's large and growing mailing list received this press release, including the local and national press corps.

Kameny had found the perfect test case years before, and it became his first important victory. Bruce Scott had a bachelor's degree in political science from the University of Chicago when he joined the civil service in Washington before the U.S. entered World War II. He left his job to join the Army and returned to it when he was honorably discharged. In the mid-1950s, however, he was fired on suspicion of being gay. Then in 1956—when he was 45 years old, unemployed, and beyond desperate for work—he saw an article about Kameny in the *Washington Star* and called him for advice. Once Kameny had Washington's ACLU branch behind him, he realized that Scott would be an ideal plaintiff, a decorated veteran whose record at the Labor Department was spotless. Kameny told him then to apply once more for a job in the Labor Department, wait for them to turn him down, "and then we'll fight them."

They did so with the help of one of Kameny's ACLU cofounders, David Carliner, a top civil rights attorney known for his work against segregation in the South. In 1963, *Scott v. Macy* ended in a ruling by the D.C. Court of Appeals that his firing had been capricious and that even asking a U.S. citizen about his or her sexuality was a violation of the right to privacy. By then, Scott had returned to his native Chicago, where he had found a job with the state of Illinois, but his victory became the basis for others.

Kameny had another major victory in 1963, thanks to the ranking member of the House's D.C. oversight committee, conservative Democrat John Dowdy of Texas. Dowdy noticed a story in the *Washington Star* complaining that "deviates" had organized a nonprofit and were raising money under a charity license. Incensed, he drafted legislation that would deprive them of it and called Kameny to testify. Kameny was thrilled at the prospect of a congressional forum, and he quickly prepared for what he assumed would be questions about the Washington Mattachine Society's charitable status. Instead, he was asked to defend what Dowdy called the "revolting" behavior of homosexuals, which was "banned under the laws of God, the laws of nature, and . . . the laws of man."

Kameny answered every question directly and logically—infuriatingly so to Dowdy, who pounced when Kameny supported "consensual behavior among adults." How many adults, Dowdy wanted to know. "Five? Fifteen? Fifty? Five hundred?"

What about animals, another committeeman broke in. "You forgot animals."

Dowdy also asked Kameny about "a newsletter put out by some bunch of perverts which mentioned the fact that somebody was gaining weight on a diet of semen." Was that the kind of thing Kameny supported?

Kameny was badgered for four hours and not only emerged unscathed but managed along the way to demolish the reasoning behind Dowdy's proposed bill. Sometime after the hearing, he learned that he had no need of his charity license anyway. Donations of less than $1,500 a year did not require one, and he had never received one for nearly that much. But the hearing got more publicity than he or his cause had ever had, including heartening signs of support in the Washington press. Kameny papered Washington with a press release declaring victory—including of course a copy to J. Edgar Hoover, who stayed on the Mattachine Society's mailing list until he died in 1972.

If Bruce Scott and John Dowdy were two steps forward, Kameny's one step back came in August, at the first convention of the East Coast Homophile Organization, a coalition of gay and lesbian groups in Washington, New York, and Philadelphia, which he had helped to organize. Invitations to speakers at the convention were sent without consulting him, and he was not pleased. There were "experts" among them, which exposed the schism that would soon cost Kameny the Mattachine Society's presidency, just as it had cost Harry Hay and his cofounders their leadership: a submissive approach to social acceptance at the expense of direct action for gay rights.

The banquet speaker on the first evening was the eminent psychiatrist and author Dr. Albert Ellis. So many psychologists from a nearby APA convention came to hear him speak that some of them had to be turned away. At the time, Ellis was writing a book whose title could have been that of his speech, *Homosexuality: Its Causes and Cures*. For an hour, he talked about the homosexual as a psychopath—perhaps afflicted by some genetic strain but in any case a poor soul in need of treatment. For once, however, at the end of his speech, a woman in the audience rose to object: "Any homosexual who would come to you for treatment, Dr. Ellis, would *have* to be a psychopath."

Kameny was furious about Ellis's address and those of other so-called experts among the speakers. "There was absolutely nothing whatsoever that anybody heard at any time, anywhere, that was other than negative," he said later. "Nothing! We were sick. We were sinners. We were perverts." Kameny called it "drivel. We are the experts on ourselves, and we will tell the experts they have nothing to tell us." What the gay rights movement needed, he said, was "an activist militant organization . . . dirty words in those days."

The day after Ellis's speech, Kameny gave his own, titled "The Homosexual and the U.S. Government." His talk was an attack on everything that Ellis and the convention's likeminded speakers had to say. Their responsibility was not to change themselves, he said, but to gain their rights as citizens and to win from society the respect they were owed and owed to themselves.

Sitting in the audience was a young woman named Barbara Gittings, who had recently been named editor of *The Ladder,* the monthly magazine of the Daughters of Bilitis, a lesbian organization founded in San Francisco in 1955. She too was uncomfortable with the disease model of homosexuality, but she had yet to articulate her discomfort. Her organization's insistence on heeding expert opinion seemed reasonable to her, not so much because she believed lesbians were, in some sense, "abnormal" but because their self-defense would be dismissed as denial.

Hearing Kameny's outright denunciation of the disease model that day was literally life-changing for Gittings. "There was a fantastic man," she recalled thinking, someone whose "clear and compelling vision" was "the most radical idea that had come down the pike. . . . He believed that we should be standing up on our hind legs and demanding our full equality and our full rights, and to hell with the sickness issue. They put that label on us. . . . Let them do their justification. We were not going to help them."

After the convention, the Daughters of Bilitis continued its conservative policy of friendly accommodation and gradualism, while Gittings started taking *The Ladder* in Kameny's direction. Without asking, she added a frank subtitle to *The Ladder*'s intentionally anodyne name: "The Lesbian Review." (The board showed its irritation by insisting that she add "for adults only" to the cover, despite their lawyer's insistence that it was not necessary.) She asked Kameny to write an article stating his case, along with a retort by the Daughters of Bilitis's research director, but she also gave Kameny the last word. She wrote editorials arguing forcefully against the view that lesbians were in any way "sick," one of them an open letter to physicians chiding them for failing to take account of recent research. Her case in point was a study by Dr. Evelyn Hooker of UCLA that was funded by a grant from the newly established National Institutes of Mental Health, where it was referred to as "the fairy project."

Hooker's method was to give gay and straight men the same battery of psychological tests, including the Rorschach, Thematic Appercep-tion (TAT), and MAPS (Make a Picture Story) tests. She gave the blind results to a panel of the nation's top psychologists and psychiatrists, including the two men who had created the TAT and MAPS tests. All of them expressed confidence at the outset that they would be able to correlate the responses to sexual preference, but Hooker's study showed otherwise. To their unanimous disbelief, none of them could do better than chance. One of them insisted on a second attempt and failed again.

Despite being proved right, their open contempt for the disease model of homosexuality got both Gittings and Kameny fired—she from *The Ladder*, he from the Mattachine presidency. Her end came as she and Kameny plotted a picketing campaign, which the Daughters of Bilitis let her know it could never advocate without public support. With his usual tact, Kameny wrote the DOB board and called their position "arrant nonsense. When one has reached the stage where picketing is backed by the larger community, such picketing is no longer necessary."

At the convention of 1964, Kameny heard perhaps the most disappointing speech of his life, when Edward Sagarin, formerly known as Donald Webster Cory, placed himself clearly among those who considered homosexuality a disease. He denounced gay activists like Kameny for having cut themselves off from reality by their "defensive, neurotic, disturbed denial" of science. What was needed was a cure, he said, perhaps one like Alcoholics Anonymous, which attacked the disease quietly and anonymously, without requiring its members to be exiled from polite society. Two years later, Sagarin submitted a doctoral thesis titled "Structure and Ideology in an Association of Deviants," which used the Mattachine Society as his principal example. He was even more explicit in his criticism of the Mattachine Society in a book he published years later, which had a chapter titled "Homosexuals: The Many Masks of Mattachine."

After the Daughters' convention—a group whose formation Cory/Sagarin had encouraged—Kameny wrote him a blunt goodbye.

[Y]ou have left the mainstream for the backwaters . . . you have become no longer the vigorous Father of the Homophile Movement, to be revered, respected and listened to, but the senile Grandfather of the Homophile Movement, to be humored and tolerated at best; to be ignored and disregarded usually; and to be ridiculed at worst.

Kameny lost his hold on the Mattachine group he started in part because he insisted on putting direct action for gay rights ahead of service work, including health education and counseling. But leaders and members had also wearied of his autocratic style. "Giving all views a fair hearing didn't suit my personality," Kameny said later. "And the Mattachine Society of Washington was formed around my personality."

Perhaps that armor of self-certainty was required for Kameny to be true to his convictions against such long odds for so long, as it seemed to be for Harry Hay. Like Hay too, being voted out of the group he started was exceedingly painful, even as it freed him to become more active and even more successful on his own.

Harry Hay's greatest disappointment was that he had failed to make gay rights part of the civil rights agenda, though in truth that ambition had never had a chance. After four years, Kameny shared that sense of failure. His Mattachine Society had only a few women and exactly no Black members. Three weeks after the Dowdy hearings, at the March on Washington, Kameny picketed with just four other white men in a crowd of 250,000, very few of whom would have known the meaning of the word "Mattachine."

One who did was the March's chief strategist and organizer, Bayard Rustin. In 1953, when Pasadena police spotted him in a parked car committing a "lewd and lascivious act," a friend had reached out to Harry Hay's Mattachine Society for help. Civil rights leaders, however, had no interest in the rights of gays, lesbians, or women in general. At the March, Rustin was allowed less than a minute to introduce two women at the forefront of the movement, one of whom was Rosa Parks, who got only seconds at the podium.

Kameny and Gittings tried their best to be inclusive. The first gay and lesbian picket line at the White House, which took place in April 1965, had only 10 marchers, but three of them were women. Two months later, at the Civil Service Commission, there were 25 (17 men and 8 women), and back at the White House in October there were 45, including more than a dozen women. John Macy, chairman of the Civil Service Commission, remained unmoved, but Kameny would have the last word.

*   *   *

Harry Hay and Frank Kameny were hardly two of a kind, in style or substance. Harry's presentation of himself was scrupulously defiant.

At a time when any sign of gender transgression was dangerous, he wore scarves, earrings, and pearls with his favorite longshoreman's hat, and his wardrobe's color palette was resplendent. Frank, despite his disdain for convention and assimilation, was all white shirts, dark suits, and ties. Their differences, like their achievements, were great.

Harry survived his relationship with Jørn as he had weathered his "years of terror" with Anita, by diving deep into historical research—work that to Frank Kameny would have seemed just as profoundly boring and irrelevant as the questions Harry had been asking since he wrote his first manifesto: "Who are we? Where did we come from? What are we here for?" In the 1960s, Harry found answers in the pueblos of the Southwest, where he studied indigenous people whose expressions of sexuality and gender took their place in his gay family tree. They were called the "berdache" by the first Jesuit missionaries, a pejorative later amended to "Two-Spirit" people. Neither term described the scope of variation in North America's many tribal cultures, but never mind: To Harry, they were early-American Mattachines. They wore unique costumes. They had a helping, spiritual, and ceremonial role in their communities. And they confirmed in Harry Hay, as had the masked performers of medieval France, the belief that people were not incidentally, accidentally, or voluntarily lesbian, gay, bisexual, transgender, or queer. That was just who they were. In time, he would come to feel that at least part of their collective mission was to free heterosexuals from their own socially enforced gender roles, to free sexuality from reproduction, and to restore sacred meaning to conscious acts of love.

Frank would have been mystified by all that. The point was to change the law. The rest was, if not irrelevant, distinctly secondary.

Harry was a romantic, exuberantly promiscuous while wholly committed to his partner, John Burnside, whom he met not long after breaking up with Jørn. Harry later joined his "Two-Spirit" study to the counterculture by cofounding the Radical Faeries, an anarchistic, communitarian, back-to-the-land movement. Burnside was his partner in the Radical Faeries and in everything else, from their work with the post-Stonewall Gay Liberation Front to their support for draft resisters during the war in Vietnam.

Frank kept his love life resolutely private, a mystery even to his closest friends. Timothy Clark, a tenant and caretaker with whom Kameny spent his last 20 years, was unknown to them until Kameny died and Clark struggled unsuccessfully to keep the ashes from those who wished to give his remains a memorial gravesite.

Harry Hay could be a very sharp thorn in the side of the gay-rights movement after Stonewall, complaining of tactics and goals he considered heteronormative—discrimination against effeminacy, for example, and the ambition for public office.

In 1971, Kameny became the first openly gay man to run for a seat in Congress, as a nonvoting delegate for D.C. After a loss that shocked no one, he transformed his campaign into the Gay Activists Alliance, which in 1973 helped to pass one of the first laws in the nation to ban discrimination on the basis of sexual preference. In the same year, thanks in part to persistent lobbying by Kameny, Gittings, and others, the American Psychiatric Association deleted homosexuality from the forthcoming edition of the *Diagnostic and Statistical Manual of Mental Illness*, effectively admitting its decades-long error and distancing the APA from those in its ranks who persisted in it. Kameny's wry reaction: "In one fell swoop, 15 million gay people were cured!"

He kept up the fight in the 1980s and later. His paralegal practice came to the defense of untold numbers of people in danger of losing security clearances and being discharged from the military because of their sexuality. He appeared as cocounsel at discharge hearings for men in every branch of the service, and he coined their legal strategy: "Say nothing, sign nothing, get counsel."

He was still winning battles in the 1990s—for example, when President Bill Clinton issued an executive order banning sexual orientation as a condition of security clearances. Clinton's "don't ask, don't tell" policy, on the other hand, left him cold. "I am proud of my military service," he said, "but I have resented for 64 years that I had to lie to my government in order to participate in a war effort which I strongly supported."

Kameny was a soldier for gay rights, a legal and political leader with no illusion and no fear about how bloody the fight could get. In the pre-Stonewall years, when forward progress faltered from defeat to hope and back, many gave up, but Kameny grew more determined with every battle and every inch of ground he won, neither tiring of the fight nor changing his plan of attack until old age forced itself on him in the early years of the twenty-first century.

By then he had seen many of his dreams come true. Federal job prospects were no longer asked about their sexuality, and Washington's long-standing sodomy law was repealed. Security clearances and jobs were restored, vice squads disbanded, and arrests for solicitation by undercover police ended by statute, transforming entrapment from a tool of law enforcement to a successful defense.

Among his favorite vindications came in 2009 when he sat onstage before an audience at the U.S. Office of Personnel Management, a descendant of the Civil Service Commission. There, he was presented with a letter in which director John Berry apologized for the Civil Service Commission's "shameful action" in firing him and thanked him for his refusal to let the injustice stand. "With the fervent passion of a true patriot, you did not resign yourself to your fate or quietly endure this wrong," Berry wrote, conveying "the gratitude and appreciation of the U.S. Office of Personnel Management for the work you have done to fight discrimination and protect the merit-based civil service system." Kameny stood when Berry was finished and said simply, "Apology accepted."

Looking back, Kameny said he felt pretty sure that people were better off for the fact that he had lived, which was "a very good feeling to have." He made that statement during another ceremony, this one at the Smithsonian's National Museum of American History, which had persuaded him to donate the picket signs from his first demonstration at the White House. Brought over from his attic, they were placed on a platform among other notable objects: the desk where Thomas

Jefferson wrote the Declaration of Independence; the inkwell Abraham Lincoln used when he signed the Emancipation Proclamation; and the "Jailed for Freedom" pin that suffrage leader Alice Paul wore when she left prison in 1918. To make sure he understood his pickets' value, or perhaps just to make sure the audience did, curator Harry Rubenstein said, "Frank, this is where the pickets fit into American history."

It was one among many honors. A street was named for him, his home was made a historic landmark, and in the first year of the Obama administration he was invited to the White House more than once. He stood by the president's side at the signing of a measure that extended federal employees' health benefits to gay partners. Twelve days later, he was back for the fortieth anniversary of Stonewall, and the following year he returned again for a ceremony to mark passage of the Don't Ask, Don't Tell Repeal Act. In an audience of hundreds, a place was reserved for him in the front row, and he wore his Combat Infantryman's Badge for the occasion. A few weeks after the repeal took effect, on National Coming Out Day, Frank Kameny, 86, died in his sleep.

In the Oval Office a year before he died and after a half-century of struggle, Frank Kameny received warm applause and a pen President Obama had just used to extend federal employees' benefits to their same-sex partners.

Frank Kameny, Harry Hay, and their known and unknown cohorts left their country a priceless legacy. They lifted the burden of shame from millions of people whom the medical profession called psychopaths, the church called wicked, and the state called felons, and they replaced that burden with every citizen's birthright: self-respect and the respect of others. No one in the early "homophile" movement got more recognition in their lifetimes than Harry Hay and Frank Kameny, but what deserves celebration as much as the victories they and their compatriots won is the model they left behind. The poet E. E. Cummings famously wrote: "To be nobody but yourself in a world which is doing its best day and night to make you everybody else means to fight the hardest battle which any human being can fight. . . ." That is what they did.

Meet Jane Crow

How Pauli Murray, Gerda Lerner,
Fannie Lou Hamer, and others imagined
a movement beyond the Second Wave

———

Be nobody's darling;
Be an outcast.
Take the contradictions
Of your life
And wrap around
You like a shawl,
To parry stones
To keep you warm. . . .

—Alice Walker,
"Be Nobody's Darling,"
Revolutionary Petunias, 1973

The light in the eyes of Pauli Murray, an undergraduate at
Hunter College for Women and a political activist in the early 1930s,
was shining when she was just a toddler.

A nna Pauline Murray was three years old when her mother died. Neighbors whispered that it was probably suicide, that she must have been driven to it by her husband, Will, whose deep depressions and violent "fits" had taken him to a hospital more than once. In fact, she died after a cerebral hemorrhage, but the facts of her life suggested a major contributing factor: She was in the fourth month of her seventh pregnancy in 11 years; she was married to a clearly sick man; and she was overworked as a nurse and mother of six. After she died, Will came apart, and relatives committed him to an asylum near their home in Baltimore for what turned out to be the rest of his life. The children went to relatives. Anna Pauline was sent alone to Durham, North Carolina, to live with her mother's parents and the relative she knew best, her mother's sister and her namesake, Pauline Dame, who legally adopted her and whom she came to call Mother.

The next time Anna Pauline saw her father she was almost nine. She could not wait to see him. Her relatives by then had told her why her mother had fallen in love with him, though little of the rest. Her picture of him was of a dashing, intelligent, Howard University graduate: a natural athlete, teacher by profession, pianist, poet, and omnivorous reader—a man with a seemingly endless appetite for intellectual growth. Anna Pauline admired that drive and wished to let her father know she had it too. "I could not wait to see him," she wrote later. "I knew exactly how he would look, and I knew he would remember me because people said I looked so much like him and had his quick mind. I was bursting to tell him all about school and that I was on the Honor Roll in my class." The haggard, unshaven man brought out to see her, however, was nothing like the father she thought she knew, and he clearly did not know who she was. That was her last living memory of him. The next time she saw him was a few years later, at his funeral, after he was beaten to death by a white orderly who found him "uppity."

Anna Pauline Murray spent a great deal of her life as she spent her childhood, among disorienting losses and fissures in what she called a "confused world of uncertain boundaries." Until her mother's death and then at her grandparents' home, she was raised in relative comfort, a child of the Black middle class. Her family were nurses, teachers, landowning professionals, and members of the Episcopal church. They had some of the advantages that came with light skin, but their distinctions of complexion, class, and ancestry also made for confusion. Her grandparents, Robert and Cornelia Fitzgerald, were descended from both slaves and slave owners, from Quakers and rapists. Robert had fought for the Union in the Civil War, while Cornelia was actually proud of her Confederate heritage—this despite the fact that her mother was a slave raped repeatedly by her owner's two sons, one of whom was her biological father. For Anna Pauline, to live with these grandparents was to witness "a tug of war between free-born Yankee and southern aristocrat," between a man who had been willing to give his life to end slavery and a child of rape who was proud that her father could afford 30 slaves. Murray herself was what she described later as a "borderline racial type," darker than her grandparents but light-skinned enough to be resented and taunted by her Black schoolmates. "In a world of black-white opposites," she wrote later, "I had no place."

She lived with a more agonizing ambiguity as well. In her teens, she became convinced that something was physically wrong with her—that she was born to be a man. Over the years, she wrote to one physician after another seeking a medical reason for her confused gender. She could not identify as a lesbian because she was attracted most often to heterosexual women, which meant suffering a series of painful rejections. Among the ways she dealt with her conflicted gender was to try and embrace it. She changed her name to the gender-indefinite "Pauli," and among her papers she left pictures of herself in her twenties in various poses and outfits, captioned "the Imp," "Pixie!," "the Dude," "the Crusader," and "Pete," perhaps trying on identities, perhaps for self-assertion, perhaps both.

Her lack of certainty about race and gender defined the most intimate challenges Pauli Murray faced during her life. They also prompted the advances she made for civil rights and women's rights during her long legal career, including the argument that ultimately persuaded the Supreme Court to outlaw discrimination on the basis of sex. Like other feminist pioneers at the time, her life was a hero's journey decades long but little noted until the late twentieth century, when scholars began to retrieve a history that was missing in the Second Wave urtext, Betty Friedan's *The Feminine Mystique*.

*　　*　　*

As the name implied, Second Wave feminism was taken to be the first upsurge of activism for women's rights since 1920, when the suffrage movement and ratification of the Nineteenth Amendment gave women the right to vote. Forty years later, Friedan detected a resurgent impulse for liberation among women, which she described as "buried, unspoken," confined to "a strange stirring, a sense of dissatisfaction" that was nowhere evident "in the millions of words written about women, for women. . . ."

In fact, the oppression of the "happy housewife" was a central message in numerous articles by the Columbia University sociologist Mirra Komarovsky and in her *Women in the Modern World* of 1953, which was also the year Simone de Beauvoir's *The Second Sex* was published in English. Almost a decade before those books, the connection between gender and racial discrimination was discussed in an appendix to Gunnar Myrdal's historic study of racism, *An American Dilemma*, and in 1956 the plight of the educated woman was confronted directly by his spouse, Alva Myrdal, in her collaboration with Viola Klein, *Women's Two Roles: Home and Work*. Three years later, Eleanor Flexner published her groundbreaking *Century of Struggle: The Woman's Rights Movement in the United States.* Given all that had been written already about "the woman problem," the publisher of *The Feminine Mystique* actually worried that Friedan's book would have to "fight its way out of a thicket." Unlike those writers, however, Friedan was a practiced and articulate polemicist who was also used to writing for a mass audience, and she was not above a little cosmetic overstatement. "To women born after 1920," Friedan wrote, "feminism was dead history."

She knew better than that. As her biographer Daniel Horowitz disclosed in his 1998 biography, she had been advocating for the rights of women for almost 20 years before *The Feminine Mystique* was published. From her first job after graduation from Smith College in 1942, she was a journalist for left-wing unions that promoted Rosie the Riveter during the war, and she protested Rosie's demotion to homemaker and domestic worker when the veterans came home and took her jobs. One of Friedan's first articles in that first job was a salute to Elizabeth Hawes, a fashion designer turned UAW organizer and author of the new book *Why Women Cry: Or, Wenches with Wrenches.* "Men, there's a revolution cooking in your own kitchens," Friedan wrote in 1943, "a revolution of the forgotten female, who is finally waking up to the fact that she can produce other things besides babies." Her position in *The Feminine Mystique* had been clear 20 years earlier in the way she spoke for Hawes:

> No woman on God's earth . . . wants to have her entire life swing around a solitary, boring, repetitive business which means exhausting herself washing the same dishes and clothes day in and day out—cooking food for the same people, seldom seeing a living soul other than a tired husband and her own children for more than a very short time.

At the Federated Press and later at the news service of the United Electrical, Radio, and Machine Workers of America, Friedan's writing on women's issues was as radical as her employers would allow it to be.

In 1952, pregnant with her second child, Friedan was laid off, as was the only other woman on the writing staff. After that, she softened her rhetoric in articles for mass-market women's magazines but even then advocated for the right of women to pursue fulfillment in the world of work and to defeat whatever stood in their way, including chauvinist husbands. Yet in 1972, a decade after finishing *The Feminine Mystique*, she wrote in the *New York Times*: "Until I started writing it [in 1957], I wasn't even conscious of the woman problem."

*   *   *

Years before Daniel Horowitz disclosed the early career of Betty Friedan, scholars were already beginning to rewrite the history of feminism, particularly the role played by distinctions of race and class. Any short list would omit many important works, but a historic beginning was made by Gerda Lerner, née Kronstein, the privileged daughter in an Austrian Jewish family who barely escaped Nazi-occupied Vienna. In 1939, at the age of 19, she managed to reach exile in the U.S., where her experience of anti-Semitism and identification with other oppressed people would lead her to the study of racial, ethnic, gender, and other discriminations. By the time *The Feminine Mystique* was published, she was teaching the first college course in the U.S. devoted to women's history. She read Friedan's book just days after it was published and decided immediately to include it in her course. She wrote Friedan to compliment her on her "splendid" book but also to point out what she considered its greatest flaw. "[I]t addresses itself solely to the problems of middle-class, college-educated women," she wrote.

> This was one of the pitfalls of the suffrage movement for many years and has, I believe, retarded the general advance of women. Working women, especially Negro women, labor under . . . disadvantages imposed upon them by both economic oppression and the feminine

mystique. . . . To leave them out of consideration of the problem or to ignore the contributions they can make toward its solution, is something we simply cannot afford to do.

She could have been thinking of Fannie Lou Hamer, a 45-year-old sharecropper, wife, mother, and activist in the Mississippi Delta, who, in the same year Friedan's book was published, was shot at, jailed, beaten mercilessly, and thrown off her plantation for trying to vote—a woman who, through it all, held to what her mother and her church had taught her: You had to keep loving even the worst white people because they were sick, and they needed a doctor. Thirty years later, the prominent civil rights activist Unita Blackwell remembered the first time she heard Hamer saying that, because she thought it amounted to letting racists off the hook: "I was so angry that day, listening to all her stuff. . . . I said, 'This woman is crazy.'"

Pauli Murray and Gerda Lerner were crazy that way too: intuitive and brave enough to look directly at their most complex and painful challenges, to find their source, and then to act on what they saw, whatever the cost. Among other things, they saw that race, class, and gender were inseparable, mutually reinforcing sources of discrimination that could only be defeated on the basis of that understanding. Against the punishing, reactionary tide of 1950s America, they and others fought for that elusive goal with sufficient imagination, force, and foresight that, more than two decades later, a professor at the UCLA School of Law—Kimberlé Crenshaw—could articulate its legal force and give it a name: intersectionality.

*   *   *

Gerda Kronstein was 13 years old when civil war broke out around her family home in Vienna. The occupation of Austria by Nazi Germany was still four years in the future, but when Hitler declared his intention to unite all German-speaking peoples, Austria's chancellor turned away from democracy, canceled freedom of the press, ended jury trials, ignored the legislature, and put protesters in jail. With that, a scattered movement for Austrian freedom and independence rose up in armed resistance.

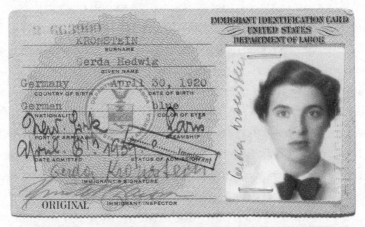

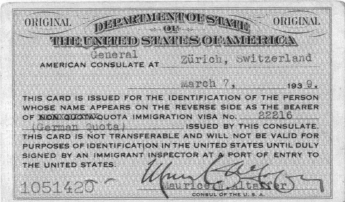

At the last moment, Gerda Kronstein's mother confessed
she would not be going with her daughter to America after all.
They never saw each other again.

Gerda would remember February 12, 1934, as the day gunfire broke out near her home. Minutes later, her father called from his pharmacy to tell them to light candles and fill the bathtubs with water. The trade unions had called for a general strike, he said, and the fighting was going to get worse. Just after he hung up, the telephone went dead, and then all the lights went out. The shooting went on all night and was joined the next morning by the sound of cannon fire. The radio played only Strauss waltzes and martial music all day long, occasionally interrupted by an announcement that the rebellion had been crushed, even as continuing gunfire declared the opposite. The artillery was aimed at the Karl-Marx Hof, a nearby housing project for workers. "There are women and children in there," she heard her mother whisper to her father. "How could they do that?"

Like Pauli Murray, Gerda Kronstein lived in ambiguous, painful, potentially dangerous territory. She was raised in luxury, but she was Jewish in an expressly Roman Catholic and increasingly anti-Semitic country. Her parents lived together and apart, their marriage literally reduced to a signed, legal agreement. They had separate apartments in the family home, and each had another home as well. Her father lived with another woman, and her mother had a painting studio where she entertained. Her mother showed little interest in women's traditional roles. She left the cooking and housework to maids and the children's care to governesses. Her passion was her art—her friends and houseguests were artists—and she dressed the part, leaving aside the fashion of the Viennese *haute bourgeois* for hoop earrings, loose-fitting blouses, colorful floor-length skirts, and sandals. Gerda was closest to her father's mother, who also had an apartment in the family home and who made no secret of the fact that she despised Gerda's mother.

In self-defense, Gerda prepared herself for life in a theater of family conflict by becoming combative herself, even as she internalized the self-image of "a misfit, a freak, an outcast." In secondary school, she began taking the long way on her walk to school, a detour through lives like those being lived in the Karl-Marx Hof. Though the families were poor, they seemed to her more vividly alive than her own. She envied even the children from the local orphanage, whom she saw laughing as they walked to school together: At least they had each other.

As Austria's Nazi movement rose in influence, Gerda helped her parents get rid of every politically sensitive book and magazine in the family library, but away from home, she studied sedition. At a time when being caught reading literature from the Communist Party underground was a criminal offense, she cherished whatever she could find or borrow from friends, which kindled her passion for politics and her ambition to become a writer herself. At night, when no one could hear, she listened to Radio Moscow on the family's shortwave radio to find out what was happening in Germany, how much worse it was there: the Nazis' all-out war on Communists, the humiliations, roundups, and abuse of Jews. Her early sympathy with Communism, she wrote later, "allowed me to find a territory of my own." In retrospect, it seemed to her "a desperate choice," but "defining myself as an outsider and moving toward danger the way the swimmer moves toward the breaking wave—these two tendencies shaped my character and being."

In March 1938, one week after Hitler's forces arrived to occupy Austria, Gerda's father left the country. He promised he would make a new life for them in Liechtenstein, and then, taking as much as he could carry, he made his way across the border. Not long after that, storm troopers came looking for him. To pressure him to turn himself in, they took Gerda and her mother to prison as hostages. Six weeks later, after the family pharmacy and other assets had been turned over, they were told they were free to go as long as they agreed to leave Austria and never return. Gerda's mother quickly sold their home and possessions for pennies, and they left Austria, lucky to be alive.

By 1939, Gerda's mother was in the South of France, having found a life like the one she left, as a painter in a community of fellow artists. Gerda managed to get a visa to the U.S. thanks to a boyfriend who had made his way there earlier and who sponsored her as his fiancée. She joined him in Harlem, where he had a steady job, but their marriage of convenience soon lapsed into an amicable divorce. At that, she sank into desperate poverty. Unable to get work in the last days of the Depression, she came close to starving. At the same time, as France fell to the Nazis, her mother's letters became increasingly desperate, pleading for help that Gerda was powerless to provide. Her mother managed to survive life in a Nazi detention camp but died a few years after the war, and Gerda never saw her again except in guilty dreams.

Her only financial support was one low-paid temporary job after another. Friendless and shunned by the anti-Semitic German community, she found herself most at home with the African American women who were her neighbors. They too were shunned and denied the standing of citizens. They too were poor and displaced people in flight from discrimination and its cruel enforcements. They were suspicious of her at first, but she felt the distance between them close as she told the story of her own imprisonment, forced emigration, and ostracism in America.

She managed to find a place for herself in the left-wing theater community, which is where she met Carl Lerner, her husband until the day he died 33 years later. They were brought together by a script she had written for New York's annual German American Day for Peace and Progress, which drew left-wing activists, including members of the U.S. Communist Party. Carl Lerner was then an out-of-work but experienced theater director, and he revised Gerda's script in ways she had to admit were major improvements. Working together led to a mutual affection that led to marriage, two children, and a life of activism together, in and out of the Communist Party.

Carl had been a member of the Party for years when they married. Gerda was not, but the difference was almost a technicality. They volunteered, went to meetings and fund-raisers together, and believed, together with thousands of other Americans, that Marxism held the promise of greater equality and justice and the hope of a better world. It seemed to them that Communism was as American as the Declaration of Independence, and that Americans had simply lost touch with their revolutionary roots.

In a few years, it would be hard to imagine there was ever such a time, but during the Depression and the wartime alliance, the story of Soviet Communism was easy to love. By dethroning absolutism, so the story went, the Bolsheviks were ending the long oppression of Russia's workers and peasants. Poverty, famine, and illiteracy were under sustained assault. The industrial base and economy of the Soviet Union were growing stronger every day, and the elite hoarders of wealth— like the rapacious U.S. financiers accused in the 1930s of fabricating the fool's-gold 1920s—were said in Russia to be gone with the czars. Americans who went to Russia to see for themselves brought home to a nation of bread lines and despair the story of a bold, young country undertaking a great experiment: a new kind of democracy, a government that was truly of, by, and for the people, and an alternative to capitalism that promised increases in both equality and liberty, including freedom from want.

It was evident even then that there were problems with that story, but as the Soviet Union bore by far the greatest cost in human lives during World War II, even such staunch anti-Communists as the publisher Henry Luce allowed his magazines to speak well of it. In 1943, in a special issue on Russia, Luce's *Life* magazine actually described Lenin as "perhaps the greatest man of modern times . . . a normal, well-balanced man who was dedicated to rescuing 140,000,000 people from a brutal and incompetent tyranny. He did what he set out to do."

Gerda finally joined the Party in a spirit of defiance, at a time when friends who had supported the Soviet-backed Loyalists during the Spanish Civil War were being investigated by the House Un-American Activities Committee as "premature anti-fascists," presumed to be Communist dupes, comrades in hiding, or both. Carl's film career was nearly destroyed by the film industry's blacklist, but even then he and Gerda both persisted in Party work because they still believed in its ideals and refused to be intimidated by fear.

Gerda's best memory of her Party work was helping to start the Congress of American Women (CAW), a branch of the Soviet-backed

Women's International Democratic Federation and the first feminist organization the U.S. Communist Party had ever supported. Before the war, the American Party had taken less than no interest in women's rights, considering it a bourgeois distraction from the class struggle. The *Daily Worker* made its position clear on the "women's page," which was full of cooking and housecleaning tips and pictures of barely clothed models under headlines such as "Mrs. New York—And She Can Cook Too!" In the late 1930s, when a book-length reexamination of "the Woman Question" made the rounds of Party publications on the East Coast, every one of them refused to excerpt it. But as the war came to a close and women began losing jobs to returning veterans, the Party's long-standing commitment to fight racism ("white chauvinism") was linked to the cause of ending male supremacy, for which the Party coined the term "male chauvinism."

At that, the *Daily Worker* transformed the woman's page from household hints and recipes into a forum for ideas. Like the Party, the Congress of American Women strongly supported legislation against lynching and racial discrimination, but its feminist agenda otherwise ran ahead of the Party's. Along with issues such as equal pay, government-sponsored day care, and job protections, CAW's feminism was joined to its commitment to interracial leadership and membership. Theirs was a feminism not separate from but inclusive of civil rights, and no one did more than Lerner to model the kind of self-examination and candor necessary to overcome racial barriers to trust, as she had learned to do during her first days in the U.S. She wrote decades later that her time in CAW was the best political experience she had ever had.

Like others, she was heartbroken when, in 1950, CAW surrendered to the fate of other left-wing organizations. A report by the House Un-American Activities Committee denounced it as "a specialized arm of Soviet political warfare" whose true mission was to render the U.S. and its allies "helpless in the face of the Communist drive for world conquest." After long debate, the board of CAW voted to disband rather than fight a prolonged, expensive, and almost certainly losing battle to avoid registering under the Foreign Agents Registration Act, which would subject its members to surveillance and charges of subversion.

Even after that, the Lerners continued for some time to brave the witch hunt and join every progressive cause and picket line—against the war in Korea, against nuclear weapons, and against the many outrages of McCarthyism. In their interracial community in New York City's borough of Queens, Gerda's activism included mobilizing her PTA to demand needed improvements to her children's school building and to replace the principal who had presided over its decline. At the same time, she worked at home on a second novel, the first having failed to find a publisher. In other words, without setting out to do so, Lerner proved that a woman could have a close family, a consuming career, and a life of activism—that she could "have it all." Besides her own fierce drive, her supports included a loving husband, a band of comrades, and the sage advice of a good friend: "If you want to be a writer, you have to be a sloppy housekeeper."

By the middle of the 1950s, however, she was near despair. Her second novel, like her first, could not find a publisher, and she thought her years of work as a writer had come to nothing. At the same time, Nikita Khrushchev's revelation of Stalin's many crimes convinced both her and Carl, with deep regret, to leave the Party and their ever fewer comrades. As she had helped her parents purge their library in Vienna, she threw every evidence of her connection to the Congress of American Women into the fireplace, and after that she did not talk about her membership or work in the Party for decades.

At this point in her autobiography, Lerner paused to remember what it was like to climb the mountains of Austria when she was young, how much more difficult it was as the climb steepened near the top. That was when weather closed in, the trail disappeared in rock, and you knew that, as near the summit as you seemed to be, the most arduous climb lay ahead. "It is then that you take one small laborious step after the other," she wrote. "Forget the goal, forget the possibility of failure. . . . This is the time when the mind forces the body to do more than it can."

She began another book, this one a historical novel based on the lives of the sisters Sarah and Angelina Grimké, white women of the South who were pioneers for racial and gender equality in the nineteenth century, several years before the suffrage movement began. The subject spoke directly to racial conflict in the suffrage movement, but when she had written eight chapters of their story as a novel, she realized it needed detail she could only collect with the tools of a professional historian. So, in 1958, at the age of 38, she enrolled as an undergraduate history major at the New School for Social Research, where she began the climb to the summit of her career.

By 1962, she was teaching women's history at the New School, which is said to be the first such college-level course taught in the U.S. Thanks to her personal history and her years in the Congress of American Women, she brought to her students a race- and class-inflected history of feminism that reached back to slavery and pointed beyond *The Feminine Mystique*. In just three years, she worked her way through both a master's degree and a PhD in history at Columbia University, where she fashioned her own curriculum to concentrate on the history of women. She abandoned her novel to make the Grimké sisters the subject of her dissertation, which also became her first published book, the first of 12 books she wrote in the field she helped develop and championed for the rest of her life.

In her first full-time teaching job, as a professor at Sarah Lawrence, she and a colleague proposed to start the first postgraduate program in women's history. "What I wanted to do," she said later, "was to tell this generation that is now teaching and the students that, first of all, nobody gave us anything. It makes me furious when I hear that they gave us suffrage. Excuse me, it took 72 years of organizing, grassroots effort. . . . [W]e had to fight every inch of the way for every advance, and against constant resistance." Lerner had to fight for the field of women's history too. The faculty of Sarah Lawrence's history department argued that there was no reason to divide history by gender, and in any case, they said, there were not enough primary sources for such a program. Columbia professor Alice Kessler-Harris, who was also early to women's history studies, recalled that, at the time, that "seemed a perfectly good explanation." As she also remembered, "Gerda would have none of it."

Thanks in no small part to Gerda Lerner's scholarship and persistence, the distinctive place of women in history would come to be well known, and there would be departments of women's history and women's studies in most major U.S. colleges and universities. Some of its leading scholars were her former students.

*   *   *

The picture taken of 20-year-old Pauli Murray as "Pete" actually appeared in *Negro Anthology: 1931–1933*, a collection of writings from the Harlem Renaissance. Her story, titled "Three Thousand Miles on a Dime in Ten Days," was the first she ever published. The byline was "Pauli Murray," but the photo, captioned "Pete," appears to show a young man sitting on a concrete block in workers' clothes and a sailor's cap, smiling broadly and leaning into the picture, hands clasped around one knee. Decades later, the story could clearly be read as a portrait of Murray's divided self. "Pete" was the hero of the story, but the narrator's voice was that of an easily frightened traveling companion, a genderless observer but one who clearly admired Pete's fearless confidence.

The story was inspired by a train-hopping cross-country trip that Murray had made with her friend Dorothy Hayden. That trip began and ended in New York City, where Murray had lived since graduating high school. In 1933, at the age of 23, she got her BA at the then tuition-free Hunter College for Women, but she also got an education where she lived, at Harlem's new YWCA, on 137th Street. The building took up an entire city block and was a center of the Harlem Renaissance. There, she found mentors for her writing in Langston Hughes and Countee

Cullen, and she became friends with women who would be leaders in the civil rights movements of the 1950s and '60s, including Ella Baker, Anna Arnold Hedgeman, and Dorothy Height. Baker introduced her to left-wing Depression-era politics by sending her downtown to the radical Worker's School and night classes with its founder, Jay Lovestone, the former leader and now enemy of the Communist Party. Lovestone taught Murray enough to know that neither the Party nor Lovestone's oppositional variant were appealing to her, even if some of their values were.

Only odd jobs kept Murray alive in the '30s, when her thoughts and free time were preoccupied by her conflicted sense of gender. She spent days and weeks in the New York Public Library, researching the subject. Even then, some of the latest books and papers were proposing that gender was not binary but a spectrum from male to female, an idea that was intellectually satisfying to her but emotionally useless against the repeated agony of her rejection by heterosexual women. She found one plausible explanation of her gender confusion in Havelock Ellis's definition of the "pseudo-hermaphrodite," which also did little to help. Her letters appealing to physicians and psychiatrists left no doubt of her desperation, but they also demonstrated a lucidity and level of detail that spoke to her fearlessness in grappling with her predicament rather than retreating into denial.

Finally, in the late 1930s, she found a job she valued for the work itself, and one that would lead directly to her future. She was hired by A. Philip Randolph's Workers Defense League to generate financial support for the appeal of a Virginia sharecropper named Odell Waller, who had been sentenced to death for murdering his white sub-landlord over his family's rightful share of the harvest. Waller claimed self-defense, and there was little evidence to contradict him, but the verdict and sentence were decided in the usual southern manner—in a matter of minutes, by an all-white jury. Like other southern states, Virginia created such juries by limiting its pool of jurors to registered voters and by imposing a poll tax that kept most

Black and poor white citizens from registering. The NAACP took on Waller's appeal as a way of attacking the poll tax, which had denied him a jury of his peers. For most of a year, Murray traveled the country with Waller's mother to plead his case, in the course of which she became fluent in arguing from the Fourteenth Amendment's promise to every citizen of "equal protection of the laws." All along their cross-country tour, she recalled later, "I kept saying to myself, 'If we lose this man's life, I must study law.' "

One night in Richmond, Virginia, she made her appeal to a meeting of Black ministers. Among the speakers, and among the audience for her presentation, were the celebrated civil rights attorneys Thurgood Marshall and Leon Ransom, who was then the acting dean at Howard University's School of Law. Intimidated by their presence in the audience but also simply exhausted from her time on the road, she remembered, "I get out two words, then just utterly collapse in tears trying to tell the story of this young sharecropper." When she recovered, she obviously made her case, because she came away with $23 from the ministers and Ransom's offer of a full scholarship to Howard's School of Law.

Being the only woman in her all-male class at Howard University School of Law gave Pauli Murray her fateful exposure to gender discrimination.

It was there, in the early 1940s, that Murray recognized the kind of discrimination she would later help to make illegal. Her graduating class was not only exclusively Black but was also, with the sole exception of herself, all male. Until then, she had traced every discrimination against her to racism. Now, as the lone female, and perhaps especially as one who identified as a Black man, she began for the first time to recognize the sting of sexism and gender discrimination. On the first day of classes, a professor remarked how strange it was to have a woman there. He guessed they would all just have to get used to it, he said, which brought out a burst of laughter that left her "too humiliated to respond." After that, she noticed that fellow students sometimes seemed to be laughing at her behind her back, and it was clear in all her classes that she was called on less often than others. At first, she thought it was the softness or high pitch of her voice, but she found that trying to make it lower and louder did not help.

What finally defined the issue for her was being told, by Ransom, that she could not belong to a professional fraternity on campus because she was a woman. He denied that the decision had anything to do with Howard. A national legal fraternity was recruiting members for a new chapter on campus, he said, and it was their policy to accept only men.

At the time, Ransom and Howard's law school were at the center of the legal struggle for civil rights. It was at Howard where some of the most important challenges to racial discrimination were devised and rehearsed. Because she respected Ransom and knew that he respected her, his response was especially, painfully meaningful. As she put it in her autobiography,

> The discovery that . . . men I deeply admired because of their dedication to civil rights, men who themselves had suffered racial indignities, could countenance exclusion of women from their professional association, aroused an incipient feminism in me long before I knew the meaning of the term "feminism."

That was her introduction to "Jane Crow," the name she adopted for a set of prejudice-based customs and attitudes that asserted male supremacy and disempowered women as surely as Jim Crow laws asserted white supremacy and disempowered people of color. For the moment, gender discrimination was too personally loaded to become her mission, and those few advocates for civil rights who paid attention to it saw it as competitive with the fight against racial discrimination. At that point, Murray herself was conflicted about that and had already taken her place in the vanguard of the civil rights movement.

In 1940, the year before she began law school and 15 years before Rosa Parks refused to move to the back of a city bus, Murray and her roommate Adelene McBean chose to go to jail rather than move to a broken seat at the back of a bus. It was an especially brave gesture given that Murray was traveling dressed as a man, which must have made for an interesting conversation when she insisted on sharing McBean's cell. When they were fined and released, Murray appealed to the NAACP, which was already looking for a case to challenge segregated seating on interstate trains and buses. The NAACP chose its plaintiffs very carefully, however, and her cross-dressing may have been among the reasons they declined.

During her last semester in law school, in the spring of 1944, she led one of the first civil-rights demonstrations based on Mahatma Gandhi's model of nonviolent resistance. With her help, seventeen years before the history-making sit-in at Woolworth's lunch counter in Greensboro, North Carolina, Howard students mounted a direct-action campaign to desegregate the restaurants of Washington, D.C.

Murray's historic contributions to the fight against both racial and gender discrimination began with her law-school thesis, which took on what even the NAACP's best legal minds believed to be invulnerable: the "separate but equal" doctrine set down in 1896 by the Supreme Court's decision in *Plessy v. Ferguson*. Until *Brown v. Board of Education*, the NAACP would take only cases in which "separate" facilities were not "equal" to those for whites, which left the issue of segregation per se unchallenged. Murray's thesis laid out an assault on the "separate but equal" doctrine based on the Fourteenth Amendment, which was passed during Reconstruction precisely to ensure that the southern states would give Black Americans the rights accorded to all whites. Her argument revisited Justice John Marshall Harlan's eloquent but as yet widely dismissed dissent in *Plessy.* In it, Harlan defined segregation as a legacy of slavery, exactly what the Fourteenth Amendment and its Equal Protection Clause were meant to prohibit. The Constitution recognized "no superior, dominant, ruling class of citizens," Harlan wrote, and it forbade putting "the brand of servitude and degradation upon a large class of our fellow citizens, our equals before the law." Murray's theory also had a contemporary source in Gunnar Myrdal's just-published study of racism, *An American Dilemma*, which cited recent research to show that segregation left a legacy of long-term psychological and practical damage to its victims and the society that perpetrated it.

Years later, as Thurgood Marshall was readying his argument in the racial-discrimination cases consolidated under *Brown v. Board of Education*, Murray's professor Spottswood Robinson remembered her thesis and gave it to Marshall, who incorporated it in his argument to the Supreme Court. By then, Murray had also finished a project for the Methodist Church, which had asked her to review the segregation statutes of all 48 states so that they could legally integrate as many of their local offices as possible. The result was her first book, a 776-page treatise titled *States' Laws on Race and Color.* It was published in 1952, more than a year before Marshall made his argument in *Brown.* He bought a copy of her book for everyone on the NAACP legal team and called it their "bible" for civil rights litigation.

*   *   *

Despite all that she had done, Murray found that getting a good job actually practicing law was nearly impossible. At the best law firms and corporate law departments, women lawyers were scarce, and Black women were invisibly few. In 1951, she found a job possibility that matched her ambition: to work under a State Department contract to help the government of Liberia develop its legal code. Just then, however, the witch hunt caught up with her. During the application process, she got a copy of Congress's just-released "Guide to Subversive Organizations and Publications." Hundreds of organizations were listed, on 150 pages of small type, and Murray calculated that she had belonged to at least seven of them. She also learned that some of her references—including Eleanor Roosevelt, Thurgood Marshall, and A. Phillip Randolph—were considered politically suspect. So she was bitterly disappointed but not surprised when she was disqualified on the basis of "past associations."

Rather than continuing to hunt for a job she would not want, she decided to undertake a project she had been thinking about for years: to write a historical portrait of race in America through the story of her grandparents and their slave and slave-owning ancestors. Her friends and mentors all encouraged her to write it, and she found an agent, Marie Rodell, who believed in the idea. On the basis of an outline and sample chapters, Harper & Row gave her a $1,300 advance.

To supplement that as deadlines came and went, Rodell found her work as a typist for some of her other clients. One of them was Betty Friedan, who by then was writing for mainstream women's magazines. Murray left no record of her reactions to what she typed for Friedan, but the magazines' main audience of suburban housewives suggests she would have been underwhelmed. Her own subject was the South in the time of slavery and, by implication, its legacies to women of color, which she could witness in person on any weekday at what were known as New York City's street-corner "slave markets." There, Black women lined up for inspection every morning with their working clothes in paper bags, hoping to be hired for housework by the hour or the day.

When her book was published in 1956, *Proud Shoes: The Story of an American Family* won lavish praise everywhere but the South, where its sale was widely banned. By then, a mentor at a prestigious law firm had managed to get her a job as an associate, but she soon tired of what she thought of as assembly-line advocacy. She left for a job in the newly independent Republic of Ghana, which had just opened a law school in Accra. There, she taught a new generation of lawyers the first course on their new constitution. She also coauthored the first textbook on Ghana's legal history and worked to bring order from the chaos of a newborn judicial system without casebooks, trained judges, or legal precedents. She left behind a curriculum, coursework materials, and the gratitude of students and faculty.

She came home not to New York City but to New Haven, Connecticut, where she had been admitted to a doctoral program at Yale Law School. Though she intended first to focus on evolving legal systems in the newly independent African states, she was diverted by the urgency of change in U.S. laws related to race and gender. In the end, her doctoral dissertation, titled "Roots of the Racial Crisis: Prologue to Policy," ranged well beyond law to examine the roots of racism in the "social pathologies" of American society. She set out to understand how the promise of equality and "inalienable rights" in the Declaration of Independence could possibly coexist with the cold-blooded barbarism visited on African Americans in the time of slavery and after. How could slave owners in good conscience have even signed their names to such a declaration? To square that with her belief in the founding principles, she arrived at a view of American democracy not as a fixed reality but as a hope and ambition, a promise whose fulfillment was the nation's reason for being. In final form, her dissertation ran to 1,200 pages in five volumes and comprised a legal and social history of the U.S. that was pointedly relevant more than half a century later.

In December 1961, at the end of his first year in the White House and Pauli Murray's first semester at Yale, President John F. Kennedy signed an executive order creating the President's Commission on the Status of Women, and he named Eleanor Roosevelt to be its chair. She and her vice-chair, Esther Peterson, recruited some of the most powerful, connected, and smartest women in the country, creating a network among them that a few years later would help to establish the National Organization for Women.

Roosevelt recruited Murray and assigned her to the committee whose job was to find the best way to establish gender equality as a matter of law. One solution was the Equal Rights Amendment, which had been bitterly divisive ever since it was first proposed by Alice Paul and the National Woman's Party in 1923. The roots of that divide went deep. Though founded by abolitionists in 1848, the early suffrage advocates had split over the Fifteenth Amendment, which gave the vote to Black men in 1870. Infuriated by the idea that Black men would have a right denied to women, some leading suffragists were outspokenly opposed. That discord in the early movement was resolved only when it became clear that new immigrants and indigenous American women would not get the vote because they were not citizens—and that Black women, like theoretically enfranchised Black men, would be kept from the polls by bureaucratic artifice and the threat of violence.

Over time, the National Women's Party and supporters of the Equal Rights Amendment became increasingly white, Christian, middle- to upper-middle class, and infected by racism and anti-Semitism—in other words, in sympathy with the southern Democrats who held power in Congress. That alliance of feminists and segregationists gave the Women's Party its best chance to pass the ERA since the 1920s, but it faced an equally awkward but powerful pair of enemies: a Congress in which male dominance was the one thing southern Democrats and Republicans agreed on, allied with a strong coalition of working women who thought the ERA could ensure equality only by giving away all the gender-specific protections they had won through long, hard negotiation. So it was that the strangest of bedfellows— abolitionists and white supremacists on one side, feminists and male supremacists on the other—conspired to divide and delay the struggle for women's rights.

When the President's Commission on the Status of Women began its work in 1962, two of the most ardent opponents of the Equal Rights Amendment were among the Commission's most powerful members— Esther Peterson, head of the Woman's Bureau in the Department of Labor, and Judge Dorothy Kenyon, a social activist since the Progressive Era and a board member of the ACLU since its inception in 1930. They were Murray's allies in the attempt to find a strategy that squared the ERA with protections for women in the workplace and that did not once again put women's rights and civil rights at odds.

During the summer of 1962, Murray researched and drafted a proposed compromise: The President's Commission would give tacit support to the ERA while pursuing an aggressive litigation strategy that would link discrimination by race and by gender. Despite some heated debate, Murray's plan made it out of her committee and was adopted unanimously by the full commission.

A month before the commission presented its final report to the president, however, it was clear that legal reform would not be enough. In the list of speakers at the upcoming March on Washington and in the delegation that was to meet with President Kennedy, there was not one of the many women who had given themselves unsparingly to the civil rights movement: no Daisy Bates, leader of the long and treacherous fight to integrate Central High School in Little Rock, Arkansas; no Diane Nash, leader of the Freedom Rides of 1961; no Ella Baker; no Rosa Parks.

Murray, among others, was furious. A week before the March, she sent her frank objection to the March's leader and her onetime mentor, A. Phillip Randolph:

> The time has come to say to you quite candidly, Mr. Randolph, that "tokenism" is as offensive when applied to women as when applied to Negroes, and that I have not devoted the greater part of my adult life to the implementation of human rights to now condone any policy which is not inclusive.

When her protests to Randolph and others elicited nothing but platitudes, she spent the day and night before the March writing an eight-page, single-spaced manifesto titled "The Role of the Negro Women in the Civil Rights Revolution." She did not rant. She built her argument carefully, beginning with the oppression of American colonists by England that led to the American Revolution. African Americans were the present-day inheritors of their righteous demand for freedom, she argued, and Black women were the most egregiously oppressed of all. They were victims of discrimination by white society as well as by Black men, including the foremost champions of civil rights. The fact that no women would speak the next day was "not an oversight," she wrote, nor was Randolph's appearance the day before at the National Press Club, where, by tradition, women were forced to sit in the balcony. "Obviously," Murray wrote, "Mr. Randolph and Company drew no parallel between the humiliating experience of being sent to the balcony and being sent to the back of the bus." Black women were now being "frozen out of the positions of leadership in the struggle which they have earned by their courage, intelligence, militance, dedication, and ability."

Her last and most pointed argument to the male leadership was that the exclusion of the movement's Black women leaders could be fatal to the drive for civil rights. Tolerance for male chauvinism in a movement against white chauvinism, she wrote, only proved that every form of discrimination was connected to every other one, and that none of them could be defeated unless all of them were.

In 1963, no civil rights campaign can be permanently successful which does not stand foursquare for all human rights. Civil rights for Negroes cannot be won at the expense of rights of labor or rights of women or by ignoring the rights of the impoverished whites and the problems of the aged and handicapped. . . . [All] non-merit discrimination is immoral and should be made illegal.

The day after the March on Washington, Dorothy Height, Murray's friend since their days together at the Harlem YMCA and now president of the National Council of Negro Women, presided over a meeting to consider how to respond to the absence of women on the March's program. The outcome was the realization that, even in a civil rights movement, women would not get their own rights without taking them, an insight Murray later said was "vital to awakening the women's movement."

Three months later, when the group met again in New York City, Murray electrified them with a speech blasting civil rights leaders for the "bitterly humiliating" neglect of the movement's women leaders, at the March and elsewhere. She framed that humiliation as the best possible evidence that "the Negro woman can no longer postpone or subordinate the fight against discrimination because of sex to the civil rights struggle but must carry on both fights simultaneously." Her speech, Height said later, began "a great debate," out of which came the concept of an "NAACP for Women," which is how Pauli Murray would later describe her vision for a women's movement to Betty Friedan.

Even then, antidiscrimination measures were circulating in Congress that would be incorporated the following year in the Civil Rights Act of 1964. As initially drafted, Title VII of the act, which established the Equal Employment Opportunity Commission (EEOC), outlawed job discrimination on the basis of race, color, religion, and national origin. Two days before the House vote, however, "sex" was added to the criteria by Rep. Howard W. Smith, a Virginia Democrat who had previously been opposed to all civil rights legislation. Some felt he was only trying to undermine passage of the bill, but in fact a plurality of those who voted for it were Republicans, along with some southern Democrats.

When the new Equal Opportunity Commission received its first complaint, however—the first of several from female flight attendants—the agency's chairman, Franklin D. Roosevelt Jr., simply ignored it. He called the sex provision "terribly complicated," and his executive director wrote it off as "a fluke," an idea "conceived out of wedlock."

Nothing did more to mobilize women in the President's Commission network to undertake a civil rights movement of their own. More in anger than frustration, Murray wrote to a close colleague on the Commission:

> What will it take to arouse the working women of this country to fight for their rights? Do you suppose the time has come for the organization of a strong national ad hoc committee of women who are ready to take the plunge?

The time had indeed come, and leaders were in place, including Dorothy Height, Anna Arnold Hedgeman, and Ella Baker. All of them had known each other since the 1930s and had worked together in New Deal welfare programs, the Workers Defense League, and Randolph's original March on Washington movement in 1941. Decades later, it was clear that they were pioneers of a new, more inclusive feminist movement, with a Wave to call their own.

*   *   *

In *The Feminine Mystique*, Betty Friedan wrote, "I never knew a woman, when I was growing up, who used her mind, played her own part in the world, and also loved, and had children." To the young women who volunteered in the South to work in the civil rights movement, that statement made no sense. They knew Fannie Lou Hamer.

"Mrs. Hamer," as they called her in a sign of respect, did not call herself a feminist. Until she was in her forties, she said, she had never even heard the word. In that, she was not unlike other women of her generation, for whom the term "feminist" was used mainly in the National Woman's Party, and even there sparingly. Elsewhere, it was sometimes called "the f-word."

Hamer had spent most of her life as a sharecropper on a cotton plantation in the Mississippi Delta, the deepest of the Deep South. The last of 20 children, she began picking cotton after school at the age of six. She was already a prize-winning student when she had to quit school after sixth grade to join her parents in the cotton fields full-time. From then on, her working day ran from first light to exhaustion, "from can to can't." The family often lived on meals of bread and onions, sometimes without the onions.

Like all Black sharecroppers, her family also lived under the threat of white violence, which could come anytime and out of nowhere. One of her strongest childhood memories was of her mother "getting on her knees to pray that God would let all her children live." Every morning when they left the house to go to work, her mother brought along a pail covered by a cloth. Fannie Lou never knew what was in it until one day she managed to take a peek and saw a 9mm Luger. "No white man was going to beat her kids," she remembered her mother saying.

Hamer's activism for civil rights did not begin until she was almost 45 years old, but she had been practicing other forms of resistance for years. Her maturity, work ethic, and good arithmetic skills led the landowner to make her the plantation's timekeeper, responsible for noting each field hand's hours worked, their daily weight in cotton, and the money they had earned. In that role, she managed to resist the owner's habit of cheating the workers by shaving down their debts to him and otherwise bending the books toward justice, somehow without detection. In that way and others, she worked to undermine the system by which plantation owners kept Black laborers in their debt. "I was rebelling in the only way I knew how to rebel," Hamer said.

She got that spirit of rebellion from her mother. "There weren't many weeks passed that she wouldn't tell me . . . you respect yourself as a Black child, and when you get grown, if I'm dead and gone, you respect yourself as a Black woman, and other people will respect you." In the Mississippi of the 1940s and '50s, the corollary to self-respect was rage at the disrespect of others, and Fannie Lou got angrier and angrier as she grew from childhood to womanhood. "It's been times that I've been called 'Mississippi's angriest woman,' and I have a right to be angry," she said. For years, she had been looking for something more than cooking the plantation's books to "really lash out and say what I had to say about what was going on in Mississippi," but even civil rights organizations were reluctant to do that. Without support, it would be worse than useless.

Her chance came in 1962, when the Student Nonviolent Coordinating Committee came to Sunflower County and her hometown of Ruleville, which made an especially tempting target for SNCC's voter registration campaign because it had a Black majority, and only one in a hundred were registered to vote.

One night in late August, at the William Chapel Baptist Church in Ruleville, where Hamer worshipped and sang every Sunday, SNCC held a meeting to recruit volunteers. They finished their talk by asking willing volunteers to raise their hands. Very few went up, but Fannie Lou Hamer's did—"as high as I could get it," she wrote later in an autobiographical pamphlet for SNCC.

> I guess if I'd a had any sense I'd a been a little scared, but what was the point of being scared? The only thing they could do to me was kill me, and it seemed like they'd been trying to do that a little bit at a time ever since I could remember.

Four days after signing on with SNCC, she and 17 others got into a school bus for the 26-mile drive to the county courthouse in Indianola, where they tried to register to vote and, as always, failed. In one of the common methods of disqualification, the registrar tested them on the most obscure passages of the Mississippi constitution. Hamer drew a blank when asked to explain the theory of "de facto" laws, which she said she knew as much about "as a horse knows about Christmas."

As they started driving back to Ruleville, they were stopped by police, whose transparent excuse was that the color of the school bus was off. The driver was taken into custody and back to Indianola. As his passengers waited to see what would happen next, they began to talk about why they needed to be home, what was keeping their driver, what they would do if he never came back, what might happen if they were put in jail themselves. As the anxiety mounted, Hamer began to sing. One of her favorites was the gospel song "This Little Light of Mine," inspired by Matthew 5:14–16: "Let your light so shine before men that they may see your good works and glorify your father in heaven."

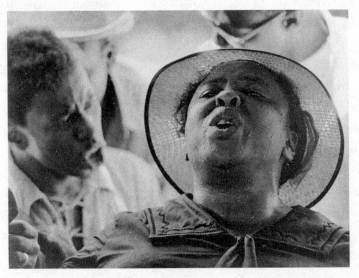

At moments of high tension like this one, at the March Against Fear in 1966, Fannie Lou Hamer had a way of quieting nerves and inspiring solidarity with a gospel song.

It was for moments like these that her voice was always remembered—a strong, low contralto that cut through tension like a sharp knife. Harry Belafonte, who sang with her many times, said he could not really describe her voice "*as* a voice" because it seemed to be more than that. It was "the voice of us all," he said, a voice that "transcended all other considerations at the moment." She sang songs everyone could sing, because they were the spirituals they sang together in church on Sundays and in the cotton fields every day. SNCC was committed to leaving local causes in the hands of local leaders, and they knew after the trip to Indianola that they had found one in Mrs. Hamer.

Her plain, no-nonsense approach to activism made the leaders of the more traditional NAACP and the Southern Christian Leadership Conference uncomfortable, which she did not mind at all. She had indelible memories of being degraded by Black men and civil rights leaders more educated than she. She was far from alone in calling the NAACP "the National Association for the Advancement of *Certain* People," and that animus remained when she took on a leadership role with SNCC. Before audiences of the powerful and the powerless, she spoke as she spoke at home, in the vernacular of a sharecropper but with the fluency and power of her singing. "I don't think there was a wasted hum when she sang," Belafonte said, and she spoke the same way—directly, without a pause or second thought, never from notes, always from the heart.

By the time she got home from trying to vote, the owner of the plantation where Hamer had worked for 15 years knew what she had done, and he gave her an ultimatum: If she would not withdraw her attempt to vote, she could no longer live or work there anymore. After talking to her husband and their daughters, she left and never went back.

Other people on the bus to Indianola paid a price as well. The bus driver was fired because his mother was one of those who tried to register. Homes whose owners were known to have taken in Mrs. Hamer and the SNCC workers were sprayed with gunfire. A farmer pulled his truck alongside two SNCC workers and threatened to shoot them if they ever came near his land.

After that year's harvest, her husband and daughters left the plantation to join her, but they had to leave Ruleville for a while because of threats against them. Perry Hamer could get only occasional work after that because of his wife's activism, but in time friends helped them to get a small house in Ruleville, and from then on they subsisted on food surplus, charity from friends and movement allies, and her ten-dollar-a-week stipend from SNCC.

Ruleville's infamous mayor Charles Dorrough did everything he could to make her life miserable. He tried to disqualify her from the federal food program. He called her to his office when she was two days late on her water bill, which was for $9,000. She said she had been wanting to ask him how she could owe that much since they weren't home most of the time and didn't have running water in the house. She fought inflated utility bills for years after that.

Despite everything, she kept up her activism with SNCC and others. She worked in the Citizenship School program of the Southern Christian Leadership Conference, which taught would-be voters what they needed to know to pass the registration tests and whatever else they wanted to learn, from reading the newspaper to filling out forms for money orders. While working to solve practical problems in her community, she attended leadership programs and spoke widely about the problems of Mississippi and the nation, and as she grew in recognition and influence she became an ever-larger target for retribution.

*   *   *

In the spring of 1963, Mrs. Hamer and other SNCC workers attended a Citizenship School in Charleston, South Carolina. On the way home, during a long layover in Winona, Mississippi, a few of them got off the bus to use the bathrooms and get something to eat. Practicing what they had learned, they sat down at the lunch counter. Then they waited. After some time, they got the attention of a waitress, who said, "We don't serve n-----s." Then the Winona police chief and a highway patrolman arrived and started poking them off their stools with billy clubs and telling them to get out. They left peacefully but then stood outside discussing what to do. When the officers saw them writing down license plate numbers, they came outside and put them all under arrest.

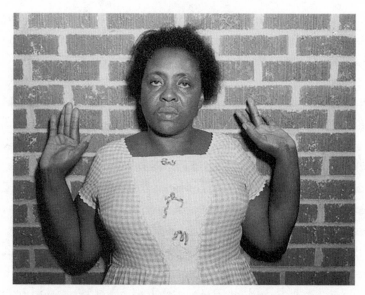

Hamer never completely recovered from the beating she took
at the county jail in Winona, Mississippi. She suffered especially
from being beaten repeatedly on areas where she had had
polio as a child. After Winona, however, her activism only increased.

At the Montgomery County jail, they were taken to individual cells and then brought out to be beaten, one by one. The first was June Johnson, then 16. The other prisoners could hear her trying to reason with the police, saying the waitress had broken the law by refusing to serve them.

"What do you think we're supposed to do about that?" one of the officers said.

"You all are supposed to protect us and take care of us."

All they heard after that was Johnson's pleading and crying, and the sounds of a long, loud beating, including the sharp cracks of a billy club against her skull. When they saw her as she was walked back to her cell, most of her clothes were torn off, her head was beaten in, her left eye was swollen shut, and there was blood all over her. After a few minutes the police returned to make her get rid of the evidence. They told her to strip in front of them, then to wash her clothes and wipe away all the blood from her body. They called in someone else to clean the blood from the floor, then brought out another SNCC worker, 30-year-old Annelle Ponder. As they beat her, they kept insisting that she say, "Yes, sir" to their questions, but she never did, and they kept beating her.

Then it was Hamer's turn. They knew who she was and told her, as she later testified, "We're going to make you wish you was dead." They took her to a room where Winona's police chief and the arresting officers were waiting. With them were two Black prisoners. One of them, who looked as if he had been beaten himself, was ordered to beat her with a blackjack. He protested at first, then began to do as he was told, and she began to scream. "That man beat me 'til he gave out," she testified. The officer who took over focused the blackjack on her head. Then others joined in, beating her all over. When they began beating her left side and left leg, which had never recovered from the polio she had had as a girl, she tried shifting her feet to protect herself, and at that the other Black prisoner was told to sit on them. Then she used her hands and arms to try to take the blows, but the beating continued, and she continued screaming and crying until she was going in and out of consciousness. Then she was literally thrown back into her cell and "just lay there crying," Johnson remembered. "All night we could hear her crying."

The beatings of the others went on for hours. When SNCC workers came from headquarters to check on them, they were arrested and beaten as well. Two days later, without a lawyer present, each of them was convicted of disorderly conduct and resisting arrest and fined $100. Before they were released, two agents from the FBI turned up to investigate. They seemed suspiciously friendly toward the police and soon left. After that, Hamer and her fellow prisoners were forced at gunpoint to sign statements saying they were beaten not by police but by each other.

The police were right to worry about the U.S. Justice Department getting involved. On the day of the arrests, Julian Bond, cofounder and then communications director of SNCC, wired Attorney General

Robert Kennedy about what was happening in Winona. Once they were released, the Justice Department filed suit to overturn their convictions and sued five of the police officers for depriving those arrested of their civil rights. Their trial at the federal court in Oxford, Mississippi, however, featured the usual jury of 12 white men, and, as expected, ended in acquittals.

On their release, Hamer was taken to a hospital in Greenwood, which sent her on to Atlanta because of the severity of her condition. Her recovery took months, and it left her blind in one eye and with serious kidney damage and an even worse limp than she had had before, but the beatings only fired her determination to change things.

Around this time, Jane Stembridge, a white seminary student who had been recruited as SNCC's first full-time employee, wrote a note to herself: "I have been thinking about this. Mrs. Hamer is more educated than I am. That is—she knows more." Watching Mrs. Hamer gave Stembridge an insight about herself: "I went into society. . . . And that is where I learned that I was bad. . . . Not racially inferior, not socially shameful, not guilty as a White southerner . . . not unequal as women . . . but Bad." Stembridge was then in rebellion against the standards forced on her as "a good southern girl," standards that she felt worked against feeling strong and whole. Hamer seemed to have no such problem, and Stembridge thought her distance from "society" had preserved her ability to be proud of herself. Without that sense of confidence, Stembridge wrote, "She couldn't get up and sing the way she sings. She wouldn't stand there, with her head back and sing! . . . She knows that she is good."

To Stembridge and to other young white women from south and north, working for civil rights introduced them to a feminism different from their mothers'. They served local people for whom the civil rights movement was not just a good cause but a very personal fight for freedom. Their most impressive leaders were brave women, young and old, married and single, some of them raising children and working outside the home while defying the threat of racist violence every day to win equality for themselves, their family, and their community. To the daughters of Betty Friedan's readers, the SNCC experience prompted less a "strange stirring" than an agenda.

*   *   *

As soon as she had recovered sufficiently from her wounds, Hamer redoubled her civil rights work, which took her into new, more ambitious forms of activism. In 1964, she dove into the voter registration project "Freedom Summer." That spring, on a campus in Oxford, Ohio, she coached hundreds of student volunteers on how dangerous their undertaking was going to be, how far to go in resisting police, how to respond to white racists, and all the many things *not* to do. Her own story was warning enough for the volunteers, who were unpaid, 90 percent white, and most of them new to the South. She advised and comforted them all through that summer of violence, which began when the Klan and local police collaborated in the kidnapping and murder of three volunteers. The search for them clouded most of the summer, but their bodies were eventually found, and decades later, those old enough to be there could remember their names: James Chaney, Andrew Goodman, and Michael Schwerner.

By the end of Freedom Summer, police had made a thousand arrests of civil rights workers and the local people who helped them. At least 67 churches, homes, and Black-owned businesses were bombed or burned out. By the end of the summer, there were only about 1,200 new Black voters in Mississippi, but national outrage over the violence of Freedom Summer led to two historic victories: It helped to convince President Lyndon Johnson to push through passage of the Civil Rights Act of 1964 and the Voting Rights Act of 1965.

Even as Hamer worked to support the volunteers of Freedom Summer, she was also active in forming a new Mississippi Freedom Democratic Party, which tried to replace the state's all-white delegation to that year's Democratic National Convention. At that, President Johnson drew the line. When she was scheduled to make that argument in a televised meeting of the Credentials Committee, he called a newsless news conference so the networks would cut away from her. That proved worse than futile, however, since all three networks responded on the evening news that night by replaying her testimony, which included a graphic account of the beatings in Winona.

After that she focused her activism on poverty in the Delta, where 70 percent of the homes were no better than shacks, most had no indoor plumbing, and the median income for Black families was $456, at a time when the national poverty line was $2,000. Periods of near-starvation were not uncommon. Malnutrition was epidemic. She also worked with SNCC to start the Mississippi Freedom Labor Union, which led local field hands and domestic workers in a series of dangerous but ultimately futile strikes for better wages.

Her most ambitious program to address the sources of poverty was the Freedom Farm Corporation, which set out to rebuild the economy of Rulesville and Sunflower County from the bottom up. Freedom Farm initiatives included buying hundreds of acres of land and making them available to former sharecroppers and others. The organization developed animal-breeding programs to increase the meat supply. It bought homes to convert rents into mortgages and turn tenant families into homeowners. It built dozens of new houses, raising more than $800,000 in FHA loans to do it. Freedom Farm gave out student scholarships for vocational schools and college. It helped develop new local businesses, which included buying buildings for a sewing factory, a fashion shop, and a plumbing operation that could put in water lines and sewers. In the end, Freedom Farm helped more than 600 families get to the point where they could help themselves. Hamer hired a manager to run the day-to-day business while she approved and helped to design new projects and traveled all over the country raising money to pay for them. While doing all that, she won a lawsuit as the named plaintiff in a lawsuit to integrate the all-white schools of Sunflower County. That victory, 15 years after

Brown, gave her the pleasure of escorting her daughter Vergie Ree into the previously all-white school in Ruleville.

Still, she was met more often by defeat than victory. In the end, Freedom Farms gave out more than it took in. She lost three races for local office, and in a race for state senator she lost by a margin so overwhelming she was probably right to call it fixed. She even failed to carry Ruleville. The Freedom Democratic Party was the only Mississippi delegation seated at the 1968 national convention, but by then Black women were no longer among the leaders. As Unita Blackwell recalled, the Party had "lost the truth . . . because all the guys were in again, the big wheels. . . ."

That Hamer won any victories at all was a demonstration of fierce determination. That was tested when her 22-year old-daughter Dorothy Jean, the mother of an infant and a toddler, suffered a cerebral hemorrhage. Hamer was with her and rushed her to the nearest hospital, but she was refused admittance because she was Black. The next closest hospital turned her away for the same reason. By the time they found a hospital that would take her, they were in Memphis, 120 miles from home, and as they approached the front door, Dorothy died in her mother's arms. Fannie Lou and her husband took in Dorothy's two children. That was the year she started Freedom Farms.

In 1971, she became one of the first leaders of the National Women's Political Caucus. In her inaugural speech she wanted them to know that she was more than just a feminist. In a way, her speech restated Pauli Murray's letter to A. Philip Randolph the night before the March on Washington. To a group whose theme was "sisterhood," she said women would never be sisters unless they joined hands in the cause of the Black man, "because nobody's free unless everybody's free."

Years later, her comrade-in-arms Shirley Chisholm remembered that Hamer's speech was "kind of harsh. A lot of women could not understand what [she was] railing about." But Chisholm and other Black women at the conference backed her up, and Gloria Steinem resoundingly joined in. At the end of the day, the organization passed a measure pledging to support candidates both male and female, Black and white, but only those committed to eliminating the linked oppressions of sexism, racism, violence, and poverty.

A few months later, Hamer collapsed during a demonstration and was hospitalized for what was called a nervous breakdown. Later she lost a breast to cancer. She was never the same after that, but her legacy was secure, and she lived long enough to see it honored in a book of writings by Black women. The scholar who collected them saved Hamer's for last. It was taken from a speech she made to the NAACP Legal Defense Fund that talked about the debt feminism owed to the civil rights movement. She talked about her empathy for white women, who had been put on a pedestal and given "this kind of angel feeling that you were untouchable." That pedestal was going to be gone very soon, she said, and when that happened, white women were "gonna have to fight like hell, like [Black women] have been fighting all this time."

She ended her speech with a kind of farewell to her generation of activists and an exhortation to the next one. It was the story of a wise old man, who was known for being able to answer even the most difficult questions.

So some people went to him one day, two young people, and said, "We're going to trick this guy today. We're going to catch a bird and we're going to carry it to this old man. And we're going to ask him, 'This that we hold in our hands today, is it alive or is it dead?' If he says, 'Dead,' we're going to turn it loose and let it fly. But if he says, 'Alive,' we're going to crush it." So they walked up to this old man, and they said, "This that we hold in our hands today, is it alive or is it dead?" He looked at the young people, and he smiled. And he said, "It's in your hands."

*   *   *

That story comes at the end of more than 150 entries in Gerda Lerner's groundbreaking collection of primary-source documents, *Black Women in White America*. There had never been a book like it. The title page read "edited by Gerda Lerner," but it more accurately might have said "flung by Gerda Lerner," because it gave the lie to all the university historians who had insisted there was not enough evidence that women, much less Black women, deserved a separate discipline of history. To find her sources, Lerner scoured old newspapers, public hearings, trial transcripts, libraries, files, and personal papers that she found gathering dust in churches, attics, local libraries, and courthouses all around the North as well as the South.

Her work accomplished its purpose. The year the book was published, after a struggle with faculty and administration at Sarah Lawrence that had gone on for years, she realized her dream of starting the nation's first graduate program in women's history. According to NYU professor Linda Gordon, her former student, the impact of *Black Women in White America* was "stunning, even thrilling. . . . A generation of historians of Black women felt empowered by that book." One of them was Professor Darlene Clark Hine of Northwestern University, who never forgot seeing the book for the first time. She sat with it for hours that day, and she later called it a major influence on her career as a scholar.

For Lerner, the study of women's history was her life of activism in its final form, successor to her move toward radicalism in Austria, her work for the Congress of American Women, and her advocacy of progressive causes in and out of the Communist Party. Her commitment to the field of women's history was more than academic to her. She saw it as a way of building a better world. In the program she started at the University of Wisconsin, she required her doctoral candidates to produce public lectures on women's issues, and presentations for primary and secondary school classes on women in sports, women in the workplace, women in politics. She saw scholarship as an agent of change.

Perhaps the peak of her career as a historian was a two-volume work—*Creation of Patriarchy*, which begins in Mesopotamia, and *Creation of Feminist Consciousness: From the Middle Ages to Eighteen-Seventy*—but they were two of a dozen books she wrote to lay the foundation of her field. Her last book was her autobiography, *Fireweed*. The title refers to *Chamaenerion angustifolium*, a pink wildflower that springs up to cover blackened landscape after a fire. In England during World War II, where it blanketed the craters of German bombs, it was known as bombweed. "The first things I can think of are the breaks, the fissures," the book begins. "I've had too many—destruction, loss. . . ." Fireweed was her metaphor for recovery—for failures left behind, conflicts resolved or relinquished, and the creation of a full life, complete with a loving husband, two beloved children, and purposeful work.

The autobiography itself was one of those recoveries. For half a century, she had kept her past in the Communist Party to herself. Then, in 2002, she told it all, from hope to disillusionment and back. "Whatever contributions as a feminist theoretician and thinker I have been able to make derive from my life experience, including my life as a Communist."

The book also allowed her a reconciliation of sorts with her mother. She wrote of the last time they were together, their bags packed, waiting for the bus that was to take them together to Nice, where they would stay while Gerda continued on to America and got a visa for her mother. As the bus arrived, however, her mother told her she would not be joining her after all. Gerda was stricken, but as she recalled the moment more than 60 years later, her mother explained that she simply did not want to go, that she had "never been a normal kind of mother" and thought it was "too late to start now. . . . I will paint, my best work has not been done yet. I will survive—on my own terms." The bus arrived, they embraced, and her mother pushed her away. When Gerda looked back from the bus as it drove away—or perhaps from the perspective of all the years since—she saw a woman "strong and wise and dry-eyed, shaking her head."

After starting the first PhD program in woman's
history, in 1980, Gerda Lerner became president of the
Organization of American Historians and continued
producing her own prodigious works of scholarship.

Two years before the autobiography was published, Gerda arranged
for her mother's work—abstracts, self-portraits, and landscapes—to
be acquired and exhibited by Vienna's Jewish Museum of Vienna. Her
biography of her mother for the exhibit catalogue and her autobiography pay tribute to a great artist and a woman whose unconventional
motherhood helped her survive her life's challenges: "Like the good
fairy in the tales, she equipped me, the adventurous child poised for a
long and hazardous journey, with magic sources of strength in the face
of danger." With that strength, she built a foundation for the feminism
of the late twentieth and early twenty-first century, when women of
every race, class, sexual preference, nationality, and disability had the
support of a movement of movements.

*   *   *

Pauli Murray's work toward that end was just beginning when the rights of women made their way into Title VII of the Civil Rights Act of 1964. In 1965, she and the legal scholar Mary Eastwood coauthored a paper for the *George Washington Law Review* titled "Jane Crow and the Law," which applied the equal-protection argument she made in law school to gender discrimination. When the EEOC continued to ignore such cases, Murray raised the threat of another March on Washington to force the issue. Coverage of that threat in the *New York Times* prompted a call from Betty Friedan, which put the two of them on the road to founding the National Organization for Women.

Murray introduced Friedan to all the women in her network and was among NOW's most active cofounders. In the end, though, she despaired of Friedan's "ferociousness and bloodletting" style of leadership, which left her feeling like "a stranger in my own household." NOW was clearly moving toward full support for the ERA at the expense of the aggressive legal strategy Murray advocated. She was not against the ERA, but she feared that dropping support for the constitutional challenge would deprive it of coalition partners in the civil rights and labor movements. As she withdrew her name from nomination to NOW's board, she wrote to a fellow founder about her dismay at the latest national convention, where "I saw no Catholic sisters, no women of ethnic minorities other than about five Negro women, and obviously no women who represent the poor." At that point, she said, "I cannot conscientiously invest any more time in the organization nor lend my name to its policies."

Instead, she took her litigation strategy to the ACLU, where she was supported by one of its founding board members, Dorothy Kenyon. There, she led a successful challenge to Alabama's all-white, all-male jury system. The class-action case, known as *White v. Crook*, targeted the acquittal of two white men charged with the murder of two civil rights workers, one of them a Black woman. The plaintiffs' case specifically alleged both race- and sex-based discrimination in the county's jury pools. In collaboration with Kenyon and the Civil Rights Division of the Justice Department, Murray wrote the sex-discrimination portion of the argument.

In the end, a three-judge panel of the federal district court in Montgomery ruled unanimously that the jury system of Lowndes County, which was 80 percent Black, had a long history of excluding Black men by custom and both Black and white women by statute. The fact that both were discriminated against, and that both were denied equal protection under the Fourteenth Amendment, established the link between sex and race discrimination that Murray had recognized but not yet dared to assert in law school. Her reaction to the victory was of course ecstatic. She called the decision "the *Brown v. Board of Education* for women in this country." Mary Eastwood, her coauthor on "Jane Crow and the Law," called it "the most important thing to happen to women since the Nineteenth Amendment."

The issue did not go to the Supreme Court then because the State of Alabama chose not to appeal, but it did five years later. In the case of *Reed v. Reed*, Murray's equal-protection argument prevailed once again when the Court struck down an Idaho statute that called for men to be preferred over women as administrators of estates. Murray and Judge Kenyon were listed as coauthors of the brief in *Reed*, but they actually had no part in writing it. Its author was Ruth Bader Ginsburg, who had been hired to head the ACLU's Women's Rights Project. She signed their names to it to acknowledge Murray's authorship of the equal-protection argument and to honor Kenyon for her lifelong advocacy for women at the ACLU. "We knew we were standing on their shoulders," Ginsburg said at a conference in 2011 titled "Forty Years After *Reed*." "They were saying the same things in the '50s and '60s that we were saying in the '70s."

Ginsburg did not argue *Reed* herself, and the oral argument was weak, but, as in most Supreme Court cases, it was not oral argument but the written briefs that determined the outcome. The Court's vote was unanimous, and its decision was framed as categorically as Ginsburg could have dared to hope. Chief Justice Warren Burger read the decision from the bench.

> To give a mandatory preference to members of either sex over members of the other . . . is to make the very kind of arbitrary legislative choice forbidden by the Equal Protection Clause.

With that, discrimination on the basis of gender was declared unconstitutional.

"What makes me optimistic," Ginsburg said at the conference in 2011, "is that one lives and learns." Her example was Chief Justice William Rehnquist, a conservative Nixon appointee who had long opposed both the ERA and attempts otherwise to equate men and women, which he found inimical to the traditional differences in their social roles. He considered pregnancy, for example, the result of a clear physical difference, and therefore not arguable grounds for a case of discrimination in hiring or promotion. The Court's decision in *Reed* came the year before Rehnquist joined the Court, but 30 years later he had a dramatic change of heart. In a case charging gender discrimination in the Family and Medical Leave Act, Justice Ginsberg remembered,

> Chief Justice Rehnquist explained why it was important that this leave be given to men as well as women, because men are, or should be, caretakers of the family as women are.

Though it "may have been influenced by what was going on in the world at large," Justice Ginsburg added, "I think he was also influenced by having two daughters, with children. . . . Maybe even more, he had granddaughters." He himself wrote the opinion—for a 6–3 Court—in *Nevada Department of Human Resources v. Hibbs*, which recognized unconstitutional gender discrimination in the Family and Medical Leave Act and laid down a precedent for every future case. Ginsburg recalled that when she showed the opinion to her husband, he said, "Ruth, did you write that?"

Among other things, the decisions in *Reed* and *Hibbs* vindicated Murray's career-long fight to apply equal protection of the law to every member of every affected minority group in the U.S. Many legal scholars contributed to that cause, but it seems especially just that a woman of more than one racial and gender identity would make that case.

*   *   *

Fannie Lou Hamer lived until 1977, long enough to see African American women become ambassadors, congresswomen, cabinet members, and a candidate for the presidency in Shirley Chisholm. She saw the passage of *Roe v. Wade* and would not have been surprised that Billie Jean King beat Bobby Riggs in the "Battle of the Sexes." Just before she died, she may even have heard that Pauli Murray, in her last campaign and after getting yet another doctorate, had just become the first woman from a minority population to be ordained as a priest in the Episcopal Church.

Murray reached the Church's mandatory retirement after only five years, but she had wondered since childhood why there were no altar *girls*, so she changed that too. In her last years, women became airline pilots, generals, astronauts, and chiefs of police. Before she died, Geraldine Ferraro ran on the Democratic ticket for vice president, Sandra Day O'Connor was on the Supreme Court, and an African American woman, Vanessa Williams, was Miss America.

Only Gerda Lerner lived long enough to see the assertion of Third Wave feminism. As a movement, it had no single definition—diversity, in fact, was a defining virtue—but the moment of its birth was linked to the appearance of Anita Hill before the Senate Judiciary Committee, where she accused Supreme Court nominee Clarence Thomas of sexual harassment. In 1991, during three days of televised testimony, clueless and sometimes hostile questioning by the all-white, all-male committee sparked high-temperature outrage in a new generation of feminists. Shortly after the hearings, a college student named Rebecca Walker published an article about the Thomas–Hill face-off in *Ms.* magazine. "While some may laud the whole spectacle for the consciousness it raised around sexual harassment," she wrote, "its very real outcome is more informative. He was promoted. She was repudiated. . . . Let this dismissal of a woman's experience move you to anger. Turn that outrage into political power. . . . I am not a postfeminism feminist," she wrote in closing. "I am the Third Wave."

She was also her mother's daughter. In 1972, when Rebecca Walker was three years old, Sarah Lawrence College invited Alice Walker (Sarah Lawrence class of '65) to be the speaker at their annual summer convocation. Walker's first novel and first book of poetry had already won high praise. She had not yet coined the term "womanism" to identify the unique values and experiences of Black women, but she was already deeply involved in women's studies. That fall she would be teaching a course at the University of Massachusetts on the writings of African American women, a subject that made Gerda Lerner's new book mandatory reading.

By the time Walker came to campus, Sarah Lawrence had granted Lerner her wish to start the first postgraduate program in women's studies. Walker must have known that, because her speech echoed Lerner's argument precisely. "I am discouraged," she said, "when a faculty member at Sarah Lawrence says there is not enough literature by Black women and men to make a full year's course. Or that the quantity of genuine Black literature is too meager to warrant a full year's investigation." She invoked the "countless vanished and forgotten women" who needed to be freed from "the oppression of silence forced upon them because they were Black and they were women."

In her remarks that day, by way of "sisterly advice," Walker read two poems she had written recently, perhaps for this occasion. One was "Be Nobody's Darling," whose first stanza is the epigraph for this chapter. In the other, titled "Reassurance," she offers advice to young people who would change the world. In both poems, she describes something like Keats's "negative capability," the drive to set out alone on a dark and measureless path toward some dimly imagined place of clarity.

> I must love the questions
> themselves
> as Rilke said
> like locked rooms
> full of treasure
> to which my blind
> and groping key
> does not yet fit.
> and await the answers
> as unsealed
> letters
> mailed with dubious intent
> and written in a very foreign
> tongue.
> and in the hourly making
> of myself
> no thought of Time
> to force, to squeeze
> the space
> I grow into.

CIVIL RIGHTS

The War After the Wars

*African American GIs and the
long history of Black Power*

———

What happens to a dream deferred?
Does it dry up
Like a raisin in the sun?
Or fester like a sore—
And then run?
Does it stink like rotten meat?
Or crust and sugar over—
Like a syrupy sweet?

Maybe it just sags
Like a heavy load.

Or does it explode?

—"Harlem," Langston Hughes,
Montage of a Dream Deferred, 1951

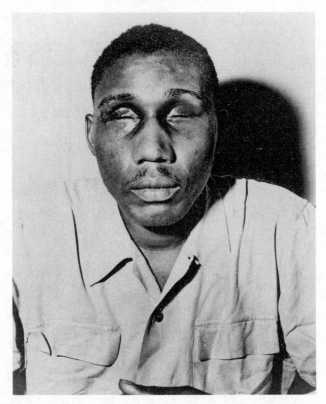

In February 1946, as he made his way home from the war, Tech Sgt. Isaac Woodard was blinded by the police chief of Batesburg, South Carolina, for failing to address him as "sir" and for looking him in the eye.

On February 12, 1946, after three years in the Army and the last 15 months in the Pacific, Isaac Woodard picked up his honorable discharge papers at Camp Gordon, Georgia. He had served with the segregated 429th Port Battalion in the Philippines and New Guinea until the end of the war. He enlisted as a private and came home as a decorated tech sergeant.

Once he had his papers, he boarded a public bus with other Black and white soldiers and a few local civilians. For the first time in three years, he was going home to Winnsboro, South Carolina, where his family had lived for generations and where his wife, Rosa, was waiting for him. They had married not long before he was drafted and had not seen each other since the day he left. He would not see her this day either, because it was his misfortune to be a Black man in full uniform, with sergeant's stripes and medals, back in the unreconstructed Jim Crow South.

A large majority of the million-plus African American troops in World War II came home to the South, where Black soldiers' homecomings were better known for insults, threats, and guns than the thanks of a grateful nation. Despite the cautionary example of Black GIs after World War I, who were given less than no credit for their service, the World War II generation thought this time would be different. The war had created bonds that crossed the color barrier, connecting Black soldiers to the people they fought for and those they fought beside. The memory of what that felt like—what General Colin Powell later called "a breath of freedom"—changed them, just as the unchanged racists in their unchanged nation expected it might.

At a stop for gas, Woodard asked the driver if he could get off and use the bathroom. Greyhound drivers were told to accommodate such requests, but this one did not. "Hell no, God damn it, go back and sit down. I ain't got time to wait." Woodard responded in kind—"God damn it, talk to me like I am talking to you. I am a man, just like you!" At that, the driver told Woodard to go ahead, but he did not leave it there. At the next stop, in Batesburg, South Carolina, the bus was met by the town's entire police force, which consisted of Chief Lynwood Shull and Officer Elliot Long.

The driver told Woodard to get off the bus to talk to them. He had just started explaining himself when Shull told him to "shut up" and hit him in the head with his police baton, a special club that came with a head filled with metal for extra weight and a spring-loaded handle for force of impact. Shull then put Woodard under arrest, twisted his arm behind him, and started walking him to the town jail. When they rounded a corner, out of sight of the bus, Shull asked him if he had just been discharged from the Army. When he said, "Yes," Shull started beating him again, saying the correct answer was "Yes, *sir*." At that, Woodard fought back and managed to get control of the club, but just then Officer Long appeared with his gun drawn and told him to drop it, "or I will drop you."

When Shull got his baton back, he beat Woodard with it harder than before, so hard he broke it and left Woodard briefly unconscious. When Woodard regained consciousness and tried to get to his feet, Shull began beating him again and dragged him to jail.

At some point during their struggle, Shull ground his baton precisely into each of Woodard's eyes, blinding him for the rest of his life. It was a particularly eloquent brutality, suggesting that Woodard had forgotten or consciously violated the Jim Crow code that prohibited looking white people in the eye. In any case, Shull's intent was clear, as a later ophthalmology report concluded: There was hemorrhaging and pus behind both of Woodard's eyelids, but his nose was undamaged. The prognosis for the return of his eyesight was unequivocal: "hopeless."

Before taking him from his cell the next morning, Shull wiped all the dried blood off his face, then walked him to the courtroom of Judge H. E. Quarles, who was also the mayor of Batesburg. Woodard was charged with "disorderly conduct." He had no lawyer or witnesses with him that day, and the word of a Black man carried less than no weight against that of a police chief. As soon as Shull told the judge that Woodard had grabbed his police baton, the judge declared him guilty ("We don't go for that kind of thing around here") and said he could pay a $50 fine or serve 30 days in jail. Woodard had $44, the judge waived the $6, and with that he was free to go, except of course he was blind. On a doctor's advice, Shull dropped him off at the Veterans Administration hospital in Columbia, South Carolina, where he spent the next two months. His wife left him as soon as she learned that he was blind, and when he was able to leave the hospital, his sisters picked him up and brought him to their father's house in the Bronx.

What Woodard suffered after the war was not the worst violence that met African American soldiers, who came home hoping more for than just a breath of freedom. The betrayal of that hope prompted every response Langston Hughes imagined in 1951: It festered, it stank, it exploded, and it did so with special force because it had happened more than once before. After Emancipation in 1863, Black men enlisted for the Civil War by the thousands. Frederick Douglass heartily approved: "Once let the black man get upon his person the brass letters, U.S., let him get an eagle on his button, and a musket on his shoulder, and bullets in his pocket, and there is not power on earth which can deny that he had earned the rights to citizenship in the United States." Reconstruction suggested he was right, but Lincoln's successor and the rise of the Ku Klux Klan helped put a violent end to that.

When the U.S. entered the First World War, NAACP cofounder W. E. B. DuBois followed Douglass's lead, urging African Americans to enlist—to "close our ranks shoulder to shoulder with our own white fellow citizens" in order to demonstrate their patriotism, their courage, and the right to equal standing in American society. Once again, that hope was crushed by violence. Inspired by D. W. Griffith's virulent

The Birth of a Nation, the Klan swelled from thousands of members to millions, and the prospect of Black soldiers emboldened by their service—in the word of the moment, "biggety"—inspired a wave of racist violence. In 1919, Black men were lynched at a rate of one every five days. No victim was a more inviting target than the Black man in uniform, who was presumed to have slept with white women in Europe and so invoked the white supremacist's nightmare vision of "social equality." Among the first to return from the Great War to Blakely, Georgia, Pfc. Wilbur Little was met by a group of whites as soon as he stepped off the train. They forced him to strip off his uniform and warned him he would be killed if he ever wore it in public again. A few days later, he was found in uniform and murdered. For all the service and lives they gave in war, as one Black newspaper put it, "It seems that the Negro's particular decoration is to be the 'double-cross.'"

On the other hand, they came home trained for war. Between the spring and fall of 1919, race riots broke out in more than 20 cities in the North and South. The first outbreak came in Washington, D.C., where Black veterans created a security cordon around Howard University and occupied the rooftops of Black neighborhoods, waiting in ambush for a band of Navy sailors who had been on a days-long spree of drunken violence, snatching Black citizens from the street and lynching them for no reason at all. In that "Red Summer" of 1919 most of the riots were started by whites—in the North most often over jobs and housing, in the South to reinvigorate Jim Crow justice and shore up white supremacy. But Black veterans were not easily cowed, and they inspired in others the determination to use force in their fight for freedom and equality.

Twenty-seven years later, driven by the same anger over their scorned sacrifices, Black veterans of World War II set out to do the same.

*   *   *

Until the late twentieth century, the story of the civil rights movement was neatly bordered by the Supreme Court's decision in *Brown v. Board of Education* in 1954 and the Voting Rights Act of 1965. By the start of the twenty-first century, however, the historians Jacquelyn Dowd Hall, Athena Mutua, Nikhil Pal Singh, and others called for retrieving a longer history of the movement. Reframed as the Black Freedom Struggle, that story included racial injustices and Black responses going back to the time of slavery and ahead to the present day.

One of the tensions resolved in this recast history was between nonviolent and violent resistance. In the classic *Brown*-to-Voting-Rights-Act timeline, they appeared to be hotly debated alternatives. In the longer view, nonviolence and armed resistance were joined in tactical alliance, which had a long history of its own. In the early 1900s, W. E. B. Du Bois, Marcus Garvey, and untold numbers of other Black citizens accepted as fact that the Klan and other white terrorists would have to be met with force. Rosa Parks was six years old when the last Black veterans of World War I came home to Alabama, and she never forgot sitting up nights with her grandfather, who kept a shotgun on his lap, waiting for the Klan. She remembered him saying, "I don't know how long I would last if they came breaking in here, but I'm getting the first one who comes through the door." She stayed up with him because "I wanted to see it," she said. "I wanted to see him shoot that gun."

After World War II, Black veterans were among the leaders in every civil rights organization in the South, from Sgt. Medgar Evers, Sgt. Aaron Henry, and Cpl. Amzie Moore of the Mississippi NAACP and Sgt. Hosea Williams of the Southern Christian Leadership Conference in Georgia to Sgt. Robert F. Williams, who actually transformed a North Carolina chapter of the NAACP into a well-trained militia. All of these and many other leaders kept guns close at hand at all times. Even Martin Luther King's home was sometimes transformed into an armory. Bob Moses, who led the work of the Student Nonviolent Coordinating Committee in Mississippi, accepted armed self-defense as a fact of life. "Self-defense is so deeply ingrained in rural southern America that we as a small group can't affect it," he said. "It's not contradictory for a farmer to say that he's nonviolent and also to pledge to shoot a marauder's head off." Among Black veterans of World War II and in the longer history of the Black Freedom Movement, nonviolence without the threat of armed resistance to racist violence amounted to surrender.

As soon as he graduated high school in 1943, Medgar Evers enlisted in the Army. He saw combat from D-Day to the end of the war in Europe, including service with the famous "Red Ball Express."

Two weeks after Woodard was blinded, a group of Black veterans in Columbia, Tennessee, took up arms against local police after an altercation between a white store clerk and a Black woman. The woman's son, a recently discharged Navy veteran, intervened, and the ensuing scuffle ended when he threw the clerk through the shop window. The son and his mother were each fined $50 for disturbing the peace, but the clerk's father insisted the veteran be charged with attempted murder.

That night, a white mob gathered in the business district where the incident had taken place. Black veterans were waiting for them, and they shot out the streetlights for cover. As four policemen approached, they were warned to stop, and when they kept coming the veterans opened fire, wounding all of them, only one seriously, but effectively eliminating half of the Columbia police force. In the next few hours, highway patrolmen and state guardsmen surrounded the area. The next morning, they moved in and indiscriminately arrested close to a hundred Black men, many more than had had any part in the standoff. Twenty-five were eventually charged with attempted murder, but only two were ever tried, and only one of them was convicted, thanks to the work of a defense team led by the NAACP's Thurgood Marshall. When the trial was over, Marshall was followed and arrested by Columbia police on a patently false charge. They drove him to a remote, wooded area, and he was saved from lynching only by a brave colleague who followed the police car close behind and was ultimately able to drive away with him.

George Dorsey, a veteran of the war in the Pacific, also became a target just after his discharge. His crime was sheltering his brother-in-law, a sharecropper who got into an altercation that ended when he stabbed the son of his landlord. The son survived, but sometime later, Dorsey, the brother-in-law, and their wives were driven into a mob ambush, and all of them were murdered. "Up until George went into the Army, he was a good n----r," one of the suspected assassins said later, "but when he came out, they thought they were as good as any white people." No one was ever convicted or accused of the murders.

In an Oval Office meeting some weeks later, the NAACP's longtime executive secretary Walter White and other Black leaders told the new president, Harry Truman, about the blinding of Isaac Woodard, the murder of George Dorsey, and other racially motivated attacks on Black veterans. Truman had been a captain during World War I in France, and the bloodshed he saw and casualties his unit took gave him a strong bond with the millions of soldiers who were just then returning from World War II. Truman was facing midterm elections at the time, and his polls were discouraging, especially in the South. Even so, he could not ignore what he heard. He was especially moved by the Woodard case, and he was never much for polls anyway. "I wonder how far Moses would have gone if he'd taken a poll in Egypt," he wrote in a memo around that time. That midterm election turned out to be diastrous for Democrats in both houses, but there is no record that Truman ever regretted his decision to respond forcefully to what he heard that day.

After his meeting with the civil rights leaders, he wrote to his attorney general, Tom Clark, saying he was "very much alarmed at the increased racial feeling all over the country, and I am wondering if it wouldn't be well to appoint a commission to analyze the situation." Later, he announced just such a commission, and the Justice Department actually leveled criminal charges against Batesburg police chief Lynwood Shull. One year later, by then facing reelection himself, Truman released his commission's ambitious, no-nonsense report, *To Secure These Rights,* and he gave his full support to its agenda, which included long-stalled anti-lynching legislation; abolition of the poll tax; laws to ensure equal access to housing, education, and health care; and an extension of the wartime Fair Employment Practices Committee, whose job was to guarantee equal access to jobs.

That won Truman few friends in his home state of Missouri or with southern Democrats in Congress. A letter from an old friend in Kansas City told him to "let the South take care of the N-----s . . . and if the N-----s do not like the Southern treatment let them come to Mrs. Roosevelt."

Truman's response was blunt. "The main difficulty with the South," he wrote, "is that they are living eighty years behind the times and the sooner they come out of it the better it will be for the country and themselves.

> I am not asking for social equality, because no such thing exists, but I am asking for equality of opportunity for all human beings and, as long as I stay here, I am going to continue that fight. . . . When a Mayor and a City Marshal [*sic*] can take a Negro Sergeant off a bus in South Carolina, beat him up and put out his eyes, and nothing is done about it by the State Authorities, something is radically wrong with the system.

*   *   *

For the 1946 midterm elections in the South, there was no issue more flammable than the right to vote. Two years before, in the case of *Smith v. Allwright*, the Supreme Court had declared the South's all-white primaries to be unconstitutional. With the Great Migration to the North, the Black vote could now theoretically swing the electoral vote in 16 states. Inspired by the Supreme Court decision and the prospect of changing the racial balance of power, Black veterans led voter-registration drives all across the South. In Georgia, more than a thousand Black veterans engaged in a statewide, door-to-door campaign whose greatest ambition was to turn out the racist three-term governor, Eugene Talmadge. By the day of Georgia's primary, July 17, they had managed to register 135,000 new Black voters, but thanks to intimidation, primary-day trickery, and illegal ballot purges, at least 50,000 Black votes were uncounted. Statewide, 98 percent of the African American vote went to Talmadge's opponents, but he won anyway, even in 33 Georgia counties where Black citizens were in the majority. In 14 of those counties there were no Black votes counted at all. The first African American who had ever cast a primary vote in Taylor County, Army Pvt. Maceo Snipes, was shot two days later and died in the hospital, having been refused a transfusion because there was no "Negro blood" on hand.

In the even more racially inflamed state of Mississippi, Army Sgt. Medgar Evers was determined to vote in that year's primary. He had been discharged only three months before, after a tour of duty that ran from D-Day to the Battle of the Bulge. Like others who survived the landing on Omaha Beach, he had waded through a sea of dead bodies, Black and white, toward a beach covered with casualties. Though he saw a great deal more bloodshed during his years in Europe, that memory would never leave him, and it fed his fury at the homecoming that he and his fellow veterans received. On his way home, with his discharge papers in hand and still in a uniform decorated for his service in combat, he had to sit at the back of the bus. On the same ride, for the first time since he had left the U.S. for France, he was refused service at a restaurant.

To understand just how deep the resentment and pain of returning veterans could go, James Baldwin wrote in *The Fire Next Time,*

> You must put yourself in the skin of a man who is wearing the uniform of his country, who watches German prisoners of war being treated by Americans with more human dignity than he has ever received at their hands. And who, at the same time, as a human being, is far freer in a strange land than he has ever been at home. Home! The very word begins to have a despairing and diabolical ring. You must consider what happens to this citizen, after all he has endured, when he returns—home: search, in his shoes, for a job, for a place to live; ride, in his skin, on segregated buses; see, with his eyes, the signs saying "White" and "Colored" and look into the eyes of his wife; look into the eyes of his son; listen, with his ears, to political speeches, North and South; imagine yourself being told to "wait."

Medgar Evers was beyond angry, and he was well prepared for a fight. He identified closely with the overthrow of colonial powers in Africa and actually began amassing an arsenal with his brother, Charles, for a war on white supremacy at home. In time, they abandoned the plan, but the anger remained.

For a Black man or woman, trying to vote in the Mississippi of 1946 was an audacious, dangerous, and likely futile undertaking. During the war, among the 900 registered voters in Evers's hometown of Decatur, not one was Black. No Black person had even tried to vote there before. The Evers brothers had been able to register only because all GIs were exempted from the poll tax that year, but in the days leading up to the election, their parents were visited by white locals warning them to get their sons to stay away from the polls on Election Day. Their parents did not try to talk Medgar or Charles out of going, but they did let them know of the threats.

Walking to the courthouse to vote, Medgar and Charles shared the fondest hope of other Black citizens in Mississippi that day: to defeat the outspokenly racist two-term U.S. senator Theodore Bilbo. Bilbo knew that, of course, and he used it to incite his supporters to keep Black citizens from voting. As the election neared, in case they missed the point, he said: "I call for every red-blooded white man to use any means to keep the n----r away from the polls. If you don't understand what that means you are just plain dumb." The best way, Bilbo added helpfully, was "to see him the night before." The *Jackson Daily News* said much the same in an Election Day story headlined simply, "DON'T TRY IT."

When the Evers brothers and a few fellow vets reached the polling place that day, they were surrounded by a group of armed white men. Among them were a few they had known as boys. Another was the doctor who had delivered them. "Dr. Jack, I'm surprised at you," Charles Evers said. "You the person that brought us here, and you're standing there trying to deny me the right to vote." The doctor's response, he remembered, was that there were just "some things that n-----s ain't supposed to do." Evers and company regrouped, went home, and armed themselves, but when they returned the crowd arrayed against them had grown. Outnumbered and outgunned, they gave up and started walking home, accompanied all the way by a carful of white men, one of whom kept a shotgun trained on them. "Around town, Negroes said we had been whipped, beaten up, and run out of town," Medgar Evers recalled. "Well, in a way we were whipped, I guess, but I made up my mind then that it would not be like that again, at least not for me."

*   *   *

In that midterm election of 1946, Congress made a hard right turn. Democrats lost 54 seats in the House and 11 in the Senate, and Republicans took over Congress for the first time since FDR's first election in 1932. Among the freshmen of the 80th Congress were Rep. Richard Nixon and Sen. Joseph McCarthy, whose witch-hunting would do so much to sharpen the edges of American politics. Yet even on that Election Day there were signs of hope.

Despite his call to threaten or murder would-be Black voters, Bilbo won reelection to a third term in the Senate by his narrowest margin yet. The NAACP led a campaign to have him disqualified for having conspired to disenfranchise Black voters, and, remarkably, a Senate subcommittee actually held several days of hearings on the issue in Jackson. Almost 200 Black veterans crammed the hearing room and were virtually all the witnesses against him, even though they knew their protest had almost no chance to prevail. Witnesses ostensibly on his side included county registrars who testified without embarrassment about how they prevented Black citizens from registering—by requiring white references, by holding them to a higher literacy standard than whites, by asking them to explain the most obscure clauses in the state constitution, or just by giving them "good advice" not to register. The outcome of the hearings was as expected, but as the historian Charles Payne noted, the Black veterans who turned out for the chance to testify represented "perhaps the most significant act of public defiance from Negroes the state had seen in decades." And in the end, Bilbo never got his third term because he died before the new Congress began—a poetically just death, some observed, from cancer of the mouth. "Few would predict in the winter of 1946 that victory was in sight," John Dittmer wrote in his luminous history of Mississippi's civil rights struggle, *Local People,* "but in that crowded federal courtroom in Jackson the shock troops of the modern civil rights movement had fired their opening salvo."

Another hopeful sign appeared that election day in Charleston, South Carolina, when, in the courtroom of Judge Julius Waties Waring, the police chief who blinded Isaac Woodard actually came to trial. What had happened to Woodard was by then a cause célèbre. He had done a national speaking tour sponsored by the NAACP, and his case had won the support of Orson Welles, who returned to the subject repeatedly on his popular radio show. The trial did not have to be held on that Election Day. The federal prosecutor assigned to the case actually petitioned Waring for a continuance, saying he had not had enough time to prepare. Waring denied his request, suspecting that the case would be dropped right after the election and had only been filed as a cynical play for Black votes. "I do not believe that this poor blinded creature should be a football in the contest between box office and ballot box," he wrote to himself at the time.

Waring was a lifelong resident of Charleston, the son of one of its first families, whose ancestors settled there in the seventeenth century. He was also a power in the state Democratic Party, at least until his rulings began to diverge from community standards, especially with regard to its Black citizens. Waring's later rulings were inspired in part by the Shull trial, which ended after the Justice Department's local prosecutor actually apologized in his closing statement to the all-white jury, saying he was just doing his job. After Waring gave his instructions to the jury, he took a long walk, just to make sure the jurors would have to wait for their acquittal. When he returned, he announced the verdict from the bench without evident disgust, but his wife, who was sitting in the courtroom, broke down in tears.

From that case onward, Waring departed radically from his friends, family, and judicial peers, doing everything he could to dismantle the formal and informal ways in which Black citizens were denied their rights. He opposed the southern states' attempt to bring back the white primary with his decision in *Elmore v. Rice*, and his shocking dissent in a key school desegregation case, *Briggs v. Elliott*, helped Thurgood Marshall frame his argument in *Brown v. Board of Education*. He also made changes in his court—hiring the first Black bailiff in South Carolina history, integrating his courtroom gallery—and in his everyday behavior, welcoming Black citizens to his home, his dinner table, and his circle of friends.

His rulings for civil rights cost him political allies, old friends, and even extended family members in Charleston. Both he and his wife became social outcasts and targets of the Klan, who firebombed their home one night as they ate dinner. They were not injured, but in 1952, when Waring retired from the bench, the couple moved to New York City, where they made their home for the rest of their lives. Waring returned to Charleston briefly in 1954 for an NAACP-sponsored celebration of the *Brown* decision but not again until he was buried there in 1968. His burial site was set apart from those of his family, and very few whites turned up for the service, but it was attended by a large crowd of African Americans.

*   *   *

By the time he tried to vote, Medgar Evers had already enrolled at Mississippi's Alcorn Agricultural and Mechanical College, where he earned his BA in business administration and showed just how ambitious he was to do more. A scholar-athlete, he made dean's list grades while being editor of the college newspaper and yearbook, playing varsity football and track, and becoming president of his junior class. While excelling at all of the above, he fell in love with a classmate, Myrlie Beasley.

Before he asked her to marry him, he told her all the reasons they should stop seeing each other—for instance, that she should keep her freedom and not tie herself down to an older man. She thought he was breaking up with her of course, and as he went on, she became furious. "How kind of you to think about me!" she said. "Is there someone else?" No, he said, "It's for your benefit." At that, she tore into him, and when she was finished, he produced a diamond engagement ring. She was still furious, but they were married shortly after.

His mother warned Myrlie that Medgar had always been "a little strange." As a boy, she said, he had always been quiet and contemplative, always somewhere else, caught up in his thoughts. "I don't want you to get upset with him if he pulls away from you," Mrs. Evers told Myrlie,

> because it won't be because he doesn't love you, but that's just the way he is. . . . He's my strange child. . . . He needs to be by himself at times. . . . Sometimes I look out the window and I see them all out there playing, and I look again a few minutes later and he's nowhere to be found and I'd go out and I'd look for him and I'd find him in his favorite spot under the house. And I asked him . . . what's wrong? [And] he'd say, "nothing, Mama, I'm just thinking."

When they graduated in 1952, Evers was taken on as a protégé of T. R. M. Howard, a wealthy physician in the Delta town of Mound Bayou. In addition to his large medical practice, Howard owned a farm, a construction firm, and the Magnolia Mutual Life Insurance Company, where he gave Evers a job as a salesman and introduced him to the world of civil rights activism. The year before, Howard had founded the Regional Council of Negro Leadership (RCNL), a group that organized itself uniquely as a civil rights group with the means for self-defense and mutual protection. Because Black men who worked for whites could not join the RCNL without jeopardizing their livelihoods, Howard recruited Black veterans who owned their own businesses to run the organization. One of them was Amzie Moore, who owned a gas station in Cleveland. Another was Aaron Henry, a pharmacist with a drug store in Clarksdale.

He hired Evers to sell insurance to Delta sharecroppers, who like all agricultural workers were ineligible for Social Security benefits. During long days making sales calls and collecting premiums, he listened to their struggles, counseled them, and brought their stories home to Myrlie. Decatur was only 175 miles from his new home in the Delta, but the plantations were a world neither of them had ever known, a world where debt kept families in bondage to the owner of the land and where entire families, including young children, worked from before dawn to after dark. The sharecroppers' children had no shoes, and their homes were not even shacks. Evers passed by many of them at first, thinking no one could possibly be living there. Families got their meager food and clothes from a local store, often belonging to the plantation owner, where they bought on the "furnish" they were given at the start of the growing season. At the end of the season, their "share" would often be calculated at whatever would keep them short of paying it back. Many were illiterate and bookkeeping was loose, so the sharecroppers' debt could be whatever the plantation owner said it was. In any case, they were in no position to argue, since there were always other Black families willing to take their place. The slightest sign of self-assertion could lead to a beating, and failed escapes could lead to the end of a rope.

After that first summer of 1952, with Howard's approval and despite the risks, Evers began spending less of his time selling insurance and more of it helping sharecroppers escape through Memphis to the North by various ingenious means, once even in a casket. He volunteered with the NAACP to sign up new members, at first with very little success, but over time he, Amzie Moore, and Aaron Henry managed to revive the chapters in Mound Bayou, Cleveland, and Clarksdale respectively.

Inspired by Jomo Kenyatta's defiance of colonial forces in the fight for Kenya's sovereignty, Evers began to fantasize again about forming a secret army of Black guerrillas in the South. At the end of 1952, Myrlie was pregnant with their first child, and he wanted a son he could name Kenyatta. He got the son in July 1953, but Myrlie named him Darrell on the birth certificate, moving Kenyatta to his middle name.

By then, she wrote later, her husband had become radicalized, at least by Mississippi standards at the time. One night at a meeting of the RCNL, he declared his intention to integrate the law school at the University of Mississippi—nine years before James Meredith finally managed to integrate Ole Miss, and then only with the aid of federal troops. Over the objections of his wife, her parents, and his own, Evers pursued admission to that bastion of the white South relentlessly. His assault made headlines in both white and Black newspapers, with special note of the fact that the NAACP's top lawyer, Thurgood Marshall, represented him in the attempt. The process dragged for more than a year as university officials manipulated the admission criteria to meet their desired end, but his persistence in the face of every barrier and threat brought him to the attention of the NAACP's national leadership. It also got the attention of the FBI.

Then, in the spring of 1954, the Supreme Court's landmark decision in *Brown v. Board of Education* ordered the South's "separate but equal" schools to be integrated, and the white South's reaction verged on hysteria. Two months after "Black Monday," as the date of the first *Brown* decision came to be known in the states of the old Confederacy, 14 men met in Indianola, Mississippi, and started the first White Citizens' Council, a Klan without robes, which spread quickly across the South and beyond. Eventually the State of Mississippi covertly funded its state council, whose gentler methods of foiling integration included tactical firings, calling in loans, and boycotts of Black-owned businesses. The measures most feared, taken in concert with the Klan, were shootings, firebombings, rape, and lynching.

Before this, the NAACP had been reluctant to have a presence in Mississippi because of the danger, but the upsurge in race-motivated crime also opened new opportunities for litigation. Five months after the *Brown* decision, Evers was rejected by Ole Miss on the basis of admission requirements newly invented for that purpose, but because of the courage he had shown in his campaign, he was appointed the NAACP's first field secretary in Mississippi. His responsibilities included building up the state's branches, reporting crimes against Mississippi's Black citizens to NAACP headquarters, and investigating the crimes as needed. That of course made him a target of the Klan and the White Citizens' Councils. After that he carried a .45 revolver with him when he traveled around the state and slept with a shotgun at the foot of his bed. He also built up a small armory at home to protect his family in the event of attack. T. R. M. Howard's property had by then become an arsenal, and Amzie Moore's house in Cleveland was another one. At times of tension, their homes were lit up like daylight all night long.

Evers opened the NAACP's headquarters in Jackson in January 1955, at the start of never-ending days trying to do the impossible. One of his jobs was to convince Black victims to bring charges against white rapists, vigilantes, and murderers: in other words, to put their jobs, livelihoods, and lives on the line as soon as their names turned up on the NAACP's membership rolls, which were published regularly in local newspapers as "a public service of the Citizens' Council." And all he could promise in return was the NAACP's legal support in cases with little chance of winning. Evers's job also included circulating petitions calling for school desegregation. Not surprisingly, most of those who signed withdrew their names after threats of economic or violent retaliation. In Yazoo City, for example, 51 of the 53 people who signed such a petition withdrew their names. The other two left the state.

What bothered Evers more than those who feared the consequences were the quislings, the Blacks in white pockets, who accepted "the way things are" and said that nothing could be done about it, that whites had always won and always would. Since the Supreme Court had now clearly denied that, in *Brown* and related cases, Evers considered this complacency a kind of racial treason.

The *Brown* decision met a wall of official defiance in the South even before the second decision in the case, which defined the standard for progress in implementation as "all deliberate speed" and called for "a prompt and reasonable start." Two months before that, more than a hundred southern members of Congress had signed what came to be known as the Southern Manifesto, which promised to defy the attempt of any branch of the federal government to override state laws on segregation. That brought "deliberate speed" to a dead stop. Two years after *Brown*, there was not a single integrated school in eight southern states.

At the same time, across the South, the White Citizens' Council and the Klan mounted ever more determined attacks on civil rights initiatives and the NAACP, which shrank dramatically as its members' homes were firebombed, whole neighborhoods were burned out, and civil rights activists were tortured and killed. Preachers and schoolteachers were beaten and murdered just for speaking well of integration. It was a time of cross burnings and night riders, a virtual 1950s remake of *The Birth of a Nation*, complete with the Klan's vivid, self-induced fantasy of rapacious Black men hungry for white women.

By the time Evers opened the NAACP headquarters in Jackson, Mississippi, civil rights activism focused on racial violence and the registration of Black voters. One of Evers's branches was in Belzoni, where the most prominent members were the Rev. George Lee and branch president Gus Courts. Lee was the first Black man since Reconstruction to become eligible to vote in that county, and between 1953 and 1954 he and Courts managed to get as many as a hundred more Black men on the rolls. None had yet managed to vote, however.

One afternoon in April 1955, after another conversation with Courts about how to change that, Lee said he had just been warned in writing to take his name off the rolls, or else. He had been warned before, but never in writing, and he told Courts he had "a feeling" that things were about to get violent. Late that night, as he was driving through Belzoni's Black neighborhood, he was hit twice by a shotgun. His car ran out of control and crashed into a shack. He managed to crawl out of the car, and a taxi driver who heard the shots came to rescue him, but he died before he reached the hospital. The next day, Courts was told face-to-face that he would be next. His response was to accompany 22 would-be Black voters to the county courthouse to ask for absentee ballots, the safer way to vote. He was shot sometime later but not killed, and with the NAACP's help, he moved to Chicago.

Not long after that, another Belzoni activist, Lamar Smith, walked out of the Lincoln County Courthouse, where he was teaching Black voters how to fill out absentee ballots. He was shot and killed on the courthouse's front lawn. There were dozens of witnesses to the shooting, including the local sheriff. Though the FBI investigated all the murders, no one was ever charged, much less convicted of the crimes.

Evers was still investigating Smith's death when, in the tiny Delta town of Money, Mississippi, 14-year-old Emmett Till bragged to some friends about having a white girlfriend back in Chicago. He said he wasn't as scared of that as they seemed to be, so they challenged him to talk to the pretty young white woman behind a store counter. Apparently he did, but it was never quite clear just what he said or what happened there. The woman, Carolyn Bryant, testified to a grand jury that he had grabbed her around the waist and uttered obscenities. (Decades later, she confessed that she was lying about that.) She also claimed she had said nothing about the event to her husband, but someone must have said something, because he responded in the worst southern tradition. He and his half-brother found Till, tortured him, tied him up, weighted him down, and threw him to his death by drowning in the Tallahatchie River.

The Emmett Till case presented Evers with his greatest challenge to date. The first was simply managing to keep the case alive when local authorities were determined to make it go away. Evers gathered evidence, found witnesses, identified suspects, and laid the basis for a prosecution. In the end, the grand jury refused to issue indictments, and a few months later, confident that they would never be brought to trial or charged again, Till's murderers sold their vividly appalling account of the crime to *Look* magazine.

Months before it was published, however, Evers had transformed Emmett Till from the pitiful victim in a sensational story to the case in point for a historic reckoning, thanks in no small part to a photo. He had seen the effect of an open casket at the funeral of Rev. Lee, where people could not mourn without witnessing firsthand the brutality of his murder. As a result, he persuaded Till's mother to leave her son's casket open to mourners and to let in a few photographers, including one from *Jet* magazine. To the nation and around the world, David Jackson's picture of Till's wrecked, bloated body became an icon of America's original sin.

The Till murder only tightened the spiral of racial violence in Mississippi. Membership in the state's White Citizens' Council swelled to 60,000 members, Klan activity surged, and Evers and other RCNL members joined hands in a virtual paramilitary force. T. R. M. Howard began sleeping with a machine gun, his home became an armory, and guards accompanied him as he embarked on a nationwide speaking tour to spread outrage at the murders in Mississippi and to raise a public outcry for some federal response.

Two weeks after the grand jury refused to indict Till's killers, Howard's tour reached Montgomery, Alabama, where he spoke to a mass meeting at the Dexter Avenue Baptist Church. The new pastor, the 26-year-old, as yet unknown Martin Luther King Jr., was there, and so was Rosa Parks, by now a seasoned investigator for the NAACP and no stranger to the most awful forms of racist violence. Howard and others spoke about the murders of Rev. Lee, Lamar Smith, and others, but Parks later remembered being particularly "disgusted" by what she heard about Emmett Till that night. Four days later, on her way home from work on the night of December 1, 1955, she kept her seat on the bus—not because she had sore feet, as the story sometimes went, but because she had had enough. As Dr. King put it on the first night of the Montgomery Bus Boycott, in his informal inauguration as leader of the civil rights movement, "There comes a time when people get tired."

*   *   *

Drafted by the Army too late to fight in World War II, Robert F. Williams enlisted in the Marine Corps ten years later. His only battles then were with his commanding officer, but he learned combat skills he would deploy against the Klan back home.

Around the time Emmett Till was murdered, Robert F. Williams had just been dishonorably discharged from the Marine Corps after a fight with his commanding officer. It was his second tour of duty, this one his solution to a long period of unemployment. He had been drafted almost a decade before, but he started his service just a month before Hiroshima, and he was mustered out within the year. By the time he joined the Marine Corps, it was desegregated in theory but not yet in spirit, and Williams's instinctive response to racial insult was to fight. As a result, that two-year stint was a series of verbal and physical confrontations that earned him months of brig time and other disciplinary actions until he was finally booted out.

Between tours, back home in Monroe, North Carolina, after V-J Day, he and some fellow veterans went to war with the Klan. A boyhood friend of theirs, Bennie Montgomery, had gotten into a fight that left his landlord dead. Arrested and spirited away by authorities to protect him from a lynch mob, he was convicted of murder, executed, and returned to Monroe for burial. When the Klan made it known they were coming for the body, Williams recruited his friends to make a stand outside the funeral home and stop them. The gunfight never happened because when the line of cars filled with Klansmen drove up, they faced 40 Black men with rifles and just kept driving. "That was one of the first incidents," Williams wrote later. "That really started us to understanding that we had to resist, and that resistance could be effective if we resisted in groups, and if we resisted with guns."

By the time Williams was released by the Marine Corps and returned to Monroe, however, the local White Citizens' Council had managed to reduce the local NAACP membership to six brave souls—and as soon as they admitted Williams, five of the six quit. The one who stayed was a World War I veteran named Dr. Albert Perry. A militant advocate for civil rights, Perry was already a prime target of the Klan. Williams made him his vice president and began looking for members.

The NAACP's most common target for membership was the Black middle class, but Williams began at the town's pool hall and barber shop. His recruits were "laborers, farmers, domestic workers, the unemployed and any and all Negro people in the area," he wrote later. He also applied to the National Rifle Association to form a local shooting club. Its first members were his fellow veterans, including three of the men who had stood beside him to protect their friend's body from the Klan. He dubbed Monroe's newest NRA chapter the Black Armed Guard. He needed that core of veterans, he said, because he needed people "who didn't scare easy."

In another cycle of progress and violence, the success of the Montgomery Bus Boycott at the end of 1956 encouraged more Black activism, which in turn invited more action by the Klan. In Monroe, the worst of the trouble began in the summer of 1957, when yet another Black child drowned in yet another local swimming hole because the one public pool was for whites only. The city refused to set aside even one day a week for Black children to use the pool, arguing that the water would have to be drained and replaced each time they used it. So Williams and Perry organized protests, which lost them the few white supporters they had.

Some of Monroe's white citizens drew up a petition declaring that both Williams and Perry should be forced to move out of Monroe "with all deliberate speed," having "proven themselves unworthy of living in our City and County." Carloads of Klansmen began shooting their way through Black neighborhoods, taking especially careful aim at Williams's and Perry's houses. The Klan caravans were invariably preceded by police cars—just to keep order, said the chief of police, who was a Klan member himself. Williams, Perry, and others in the chapter received regular death threats as Klan membership and attendance at Klan rallies enjoyed a new growth spurt. "A n----r who wants to go to a white swimming pool is not looking for a bath," Klan leader Catfish Cole told one such rally. "He is looking for a funeral."

A telephoned bomb threat to Perry's wife when he was at an NAACP meeting was the turning point. The meeting quickly adjourned, members went home to grab their guns, and after that they guarded Perry's home 24 hours a day. Eventually their number grew to 60 men, and when the next Klan motorcade came to shoot up Perry's house, they faced a withering barrage from makeshift fortifications and sniper positions. "We shot it out with the Klan and repelled their attack," Williams said, "and the Klan didn't have any more stomach for this type of fight. They stopped raiding our community."

Decades later, B. J. Winfield, one of Williams's oldest veteran comrades in Monroe, talked about the effect of his leadership, that night and later:

> The Black man had been thinking it all the time, but too scared to say it, scared to do anything. Rob Williams, after he come out of service, we thought he was talking too much. But after we found out he was getting it from the big book—I mean, it was our rights—then we went with him. After we seen him do all these things and accomplish these things, we said, "Well, he must know what he is talking about."

*   *   *

Not long after Medgar Evers gave up trying to integrate higher education in Mississippi, Clyde Kennard of Hattiesburg tried it again. He too was a veteran, having enlisted in the World War II Army as soon as he graduated high school. By the time he got to Germany the war was over, but his seven years in uniform went on to include service as a combat paratrooper in Korea, where he earned a Bronze Star and other decorations. After his discharge, he enrolled at the University of Chicago as a political science major but had to withdraw before the end of his junior year, when his stepfather died. At that, he returned to Hattiesburg to help his mother start a small chicken farm on land he had bought for her with savings from his wartime pay.

Kennard's time in the military had been relatively free of the problems faced by other Black soldiers. By the time of the German occupation, Black soldiers in Germany actually had some useful benefits, including access to secondary school classes that would serve them well in the peacetime job market. Part of Kennard's service in Germany was to teach a course in democracy to young Germans as part of the "denazification" program, and by the time he got to Korea, Truman's desegregation order had begun to take effect, mainly because of the sudden need for a massive buildup of troops. The post–World War II military had shrunk to 500,000 worldwide, when more than a million would be needed in Korea alone. Training bases in the U.S. were forced to confront the fact that keeping parallel units was going to be all but impossible and so began to integrate the trainees, in bunks and mess halls as well as in classes and drills. To the pleasant surprise of Gen. Omar Bradley, first chairman of the Joint Chiefs of Staff, the transition turned out to be virtually painless, and by the end of 1951 the entire U.S. military was being desegregated.

When he returned to Hattiesburg in 1955, Kennard was a mature, accomplished 28-year-old college student, but he had not lived in Mississippi since he was 12 years old. That was when his mother, for the sake of his education, had sent him to live with an older sister in Chicago. To finish his senior year of college, Kennard decided to apply to Mississippi Southern, which was just a few minutes' drive from home. Given the volume of correspondence between him and the college, he clearly expected reason to prevail, but Southern, like Ole Miss, had been segregated since its founding.

For four years, Kennard kept applying, and the college kept inventing new reasons why he could not be admitted—changing the rules, rejecting him on spurious grounds, making false claims meant to disqualify him, and portraying him as a disruptive malcontent. By the standard of the day, he had encouraged that charge. He had tried to register to vote. He lodged a complaint when a Black school closed near his home, forcing the children to travel 11 miles to another school. He had been to NAACP meetings.

In 1959, the college president, a committee of Black leaders, and even the governor of the state met with him to urge him to give up, but he would not, and Southern had run out of reasons to deny him admission. At that point, his insurance company canceled his policy, his mortgage company foreclosed on his farm, and state investigators searched for dirt in every corner of his past, without success. Finally, the head of the Hattiesburg White Citizens' Council suggested another solution: "Kennard's car could be hit by a train or he could have some accident on the highway, and nobody would ever know the difference."

Instead, he was framed as an accessory to the theft of five bags of chicken feed worth $25, a felony that would disqualify him for admittance to Southern. The real thief, who testified that Kennard had put him up to it, got probation, but the judge gave Kennard the maximum sentence: seven years at hard labor. Evers was quoted in the press calling the verdict "a mockery of justice," for which he was cited for contempt of court, fined $100, and sentenced to 30 days in jail. Evers's conviction would be overturned, but Kennard's was not, and in November 1960 he began serving his sentence at Mississippi's infamous state penitentiary, Parchman Farm.

Kennard had been working six days a week in Parchman's cotton fields for almost a year when chronic stomach pains became increasingly severe, then debilitating. At that, he was sent to a hospital in Jackson, where the pain was traced to a lesion in his colon that was presumed to be malignant. His chance of living another five years was estimated at 20 percent, which turned out to be optimistic. No treatment was prescribed. He was returned to Parchman and to his work in the fields. As he continued to weaken and lose weight, guards made his fellow prisoners carry him out to the field and back every day.

Evers was his close friend by then and led the campaign to free him. One night he was to speak about the case at an NAACP dinner, but he had just been to see Kennard's mother, and as he began to talk about his friend, he had to stop. "Sitting next to him at the head table, I could tell he was choked with emotion," Myrlie remembered. "I prayed he'd be able to continue. Medgar had always looked on crying as a weakness in men. Over and over he had told Darrell, 'Men don't cry.' Regaining control, he started again, then stopped. It happened three times. Finally tears streamed down his face as he spoke, and he just gave way." The audience began to sing a spiritual to cover his grief.

*   *   *

Robert Williams's breaking point came at the courthouse in Monroe in the spring of 1959. He was a national figure by then, renowned for his armed standoffs with the Klan. During speaking and fundraising tours in the north and south, he had made important allies among civil rights activists, including Malcolm X, who invited him to speak at his Nation of Islam Temple No. 7 in Harlem. Later, Williams proudly quoted Malcom's introduction: "Our brother is here from Carolina, and he is the only fighting man that we've got, so we have to help him so he can stay down there."

Up to then, Williams had advocated nothing more than armed self-defense. Even that made him controversial at a time when non-violence was the defining tactic of the civil rights movement, but after witnessing court proceedings that day, he crossed a line.

The first case concerned a Black housekeeper at the Hotel Monroe who had been thrown down a flight of stairs by a white guest. The other was the case of another white man, Louis Medlin, who was accused of trying to rape a Black woman, then eight months pregnant, in front of her five young children. Several of the women in Williams's NAACP chapter told him that Medlin should be killed before he went to trial because, as awful as his crime was, he would never be convicted of it. Williams told them that if he resorted to that kind of violence, which amounted to lynching, he would be "as bad as the white people."

Black women packed the courthouse that day. The first case was dismissed, as they knew it would be. The defendant had not even bothered to be in court, knowing in advance the charges were going to be dropped. In the rape case, Medlin's wife was seated at the defense table beside her husband. As Williams swore in testimony years later to the Senate's Internal Security Subcommittee, the victim of the crime and the women in the courtroom that day had to listen to Medlin's lawyer argue this:

"Your Honor, you see this pure white woman, this pure flower of life, God's greatest gift to man, this is Louis Medlin's wife. . . . Do you think that he would leave God's greatest gift to humanity, this pure flower, for *that*." And then he pointed to the Black woman as if she [was] on trial. She broke down and started crying. . . .

As expected, after a brisk trial and a few minutes out of the courtroom strictly for show, a unanimous white-male jury acquitted Medlin. With that, the women who had wanted him killed before trial turned on Williams, saying he was responsible. A wire service reporter nearby heard his response: The time had come for African Americans in the South to "meet violence with violence."

That set bells ringing in newsrooms across the country: "NAACP Leader Urges 'Violence.'" Within hours, Williams got a telegram from Roy Wilkins suspending him as an NAACP official, but Williams became only more convinced of his position and articulated it in interviews with reporters for newspapers, magazines, and television stations.

A decade later, he explained himself in testimony to the Internal Security Subcommittee, which was still run by the shrinking segregationist remnant in Congress. The chair was Strom Thurmond, and its members included former Klansman Robert Byrd of West Virginia and Sam Ervin of North Carolina, author of the "Southern Manifesto." Williams was questioned by the subcommittee's chief counsel, J. G. Sourwine.

Mr. SOURWINE: Did you, sir . . . say that Black people must meet violence with violence?
Mr. WILLIAMS: Yes.
Mr. SOURWINE: Do you want to say anything in explanation of what you meant by that? I don't insist, but you should have the right.
Mr. WILLIAMS: Yes. Because in 1957 we had a lot of trouble from the Klan. They had come into the community, and they had shot it up. And we had a series of attacks on Black women. Fourteen Black women in one month were struck while on the streets by

objects thrown from cars by Klansmen. And also a Black woman who was eight months pregnant was beaten because she resisted a white man who was trying to rape her. . . . And they didn't take any evidence against him, and he was acquitted. . . . So then all the women who were enraged said . . . I had opened the floodgates on them, and what was I going to do. . . . And this made me realize that this was the last straw, that we didn't have as much protection as a dog down there, and the government didn't care about us. . . . [W]e had to prepare to survive. And I thought it was the American way, because when the Americans lived under British tyranny . . . they resisted it because it was wrong. . . . And I thought it would be better to be dead than to be completely subjugated in a so-called democracy under those conditions.

*   *   *

The election of President John F. Kennedy in November 1960 marked a hopeful end to the 1950s. By then, school integration had come to Little Rock and other cities in the South, raising hopes that the promise of *Brown*, if not yet realized, someday would be. A new generation of civil rights activists had emerged by then as well: The lunch-counter sit-in by students in Greensboro, North Carolina, in February 1960 prompted a wave of sit-ins in every Southern state, the founding of SNCC, and the progressive political agenda of a new generation.

Even then, to Evers's frustration, national leaders of the NAACP continued to resist the urge to activism among its youth councils, especially in Mississippi. Evers disagreed diplomatically, saying that although a sit-in might be unwise, "some form of protest was necessary" when "everyone else is protesting Jim Crow." Soon after that, 200 Black students circulated handbills calling for a boycott of white merchants on Capitol Street, who would not hire Black workers and treated Black customers with disrespect. Aaron Henry undertook a similar boycott in Clarksdale. Like Henry, Amzie Moore, who led the

Cleveland chapter, was tired of waiting for the NAACP and saw the future in SNCC. "Nobody dared move a peg [in the NAACP] without some lawyer advisin' him," he told the journalist Howell Raines later, but "SNCC was for business, live or die, sink or swim, survive or perish. They were moving, and nobody seemed to worry about whether he was gonna live or die." Evers was diplomatic enough not to let headquarters know he felt the same way, and it hurt that he could lend such activism only tacit support.

On March 27, 1961, nine students from the NAACP's youth council at Tougaloo College staged a sit-in at Jackson's segregated public library. In short order, they were arrested for "breaching the peace," and as they sat in jail overnight waiting for bail to be posted, they became a story, headlined the "Tougaloo Nine." The next day, students at Jackson State boycotted classes in solidarity and marched toward the jail, where they were met by police who drove them back with clubs, dogs, and tear gas, another trigger for their fellow activists as well as the press.

The impact of the library sit-in exceeded Evers's greatest hope. At trial, the nine were fined $100 each and given suspended sentences of 30 days in jail. That night, more than a thousand Black citizens turned out to show their support for the Tougaloo Nine, including parents who had previously told their children not to get involved in "that mess," as civil rights protest was sometimes called. A few days later, the NAACP's national headquarters joined in, authorizing an all-out campaign called "Operation Mississippi." After that there were student-led anti-segregation protests at every sort of public facility in the state, from the swimming pools of Greenville and the movie theater in Vicksburg to the Clarksdale train station and the public zoo in Jackson.

And then, in May 1961, came the first Freedom Riders, two buses full of activists, white and Black, most of them young, determined to test a recent Supreme Court decision in *Boynton v. Virginia,* which made segregation of public buses and bus terminals unconstitutional. Starting out from Washington, D.C., and bound for Jackson, the first 13 Freedom Riders made it only as far as Anniston, Alabama, where they were met and beaten by a mob of Klansmen. As the bus's tires were being slashed, the driver sped away, but carloads of Klansmen followed until flat tires stopped the bus. Klansman then surrounded it, broke open windows, and threw in a firebomb that forced out all the passengers for the beating of their lives. The Klansmen then went back to get the second bus, leaving their victims writhing and watching their bus burn. The second busload took their beatings in Anniston but met an even more vicious mob in Birmingham, where they were beaten by Klansmen organized and supervised by Birmingham's infamous commissioner of public safety, Bull Connor, who had made sure no police would be there when the bus arrived. This gang went after the riders with iron pipes and baseball bats while Connor looked on.

The call for help went out to Attorney General Robert Kennedy and activists from SNCC and the Congress of Racial Equality (CORE), who began pouring in to take over for the original Freedom Riders. Kennedy sent in an assistant, John Siegenthaler, to investigate and advise them, but another mob met the Freedom Riders when they arrived in Montgomery, and Siegenthaler was among those left lying unconscious. Kennedy then sent in federal marshals, but only enough to guard the church where Martin Luther King Jr. was speaking, while a crowd of some 3,000 whites surrounded the building, harassing and attacking Black audience members as they came and went, while local police just watched.

Given all that the Freedom Riders could face on the next stops before Jackson, Kennedy called for a "cooling-off period," but CORE's James Farmer refused. Black Americans had been "cooling off for a hundred years," he said, and the Freedom Rides continued.

Over that summer and fall, wave after wave of Freedom Riders drove through Alabama and Mississippi, taking more beatings and filling the jails along the way. At one point there were hundreds of Freedom Riders in Parchman Farm alone. One was John Lewis, the young future president of SNCC. Another was a young Howard student who would succeed him in that role, Stokely Carmichael.

By that fall, Evers was plainly suffering from overwork. Negotiating with NAACP headquarters, coordinating actions with CORE and SNCC, and helping a constant stream of people into his office who needed help of some kind, all while investigating murders and demonstrations where people were beaten and shot: He was putting in 18-hour days and drowning. His successes were also making him an ever larger target of the Klan, and he began to talk openly with Myrlie about being assassinated. Around that time, Myrlie told him he should get himself a new suit, and he said he did not think he would have time enough left to wear it.

*   *   *

That summer, SNCC's James Forman was worried less about Evers in Mississippi than Robert Williams in North Carolina. By August 1961, SNCC had sent some of its volunteers from Mississippi and elsewhere to set up pickets around the courthouse in Monroe, demanding that the city desegregate all public facilities. Every day, the demonstrators attracted a growing and ever more threatening crowd of white onlookers. Soon, picketers were being singled out and beaten. Police arrested only those who fought back, while Monroe's chief of police stood by watching. As the picketers walked home at the end of each day, carloads of Klansmen followed them, throwing bricks and bottles, brandishing weapons, and shouting death threats.

On Sunday, August 27, some 2,000 whites were waiting for the picketers outside the courthouse and attacked as soon as they began to arrive. Those who got away fled to Williams's neighborhood, which was quickly fortified. Dozens of rifles, two machine guns, and other weapons were handed out; snipers climbed trees; sentries were posted; and barricades went up. When Williams called the police chief for help, as witnesses overheard and as he later testified to the Senate subcommittee, the response was: "Robert, you have caused a lot of race trouble in this town. Now state troopers are coming, and in thirty minutes you'll be hanging in the courthouse square."

That was the night Williams, his wife, and their three sons fled Monroe. He thought their time away would be temporary, a cooling-off period, but the chief confected criminal charges, and they did not return for seven years.

By the time the FBI's wanted poster was in circulation,
Robert F. Williams and family were living in Cuba.

They made their way first to Canada and then, at the invitation of Fidel Castro, went on to Cuba. During four-plus years there, Williams broadcast a radio show to the U.S. called "Radio Free Dixie," a mix of rock, avant-garde jazz, and commentary on the latest civil rights news. All was well in Cuba for a time, but, as his wife, Mabel, put it, "Rob never stopped being Rob." At a meeting with the Cuban foreign ministry, he noticed that all the staff were white and said, "It looks like Mississippi in here." After that, she felt they were lucky to be able to leave. "I thought they would shoot him for sure."

The Williams family's next destination was a brief stop in North Vietnam on the way to China, where Mao Tse-tung gave the family a comfortable asylum. Williams was by no means forgotten in the U.S., however. In his absence he was lionized by the leaders and ground troops of the Black Power Movement. But when he finally returned, in 1969, his admirers would be sorely disappointed.

*   *   *

For all the hope of progress the presidency of John F. Kennedy inspired, his administration tried for three years to discourage the activism and so stop the bloodshed of the civil rights movement, to no avail. On May 2, 1963, some 700 school-age children streamed out of Birmingham's Sixteenth Street Baptist Church to demonstrate against segregation. Trained in the principles and techniques of non-violent resistance, they were beaten, arrested, and imprisoned. The next day, hundreds more took their place. This time Bull Connor turned his police loose on them and stood by watching as they were hit with high-powered fire hoses, beaten with clubs, and set upon by police dogs snarling and straining at their leashes. Hundreds more were arrested that day, but televised coverage, newsreel footage, and especially still images of German shepherds about to sink their teeth into young students, had an effect on the country like no civil rights demonstration had had before. President Kennedy dispatched federal riot control troops to bases near Birmingham and promised to keep the peace, but there was no peace.

Two weeks later, Governor George Wallace made his infamous "stand at the schoolhouse door," a confrontation with federal troops in which Wallace made a show of trying to stop two Black students from integrating the University of Alabama. Several hours passed as he refused to step aside, but then Kennedy federalized the Alabama National Guard, whose troops dutifully escorted the first two Black students, Vivian Malone Jones and James Hood, into the university.

A few hours later, Kennedy spoke to the nation from the Oval Office and finally placed the full force of his administration behind the cause of civil rights. His speech seemed at times to be almost quoting from Dr. King's just-published "Letter from Birmingham Jail." "It ought to be possible," Kennedy said, "for American students of any color to attend any public institution they select without having to be backed up by troops. . . .

> We preach freedom around the world, and we mean it, and we cherish our freedom here at home, but are we to say to the world, and much more importantly, to each other, that this is the land of the free except for the Negroes; that we have no second-class citizens except Negroes; that we have no class or caste system, no ghettoes, no master race except with respect to Negroes? . . . [T]he time has come for this Nation to fulfill its promise. . . We cannot say to ten percent of the population . . . that your children cannot have the chance to develop whatever talents they have; that the only way that they are going to get their rights is to go into the streets and demonstrate. I think we owe them and we owe ourselves a better country than that.

Dr. King was stunned as he watched Kennedy speak. When it was over, he said, "Can you believe that white man not only stepped up to the plate. He hit it over the fence!"

Yet no day's events went further in proving how inextricably bound together wrong and right could be: Wallace's stand for white supremacy in the afternoon, Kennedy's forceful commitment to social justice at 8 p.m., and, just after midnight, the assassination of Medgar Evers.

Evers watched Kennedy's speech at his office, and after that he had the usual deferred, end-of-day work to finish. People who saw him that night described him, despite Kennedy's speech, as "very sad and very tired." He was all but finished with the NAACP, which continued to favor legal challenges over direct action. Even so, he could look back on major accomplishments. He had realized his long-held dream of integrating Ole Miss by helping Air Force Sgt. James Meredith fight the yearslong battle for admission. Whenever Meredith's resolve faltered, Evers was there with moral support until the night he was killed, three months before Meredith's graduation. Among the last victories Evers got to see was another, larger boycott of the merchants on Capitol Street in Jackson, which turned students into seasoned activists, who in turn inspired the older generation that had so disappointed Evers before. On the last night of his life, Evers could feel that the Black community of Jackson was more united than it had ever been.

Looking back on that day, Myrlie Evers said her husband seemed to know what was coming. After breakfast he came back into the house twice before he left. "Myrlie, I don't know what to do," she remembered him saying. "I'm so tired I can't go on, but I can't stop either."

It was just after midnight, four hours after Kennedy's speech, when he pulled into his driveway, got out of his car, and was killed by a shot in the back from a high-powered rifle. Byron De La Beckwith, who had fired from bushes across the street, was tried twice for the crime, his defense secretly funded by the state of Mississippi, but the all-white juries in both trials failed to reach a verdict. Finally, in 1994, with the same physical evidence but this time presented to eight Black and four white jurors, Beckwith was convicted of first-degree murder and sentenced to life in prison. He died in jail seven years later at the age of 80.

Evers's death at 37 was a seismic event whose aftershocks were felt nationwide. An enormous crowd gathered outside the funeral in Jackson and defied an order of silence when someone started and the rest lifted their voices in "Oh Freedom," then "This Little Light of Mine." After the church service, they marched downtown, where they were met by fire trucks, police dogs, and a line of heavily armed police, who charged when someone in the crowd began throwing rocks. The outcome would have been far worse than the arrests and minor injuries that followed if John Doar of the Justice Department

The volley from a high-powered rifle that killed Medgar Evers in his
driveway also hit his car and his home, where his wife and children
were waiting up for him. Four days later, at the funeral, Myrlie Evers
tried to comfort their son Darrell Kenyatta Evers.

had not risked his life by coming between them and shouting at both
sides: "My name is John Doar. D-O-A-R. I'm from the Justice Department in Washington. And anybody around here knows that I stand for
what's right!" Then he asked for the crowd to disperse, and for some
reason, perhaps his show of courage or the solemnity of the moment,
they did. Evers's body was taken by train to Washington, D.C., where,
thanks to his service in World War II, he was buried with full honors
at Arlington National Cemetery.

*   *   *

The day Evers was killed was the thirty-sixth birthday of Clyde Kennard,
who died three weeks later. To avoid the publicity that would follow if
he died in Parchman, Governor Barnett had released him four months

before. Free to seek medical care, he flew to Chicago for emergency surgery, but it was too late to slow the advance of his cancer. When the author John Howard Griffin visited him just days before his death, he weighed less than a hundred pounds. During their visit, he kept "a sheet pulled up over his face so no one could see the grimace of pain," Griffin wrote. Kennard told him that all his suffering would be worth it if his story "would show this country where racism finally leads, but they're not going to know, are they?" His service would have qualified him for Arlington as well, but he chose to be buried in Hattiesburg.

In late August 1963, the Black veterans of World War II and Korea performed another service to the civil rights movement, providing security for the March on Washington. The Kennedy administration had tried to get the organizers to call it off to prevent the violence that seemed all but inevitable. The veterans knew there would be police in riot gear, and they knew that that sight alone could be an incitement. To ensure the March would not end as feared, the veterans used what they knew. They formed a regiment of three battalions, five companies in each. Company commanders guarded the route, keeping in touch by radio with each other, their headquarters, and the D.C. police; and in a demonstration by some 250,000 people, they kept the peace. The day was, in fact, so peaceful that the Voice of America later broadcast the speeches in a dozen languages, and the U.S. Information Agency (USIA) made a documentary of the event for export.

Not everyone found that coverage useful. SNCC's Michael Thelwell was sickened when he went by the USIA tent and saw the propaganda in progress. "So it happened," he wrote later, "that Negro students from the South, some of whom still had unhealed bruises from the electric cattle prods which southern police used to break up demonstrations, were recorded for the screens of the world portraying 'American Democracy at Work.'"

Celebration was indeed too soon, arguably by decades. In the five weeks before and after Evers's death, according to Martin Luther King's biographer Taylor Branch, there were 758 racial incidents in 186

American cities, none more moving than the murder of four young Black girls in Birmingham, who were dressed in white for the Sunday service at the Sixteenth Street Baptist Church when the bomb went off. But neither the many murders of known and unnamed civil rights advocates nor the Civil Rights Act of 1964 nor the Voting Rights Act of 1965 led to "democracy at work" for Black Americans. Neither would Malcolm X's assassination and the Watts riots in 1965 nor the founding of the Black Panther Party in 1966, nor all the the many other peaceful and unpeaceful initatives that followed.

After Malcolm X was murdered, Robert F. Williams was the most prominent living standard-bearer for militant activism. He was named in absentia to honorific posts with the Black Panthers and the Revolutionary Action Movement. He was also named president and minister of defense in the Republic of New Afrika (RNA), whose agenda included establishing a Black nation in the Deep South with its own army, funded by reparations for slavery. Williams was nothing if not realistic. His willingness to take on the group's presidency must have come from a motive apart from commitment to its cause, and speculation about that was the talk of the RNA at the time.

He seemed to be a changed man when he came home in September 1969, and the fact that he was arrested when he got off his chartered plane but immediately released suggests advance negotiations with the U.S. government. He clearly brought useful intelligence with him, having established relations with Mao, Deng Xiaoping, and other leaders of the Chinese Communist Party. In no time, he was being debriefed by the Office of Asian Communist Affairs and by Secretary of State Henry Kissinger's briefers on what he had learned in China, including its role and intentions at the height of the Vietnam War. Williams was also given a job teaching in the University of Michigan's Center for Chinese Studies, a position funded by the Ford Foundation.

Following a press conference two days after Williams got home, a story in the *Washington Post* noted that Williams had taken "gentle exception to the emotional appeals of some Black nationalists." Two months later, Williams quietly resigned from one such group, then another. "I had always considered myself an American patriot," he said at the time. "They didn't see it that way. I always stressed that I believed in the Constitution of the United States and that I thought it was the greatest document in the world. The problem is that [people] didn't respect it."

Later, he was more direct: "They have a lot of young teenagers who might have looked at *The Battle of Algiers* or something, and they get combat boots and berets, and they grab a gun and go out and say, 'Off the pigs.' We had veterans who had been trained to use military equipment. . . . We always tried to avoid a fight. [They] think a weapon is the first alternative."

For the next twenty-five years, Robert and Mabel Williams lived in tiny Baldwin, Michigan, a vacation spot tucked into a national forest in the western part of the state. Mabel became a social worker and later project director of a program for seniors. Robert gave some paid speeches at first, then worked with inmates at a nearby prison. Among other things, he urged them to follow the model of Malcolm X, who used his prison years to read and reinvent himself.

Robert's son Dr. John Chalmers Williams was grateful for his father's decision to keep a low profile and give to his family the protection he had given to the Black community in Monroe. "The Black leaders our youth know most about—Malcolm X, Martin Luther King, Medgar Evers—died young," Dr. Williams told one interviewer. "The message is like, if you choose to follow these people's path, this is what happens to you in America. My dad chose to live."

His family was around him and Mabel was holding his hand when he died of Hodgkin's disease at the age of 71. Fittingly, he was laid to rest in Monroe after a funeral service at the Central Methodist Church, and the eulogy was delivered by Rosa Parks. She knew very well how Dr. King's nonviolence and Williams's armed resistance helped each other, and she praised Williams unreservedly for "his courage and commitment to freedom." In closing, she said, "The sacrifices he made, and what he did, should go down in history and never be forgotten."

* 　 * 　 *

The same could be said for Isaac Woodard, who was all but forgotten after the acquittal of Police Chief Lynwood Shull. The rest of his life was a remarkable story of recovery, a story little known until 2019, when U.S. District Judge Richard Gergel published *Unexampled Courage: The Blinding of Sgt. Isaac Woodard and the Awakening of President Harry S. Truman and Judge J. Waties Waring.* The author serves in the same Charleston courthouse where Judge Waring heard all his local cases, including the trial of Lynwood Shull.

Because he was blinded after his discharge, Woodard received a stipend of only $60 a month. Later it was more than doubled, to $135, which still left him living hand to mouth, but he was able to buy a house with proceeds from a benefit concert sponsored by the *Amsterdam News.* When the city bought him out to build a new housing project, he used the money to buy a commercial space that held several businesses, and family members helped him collect rents and maintain the place.

Ten years after the incident in Batesburg, *Jet* magazine caught up with him. Their article, titled "Isaac Woodard: America's Forgotten Man," showed him walking and talking to friends in his neighborhood and taking care of his aging parents. "I make out all right," he said. "I just can't see."

In 1964, he was evaluated by a social worker from the Veterans Administration, who visited him in his third-floor, five-room apartment and judged that he was capably running the household and caring for his family, which included his 80-year-old father, who had cancer; his 69-year-old mother; and his two young sons, Isaac III (whose mother was Woodard's partner, Mildred Lovejoy) and George, whom he adopted. The social worker said that Isaac was proud that he could take care of them and that he also seemed "shrewd in many respects." A devout Christian, he loved listening to Sunday services on the radio, but the social worker said that when asked about what had happened in Batesburg 18 years before, he had "an intense emotional reaction."

Woodard died in 1992, at the age of 73, never knowing all that followed from the day he was blinded. He did not know that President Harry Truman had intervened on his behalf or how his case helped to inspire Truman's civil rights agenda. He did not know how much Lynwood Shull's acquittal had infuriated Judge Waring and affected Waring's course on civil rights, nor how that effect on Waring's advice to Thurgood Marshall influenced the winning argument in *Brown v. Board of Education*.

*   *   *

Passage of the Civil Rights Act and the Voting Rights Act were giant steps forward. Racial discrimination and segregation in schools and public places were outlawed. The Equal Employment Opportunity Commission was founded to ensure fairness in hiring. All the various pretenses that kept Black citizens from voting—poll taxes, literacy tests, and other tricks—were outlawed, and voter registration and elections in the South were subjected to federal oversight, at least until the Supreme Court reversed itself in 2013.

Many people contributed to the successes of the civil rights movement, prominently including women such as Ella Baker, Septima Clark, Jo Ann Robinson, Daisy Bates, Diane Nash, Fannie Lou Hamer, and a host of others, known and unknown. In part because of the movement's determined emphasis on nonviolence, however, less attention has been paid to the Black GIs whose wartime experience lent the movement tactical support and resiliency. Among the best known are Air Force Sgt. James Meredith; Sgt. Floyd McKissick, longtime president of CORE; Air Force Capt. James Forman, who led SNCC from 1961 to 1965; Army Staff Sgt. Hosea Williams, who led the bloody Selma-to-Montgomery march of 1965; and Lt. Jack Robinson, who was court-martialed in 1944 for refusing to move to the back of a bus and later integrated major league baseball.

Robinson was a member of the 761st Tank Battalion, a unit known as the "Black Panthers." The 761st was the first African American unit to see action in World War II, and they brought home every medal soldiers could get, including almost 300 Purple Hearts, 70 Bronze Stars, 11 Silver Stars, and a Congressional Medal of Honor, awarded posthumously by President Bill Clinton. After bloody frontline battles through France, Belgium, and Germany, the 761st were in the vanguard that met the Soviet Army in Austria at the Steyr river, and they continued to fight the war on the homefront, as did untold numbers of other Black soldiers.

It is no stretch to call their homecoming another war. Many of its frontline troops—from veterans of the 761st and those who stood their ground in Columbia, Tennessee, to the members of Robert Williams's Monroe, North Carolina, gun club—risked their lives to claim for African Americans their constitutional rights as U.S. citizens. Some in this fight too were killed in action; many were wounded, physically and otherwise—jobs lost, homes foreclosed and bombed, families threatened and killed—and all of them bore the risk of these and other consequences. Despite that, they gave a semblance of that "equal protection of the laws" which Black Americans had been denied for so long, and they stood their ground until the legislation of the mid-1960s affirmed their legal claim to it. Along with those brave enough to use passive resistance when attacked by Klansmen, police, and attack dogs, those who raised the price for such crimes earned their place in history.

The 1955–1965 civil rights movement takes its place in U.S. history as a time when white supremacy and racism in America were indelibly exposed, live on television for all to see. Thanks in no small part to the veterans and others who provided armed self-defense as a substitute for legal protection, the civil rights movement could hand the Black Freedom Movement back to the future. And for all that, what Marcus Garvey had said in the early twentieth century, which Earl Little often quoted to his young son, was still true. The Black Freedom Movement "is in the wind," Little told the future Malcolm X. "It is coming. One day, like a storm, it will be here."

Before We Knew

Rachel Carson and Norbert Wiener
declare the interdependence
of nature and humanity

———

We shall not cease from exploration
And the end of all our exploring
Will be to arrive where we started
And know the place for the first time.

—T. S. Eliot, "Little Gidding,"
from *Four Quartets*, 1943

During her childhood and in later life, Rachel Carson
was rarely without a book to be read and a beloved pet,
this one the family dog, Candy.

Maria Carson's other children were 11 and 6 years old when Rachel came along. In a diary, Maria described her third child as "unusually pretty . . . a dear, plump, little blue-eyed baby," quiet and well-behaved even as an infant. She was a welcome addition to an otherwise less than happy home. Maria's husband, Robert Carson, was a marginal provider, a sometime traveling salesman, and in other ways too a distant presence. The family's main asset was its property, a 64-acre farm in Springdale, Pennsylvania, 17 miles northeast of Pittsburgh. Robert had bought it hoping to sell off lots, but the family was still land poor when the Depression hit. Their house was an updated log cabin, still without indoor plumbing or central heating, now divided into four small rooms and sided with clapboard. It was crowded, hot in summer, and cold in winter, but it came with an apple and pear orchard and a landscape rich with vegetation and wildlife.

Maria was a teacher by profession, at a time when women were expected to leave the classroom after marriage. Her pupils after that were her children, none more so than Rachel. Maria began taking her on expeditions through the family's fields and woodland almost as soon as she could walk, and the outdoors became Rachel's home away from home until she left for college.

With the other Carson children in school during the day, Maria was alone with her youngest, but Rachel was a pensive, self-directed child, someone with whom it was unusually easy to be alone. In her early school years, Maria chose to teach her at home for weeks at a time. The friends from school who came to Rachel's house remembered her mother as a haunting, discouraging presence, as if they were coming between her and Rachel. When Rachel left home for the Pennsylvania College for Women (now Chatham University) in Pittsburgh, her mother came to visit so frequently and so occupied Rachel's time and attention that some of her dorm mates felt excluded.

For better and worse, her mother lived with Rachel for the rest of her life, cleaning house, doing the shopping, and typing her manuscripts, but also preempting Rachel's other relationships. The arrangement was useful for them both, but it had the effect of narrowing Rachel's world to her work, which meant more than anything else to her, just not everything.

Maria's earliest influence on Rachel was indisputably a great gift. Her years as a classroom teacher came at the height of the Nature Study movement, which applied John Dewey's pragmatic, learn-by-doing philosophy of education to the teaching of natural science. The movement's motto was "Study Nature, Not Books," and the book that popularized this approach—*Handbook of Nature Study,* by Cornell professor Anna Botsford Comstock—was Maria Carson's teaching guide, in the classroom and with Rachel. As Comstock summarized it, "Nature study cultivates the child's imagination, a regard for what is true, and the power to express it." In Rachel Carson, Nature Study found its most eloquent voice.

Her first surviving work, as a budding eight-year-old writer, was a story about "Mr. Wren," who discovered in a "dear little brown house" the perfect nest for himself and his family. The writer herself had no such home. Long before the Depression, her father's chronic under-employment and ill health exposed the family to a series of financial crises. Rachel shared a bedroom with siblings old enough to be strangers, and when she was 12, they were joined by her sister's newlywed husband, who one day simply disappeared. Money troubles, cramped quarters, rural isolation, and frequent absences from school discouraged friendships, as did her mother, who had found in Rachel the best part of her life and held on to her as if to life itself.

As she grew older, Rachel found her refuge increasingly in solitude, where she learned to write, and in the outdoors, which became her subject. Her mother subscribed to the children's publication *St. Nicholas* magazine, where F. Scott Fitzgerald and Edna St. Vincent Millay made their childhood debuts and where Rachel made hers at age 11. The last of her *St. Nicholas* pieces announced the emergence of a gifted and careful writer, age 14. In it, she told the story of a day spent with her dog, Pal, in the woods around her home, "the sort of place that awes you by its majestic silence. . . ."

> Near at hand we heard the cheery "witchery, witchery" of the Maryland yellow-throat. For half an hour we trailed him, until we came out on a sunny slope. There, in some low bushes we found the nest, containing four jewel-like eggs. . . . Countless discoveries made the day memorable: the bob-white's nest, tightly packed with eggs, the oriole's aerial cradle, the framework of sticks which the cuckoo calls a nest, and the lichen-covered home of the humming-bird. Late in the afternoon a penetrating "Teacher! *Teacher!* TEACHER!" reached our ears. An overbird! A careful search revealed his nest, a little round ball of grass, securely hidden on the ground. [Then the] cool of approaching night settled. The wood-thrushes trilled their golden melody. The setting sun transformed the sky into a sea of blue and gold. A vesper-sparrow sang his evening lullaby. We turned slowly homeward, gloriously tired, gloriously happy!

As much as her grace as a writer, all her work would demonstrate the skill of sharply focused observation she learned first from her mother, the faculty one Nature Study advocate described simply as "seeing the things one looks at."

*   *   *

Norbert Wiener was 12 years old when Rachel Carson was born, but he was a most unlikely 12-year-old. While others his age were in fifth or sixth grade, he was entering his freshman year at Tufts University. In 1906, a long front-page profile in the Sunday magazine of Joseph

Pulitzer's newspaper the *New York World* named him "the Most Remarkable Boy in the World," and it is hard to imagine anyone who could better justify that title. He told the *World* reporter he had learned much more from reading Ernst Haeckel's *The Riddle of the Universe* in German than Homer in Greek, since Homer was just "telling stories." Yes, he said, of course he loved to have fun. "Swimming is my forte. But I like to study too. When I have participated in the boys' games I turn to my Huxley or my Spencer. I get suggestions from them which lead my mind to think of greater things." Like Carson, he got his most influential schooling at home, and there the similarity in their upbringing ends.

Norbert Wiener, "the most remarkable boy in the world," age 9.

Norbert's homeschool teacher was his father, Leo Wiener, a Russian émigré who lectured at Harvard beginning in 1896 and developed the first college-level course in Slavic culture in the U.S. He was the child of Jewish parents but converted to Christianity as a young man. His saint was Leo Tolstoy. When he left Russia, his plan was to start a vegetarian commune in Central America based on Tolstoy's anarchist-pacifist brand of Christianity. Norbert did not even know his father's parents were Jewish until he discovered it accidentally when he was 15 years old. He was surprised but determined not to renounce Judaism as his father had done, and he valued especially his father's assertion that their lineage reached back to Maimonides.

Leo Wiener was said to be fluent in more than three dozen languages, and he published 40-plus books, including a 24-volume English translation of Tolstoy's complete works, a three-volume *Africa and the Discovery of America*, a book titled *Gypsies as Fortune-Tellers and as Blacksmiths,* and another titled *Commentary to the Germanic Laws and Mediaeval Documents*. He expected no less of his son, who as a result was reading English at the age of 3, Latin and Greek at 5.

Little Norbert was a genius, which was lucky. A lesser mind might have cracked under the strain of his father's teaching method, which relied on relentless, brutal criticism. His father's lessons usually began in "an easy, conversational tone," Wiener wrote in the first volume of his autobiography, titled *Ex-Prodigy*. "This lasted exactly until I made the first . . . mistake. Then the gentle and loving father was replaced by the avenger of the blood." Sharply cutting rebukes naturally made for more mistakes, which fed his father's anger, and so on. At the end of a typical lesson, "Father was raging, and I was weeping . . . morally raw all over." He loved his father and in time forgave him—"my task-master was at the same time my hero," he wrote—but their lessons took a toll on his emotional well-being even as they gave him tools of wizardry.

When he was 8 years old, the family doctor told his father that Norbert's eyes were being over-strained, that he was becoming increasingly nearsighted, and that he should not be asked or allowed to read anything for at least six months. His father's solution was to keep advancing his studies in mathematics, physics, zoology, and languages by having graduate students read to him and talk him through his lessons. His father would then test his memory and his ability to solve problems in his head. As arduous as that solution was, Wiener later told one of his students, it was then that he "relearned the world. My mind completely opened up. I could see things I never saw before." As a result, he was known to perform mental acrobatics that even he found "totally astonishing." Also as a result, as a classroom teacher he was notorious for skipping over steps to complex solutions on his blackboard. When he was asked to repeat the solution, he would still skip over steps, the same ones or others.

By the time his profile was published in the *World*, he had just finished his high school "graduation essay," which was titled "The Theory of Ignorance." In it, he attempted to fill in a gap in Socrates's self-defense at the trial for "impiety" that led to his execution by hemlock. After hearing he had been named the wisest of men by the Oracle of Delphi, Socrates had set out to study the question. His conclusion, as recorded in Plato's *Apology*, was that he was indeed different from other men, but only because he knew that he knew nothing, whereas others knew nothing but did not know it. In his essay, Wiener set out to do what he felt Socrates had neglected to do: He devised logical proofs for the assertion that all so-called knowledge was uncertain, using examples from the fields of paleontology, philosophy, religion, physics, and mathematics. He was then 11 years old.

Three years later, he graduated from Tufts with honors, and by the time he was 19, he had an MA and PhD in philosophy from Harvard, where he concentrated on the logic of mathematics. His dissertation focused on Ernst Schröder's recently published three-volume *Lectures on the Algebra of Logic, 1890–1905,* which Wiener found superior in several ways to the recently published three-volume *Principia Mathematica* of Alfred North Whitehead and Bertrand Russell. He then did a postdoctoral fellowship at Oxford with Russell, to whom he presented his dissertation for comment. Russell, who was his senior by more than 20 years and by the measure of his life's work, was tactful in his criticism, but Wiener was having none of it. To Russell's two pages of criticism, Wiener, then 19, responded with three. Fortunately for him, Russell knew the trials of Wiener's hard-driven academic life thanks to a letter he had received from Leo Wiener, whose description of his son's education inspired Russell's wry comment in the margin: "Nevertheless he turned out well."

In letters home, Wiener called Russell "an iceberg" and his courses "the acme of superficiality," but years later he was more generous, crediting Russell with teaching him "almost every issue of true philosophical significance" in mathematics, far more than he had learned at Harvard. When their work together came to an end, Wiener took Russell's suggestion to continue his study of mathematics with the elite faculty and fellows of the University of Göttingen, after which he returned to the U.S. and studied philosophy once more, this time under John Dewey at Columbia. At 21, he got a one-year job teaching philosophy at Harvard, then taught math at the University of Maine, and landed eventually at MIT, where he spent the rest of his working life and earned his twin reputations as the most accomplished and most eccentric of mathematicians: a man of stunning genius and a human being with less than no social skill who was subject to flagrant mood swings and the daily ordeal of simply being himself, convinced at one moment that he was "the most remarkable boy in the world" and at the next that he was the error-prone failure his father had taught him to fear he would become. He cycled between the poles of elation and despair for the rest of his life.

*   *   *

In temperament and personal history, Rachel Carson and Norbert Wiener had nothing in common, and there is no record that they ever met. They practiced wholly separate disciplines. The many hours she spent on her Nature Study walks anticipated a lifetime spent focused on the smallest details of natural life, sometimes through microscopes and binoculars, more often along shorelines, knee-deep in tide pools. Wiener loved biology but had to abandon it because he was beyond clumsy in fieldwork and the laboratory, and so chose the more cerebral spheres of philosophy and mathematics. Carson's life was rooted in a pastoral, imaginative childhood and defined by habits of solitude and discipline. Wiener's interests were polymorphous, and his life was a trial by fire from early childhood to the end of his life, a torment at work and at home. He would surely have envied Carson her freedom from his demons. She would have found his life literally uninhabitable.

More important than their differences, however, were the ideas they expressed in their defining works. From their very different perspectives—she in the living world, he in the electrical, mechanical, and metaphysical one—they converged on the heretical, even subversive idea that the assertion of mastery over the natural world was based on an arrogant fantasy that carried the potential for disaster.

In their time, that idea defied history and common sense. The notion that humankind's place on Earth was above and beyond that of other species was a principle as American as Thomas Jefferson and as old as God's directive to Adam and Eve:

Be fruitful, and multiply, and replenish the earth, and subdue it: and have dominion over the fish of the sea, and over the fowl of the air, and over every living thing that moveth upon the earth. (Genesis 1:28)

Such dominion had never seemed more achievable than in the early twentieth century, when world-shifting, life-saving discoveries came one after another: special and general relativity, quantum mechanics, antibiotics, X-ray imaging, the structure of DNA, universal expansion, the Big Bang. An understanding of nature at the atomic and subatomic levels was giving quantum chemists, molecular biologists, and particle physicists the ability to imagine entirely new forms of matter and energy, while new applications—telephones, radios, airplanes, "talkies"—were enriching everyday life. In the depths of the Great Depression, science's seeming monopoly on good ideas inspired a technocracy movement, which proposed running all national policies and programs through engineers and others schooled in a new science of "geo-mechanics." These "social consultants" would alone determine nothing less than "how to operate large areas of this earth's surface, beneath and above." Money was to be replaced by energy certificates, distributed equally to all citizens, who would accomplish every necessary task in assigned jobs that would take no more than four hours a day, four days a week. That desperate illusion was short-lived, but World War II continued to give new evidence of scientific mastery in jet propulsion, missile guidance, rocketry, loran, and radar.

The promise of practical omniscience had no more persuasive support than the last act of World War II, for which the physicists and engineers of the Manhattan Project managed to create the most powerful and lethal bomb in history, an almost unthinkable feat of basic and applied science that put an end to the bloodiest war in human history. To the soldiers who had survived the fighting in Europe and Asia only to face the possibility of a ground war against a suicidally committed enemy, the bomb literally meant the difference between life and death. U.S. policy makers were quick to note that it also marked a major increase in national prestige. Having proved invaluable to national security and the projection of national power, government funding for military science would continue to climb even when the war was over.

The more persistent legacy of the bomb, however, was deeply ominous, and to no one more than some of its Manhattan Project architects and other nations' wartime scientists, who, after all, had equipped all sides with weapons that helped to take the lives of some 75 million people, a majority of them civilians. Scientists in Nazi Germany were responsible for supplying the cyanide-based pesticide Zyklon B and other means of killing more than ten million gays, gypsies, Poles, and

Jews in the death camps. The U.S. Chemical Warfare Service reinvented fire as a weapon of war, mixing aluminum naphthenate and aluminum palmitate with gasoline to make a gel, called napalm, that soaked cities and their citizens in gluey streams of fire. General Curtis LeMay, who directed the campaign of fire-bombing that preceded Hiroshima, estimated that it had killed between 50 and 90 percent of the people in the 70 cities on his target list. He also admitted that, if the Allies had lost the war, he would have been prosecuted as a war criminal. Some of the Manhattan Project's senior scientists were tortured by the thought that they had created a weapon that for the first time made it possible for the human species to commit suicide and take other life forms with them.

After the war, for those inclined to look, the perverse effects of applied science and advances in technology were all around. Power plants, refineries, steelworks, and other smokestack industries, as well as exhaust from leaded gasoline in newly muscular cars, were filling the air with sulfur, carbon dioxide, hydrocarbons, and nitrous oxides. During the war, Los Angeles experienced a series of thick, yolky smogs, at least one of them so suffocating it was mistaken for a chemical attack. Nonreturnable soda bottles and other immortal plastics were piling up in landfills. There were traces of the new toxic pesticides on grocery produce. Life in lakes and streams was being choked by runoff from homes using new laundry detergents and from farms using new synthetic fertilizers. The temperature of the oceans was rising as well, for reasons yet unknown. Most alarming of all, fallout from nuclear bomb tests began turning up far from the times and places where it was released, with health effects that were especially frightening because radiation's remnant was invisible, while its danger was palpable even before it was proved.

Most of these and other contaminants were protected by powerful corporate and political interests. The nation's chemical and oil industries had every reason to suspect they were releasing toxins into the air and water, and even after they knew it for a fact, they organized to disprove it. In 1946, executives of the major oil companies formed a joint "Smoke and Fumes Committee" and hired a public relations firm to sow doubt about incriminating research. Beginning in the mid-1950s, the same tactic would be used by the major tobacco companies to escape responsibility for lung cancer, as it would be used later by the fossil-fuel industry to discredit climate science.

Military scientists, who were used to wartime secrecy, used national security in peacetime as a blind for all sorts of dubious projects. Given the nuclear standoff that passed for peace, forward-looking research required preparing for the most terrible eventualities, which justified the pursuit of some fabulous grotesques: deploying flocks of napalm-bearing bats to incinerate enemy armies or populations, for example, and saturating an enemy's water supply with LSD, which would render its people passive and unable to resist invasion, even save lives!

More questionable were some of the military's efforts to weaponize radiation. Even before the war ended, military and other government-subsidized scientists began to study how lethal doses of radioactive isotopes could be delivered undetected into the enemy's drinking water, food supply, and breathed air. Egregiously unethical studies, carefully disguised, exposed many hundreds of thousands of unsuspecting American citizens to radiation in order to measure the effect of lower and higher dosages. The first serious attempt to expose these experiments came during the Clinton administration, when it was discovered that, 20 years before, virtually all the relevant records at the National Personnel Records Center in St. Louis had been destroyed by fire, likely on purpose. Other such studies remained classified even in 2021.

Carson, Wiener, and others who advocated for precaution and transparency in the practice of science had no idea just how far the lack of it had gone. And to the extent they knew enough to protest, they were badly overmatched by the major offenders: a confluence of corporate, political, and military interests known as the "Iron

Triangle," whose powers of persuasion included lavish budgets for cooperative scientists and universities, withdrawal of funding for uncooperative ones, and the cruder tools of McCarthyism. Despite that, at a time when dissent was punished and prosperity followed from compliance, Carson and Wiener exposed the general public to an open and deeply fraught question from which they would not or could not turn away.

The question was whether the world was best understood mechanistically, as a collection of separable parts, or as a highly complex unity no part of which could be understood apart from everything else. The question was not new. From antiquity, there were those who assumed that the universe operated in a perfect, machinelike order that unfolded in predictable lines of cause and effect, like clockwork. Anything that appeared to be an imperfection was a physical part or mechanism not yet understood, something—some *thing*—for science to take apart and identify. Others conceived the universe as an organism that is always in a state of becoming. In this world, cause and effect blurred. Causes became effects and effects became causes in a multidirectional chain of "circular causalities." This world grew and evolved but always as a single, indivisible system, and to understand it required studying not what things are but what they do, how they affect each other.

This was a view on which Carson and Wiener converged. Wiener saw humanity's potentially fatal role in the natural world years before Carson, who found it all but impossible to relinquish the notion that nature was God's creation and therefore invulnerable to human error. Wiener's life did not tempt him with that idea. Yet in the end, she in her field and he in his were as one and uniquely influential in refuting the notion that humankind was somehow above or apart from nature. By confronting the effects of science practiced mainly in the pursuit of power and profit, and by calling for scientific innovations to be accessible and understood by politicians, policy makers, and the general public before they were deployed, Carson and Wiener advanced a compelling argument: that nature was neither a thing apart from humankind nor any longer even wholly "natural," since its anointed masters were ever more assertively rearranging the Earth. As evidence of the dangers inherent in that mastery, they shined a very bright light on the masters at work.

*   *   *

Rachel Carson imagined that she had given up her childhood dream of becoming a writer when she decided to make biology rather than English her college major, but she had fallen in love with hands-on laboratory work and, not surprisingly, with fieldwork. Her attachment to nature was more than intellectual: It was emotional, even sensual. "I love all the beautiful things of nature," she wrote in a guileless fresh- man essay, "and the wild creatures are my friends." Among the most cherished memories she carried with her to college were not of achieve- ments at school or family occasions but of the time she had spent exploring the fields and forests of Springdale. The outdoor world was home to her more than her house was, and college summers reminded her why. Both her siblings were still living at home—one married, the other divorced—but both now with children, which made their house's four small rooms crushingly smaller.

She also switched to biology because of its professor, Mary Scott Skinker, who was a much-admired and much-feared figure on campus: admired for her quick mind and personal magnetism, feared for her academic standards. Rachel became one of her best students and, after college, a close friend. In a letter to a friend in Springdale about her junior prom, she wrote more about Skinker than about her date. There is little evidence of other dates, and when boys were imported from nearby schools for dances, Rachel was content to stay in the dorm or venture elsewhere.

On one such night, alone in her room, she was struck by new mean- ing in a poem she had read several times before, Tennyson's "Locksley Hall." The narrator of the poem is a young man revisiting the place where he and his true love had once imagined a life together, gazing at the stars. Now the woman he loved was gone, having married a man richer than he was, in a world where everything, even love, seemed to be for sale. In his anger and disillusionment, he calls down a revolutionary thunderbolt on this wicked, mercenary world.

Let it fall on Locksley Hall, with rain or hail, or fire or snow;
For the mighty wind arises, roaring seaward, and I go.

Carson studied the life in cold tide pools for
so long that her close friend and career-long colleague
Bob Hines sometimes had to help her back to shore.

It was while reading that last line on this night, Carson said, when she felt her calling. She had never seen the ocean, never even learned to swim, but the last line "spoke to something within me, seeming to tell me that my own path led to the sea." Like college students before and after her, she had detected the way to a home after home, and that is how she wrote about the sea in all her books until her last: as the firstborn world, the family home of every form of life.

After graduation, she was admitted to the doctoral program in zoology at Johns Hopkins, but by the time she got her master's degree in 1932, the Depression was at its depth. Her mother had already sold the family china, the family was down to living on apples and pears from the orchard, and Rachel was now the most employable member of the family. Skinker suggested she take the federal civil service exams in the biological sciences, and her top score in the test for "junior aquatic biologist" led to an interview at the Bureau of Fisheries.

The timing was perfect: The agency's chief was facing the need to produce seven-minute segments for a radio series on aquatic life, and a professional script writer had just failed at the task. Taking a chance on someone who came highly recommended but whose work he did not know, he asked her to try a script or two. She ended up writing them all, and when they were done, he asked her to write the introduction to one of the bureau's usual publications, in this case a brochure on life in the oceans. She returned with it a few days later, and she watched him as he read it.

> Who has known the ocean? Neither you nor I, with our earth-bound senses, know the foam and surge of the tide that beats over the crab hiding under the seaweed of his tidepool home; or the lilt of the long, slow swells of mid-ocean, where shoals of wandering fish prey and are preyed upon. . . . To stand at the edge of the sea, to sense the ebb and the flow of the tides, to feel the breath of a mist over a great salt marsh, to watch the flight of shore birds that have swept up and down the surf lines of the continents for untold thousands of years, to see the running of the old eels and the young shad to the sea, is to have knowledge of things that are as nearly eternal as any earthly life can be.

When he finished reading, he smiled and told Carson it was not quite right for a bureau brochure. He suggested she send it to *The Atlantic*, and then he hired her.

He turned out to be right about *The Atlantic*, which published her essay in the September 1937 issue. "Everything else followed," Carson said later. When she switched from English to biology in college, "I had given up writing forever, I thought. It never occurred to me that I was merely getting something to write about."

By the time she got her job at the bureau, most of the family had moved in with Rachel, who had found an inexpensive rental in a rural community outside Baltimore. To help support her mother, her father, her older sister, Margie, and Margie's two young daughters, aged 11 and 15, she began spending her nights and weekends producing articles for magazines and newspapers. Most of her pieces were based on research that crossed her desk at the bureau, especially on marine life and oceanography, a field then enjoying explosive growth in support of submarine and amphibious warfare. That research also informed a first book, *Inside the Sea-Wind*, an exquisite portrait of marine life published in late 1941. Rhapsodic reviews did not save it from being swamped by the news of Pearl Harbor, however, and after that, the nights and weekends she had given to the book were given back to magazine and newspaper pieces.

During and after the war, she found herself increasingly frustrated in her daytime job because of her agency's changed, more circumscribed mandate. In 1940, the Bureau of Fisheries was reorganized as the Fish and Wildlife Service (FWS), an agency of the Department of the Interior that served the needs of industry as much as the public interest. That was never clearer than when she was asked to review a biological survey of Bikini Atoll, a bathtub-shaped string of coral islands on the northern edge of the Marshall Islands in the central Pacific, between Hawaii and the Philippines. The atoll's base of live coral surrounded a large lagoon, which was home to snails, crab, eels, and hundreds of other marine species. Fish and Wildlife was asked for its opinion because Bikini was to be the site of the first postwar nuclear bomb tests, and the fishing industry was concerned about effects of the tests on populations of tuna, whales, and other commercial stocks. Looking at the survey, Carson had the misgivings any marine biologist would have had at the notion of subjecting so rich a habitat to atomic bombs, but after determining that none of the most marketable species was likely to be affected, the FWS's job was to reassure the industry.

The bomb tests, code-named Operation Crossroads, proceeded as scheduled in the summer of 1946 and turned out to be military science at its most oxymoronic, less a research exercise than a life-or-death Army-Navy game. The bomb's targets were ships parked in Bikini's lagoon, surplus transports and battleships from World War II, including the venerable USS *Saratoga* and Japan's *Nagato*. Beyond testing the bomb, the Army Air Force hoped the tests would show naval warfare to be defenseless and the Navy obsolete. In the event, the tests proved nothing. The first, an aboveground test, yielded little useful information because the bomb missed its target, landing outside the range of some measuring instruments and destroying others. The second, an underwater test, was a disaster. Unlike detonation aboveground, which dispersed radioactivity into the atmosphere, water absorbed it. The result was a mile-high, million-ton column of water that came crashing back into the lagoon, setting off huge waves that painted all the ships at anchor with a thick coat of radiation and left a radioactive mist lingering over the atoll. Less than an hour after the blast, patrol boats were back in the lagoon picking up measuring instruments, and, later that day, 49 support ships joined them with almost 15,000 men aboard. A scheduled third test was canceled, and the Bikini islanders—a fishing community of 167 people who had been moved to another atoll with the assurance that their dislocation would be temporary—were told they would not be going home after all.

In the years that followed, the Marshall Islands became the proving ground for atomic weapons, and Bikini Atoll, now a UN-designated, U.S.-administered Trust Territory of the Pacific, was overlaid with concrete runways, shipyards, barracks, and laboratories, which an Atomic Energy Commission (AEC) self-promotional film described as a thrilling sign of human reinvention—"like so many science buildings on college grounds!" Carson could not have been sanguine about that, even though she still believed that nature was ultimately invulnerable to human works.

Her earliest direct confrontation of that issue came when she edited the FWS's first cautionary research on DDT, which was published in 1946. DDT was a war hero at the time. Infectious insects had been the bane of generals from the time of Hannibal, but during World War II, DDT protected untold thousands of soldiers and civilians from typhus, malaria, dengue fever, and other insect-borne diseases. Thanks in part to Hitler's personal physician, who considered the use of DDT an insult to Aryan health, the typhus-ridden German army lost the Battle of Stalingrad.

The calculation of risk from DDT in peacetime was more complicated, but if that calculation was ever made, no record of it survived. Exactly one week after V-J Day, Gimbels department store announced with a full-page ad in the *New York Times* that DDT, in a new "Aer-A-Sol bomb," was safe for use in home and yard: "Released Yesterday! On Sale Tomorrow! Gimbels Works Fast!" As a result, U.S. chemical companies were relieved of wartime inventories, more companies began making DDT, and the race was on to develop even more powerful alternatives, both new chlorinated hydrocarbons and the even more toxic organophosphates, some of which required farmers to wear gas masks and poisoned even some who did. Such research efforts were directly and indirectly supported by the U.S. Army Chemical Corps, whose Cold War mandate was to devise new chemical, biological, and radiological weapons.

The FWS's earliest DDT studies, carried out in 1945 and 1946, concluded that, in a variety of concentrations and delivery methods, DDT killed some of the species it was meant to protect and led to resistance in some of the species that were its targets. Carson used that research as the basis for a story proposal to *Reader's Digest*, saying that it raised the question "whether [DDT] may upset the whole balance of nature if unwisely used." It was an issue, she said, that "really does affect everybody." In fact, the FWS's warning was addressed not to "the whole balance of nature" but to DDT's impact on specific commercial species. She could not have known it, but just then the U.S. Army Chemical Corps was studying DDT as a lethal nerve agent against enemy armies and civilian populations. In any case, *Reader's Digest* passed on the idea.

She kept looking for jobs outside the FWS but in the meantime began to turn her nights and weekends toward another book, this one a history and portrait of life in the world's oceans. Her day job was then as demanding as it would ever be, but she spent every spare moment at the library of the Department of the Interior. Eventually she made a coconspirator of the chief librarian, who helped her find the research she needed and let her take books out overnight for return the next day. It was obvious to colleagues that she was exhausting herself with work on something more than FSW brochures, but she kept it as far from her daytime work as was possible for someone who by then was managing a staff of six and all the agency's publications. By early 1948 she was working on the book proposal and talking to potential literary agents. A year later, having taken only a few weeks' leave from her job, she had shaped an enormous amount of technical research into several chapters of vivid prose, which she delivered to Marie Rodell, her choice among several agents. Rodell had just begun her career as an agent, and Carson was one of her first clients. Both of them had made an excellent choice.

Within two months Rodell negotiated a contract with Oxford University Press for what became a beautiful and comprehensive portrait of ocean life, one that translated the best and latest science into a narrative history of life on Earth from the birth of the first single-celled organism. As with all her writing, she went over every sentence many times, reaching out to each scientist whose work she cited to be sure of her interpretation of it. She also used her mother to read her work aloud in order to correct its sonority. The result was a book that so beautifully clarified its subject's technical complexities that several magazine editors refused to excerpt it, as if its very accessibility made it suspect. Not for the last time, she was also dismissed as a woman invading a male domain. More than one man who read the book confessed to being surprised when they met her. Some expected her to be a large and domineering woman rather than the quiet, restrained scholar she was. Others actually thought that a man must have ghostwritten the book.

Fortunately for her and her readers, William Shawn, then the managing editor of *The New Yorker*, saw the book for what it was. In early 1951, *The New Yorker* bought more than half the book for excerpts that took up most of three issues that June. Published as a book on July 1, *The Sea Around Us* was on the *New York Times* best-seller list for the next 86 weeks, and its success prompted Oxford to republish *Inside the Sea-Wind*, which joined *The Sea Around Us* on the *Times* best-seller list. By the end of the year, *The Sea Around Us* had sold more than 250,000 copies. Eventually translated into 32 languages, it fulfilled Carson's most euphoric hope of success and underwrote her dream of leaving the FWS to become a full-time writer.

*　　*　　*

Six months after the bungled nuclear test at Bikini, *The Atlantic* published a letter titled "A Scientist Rebels" signed by Norbert Wiener, who by then was a legendary figure at MIT. The letter was his answer to a request from Boeing Aircraft for work he had done on weapons guidance during World War II. He refused the request and let *The Atlantic* publish his reply by way of a message to his fellow scientists.

> The experience of the scientists who have worked on the atomic bomb has indicated that in any investigation of this kind the scientist ends by putting unlimited powers in the hands of the people whom he is least inclined to trust with their use. It is perfectly clear also that to disseminate information about a weapon in the present state of our civilization is to make it practically certain that that weapon will be used. . . . I do not expect to publish any future work of mine which may do damage in the hands of irresponsible militarists.

At the time, the military was funding some of the most ambitious and well-funded scientific research being done anywhere, and nowhere more than at MIT. By the time of Wiener's letter, its famous wartime "Rad Lab" had become the Research Laboratory of Electronics and had grown from 200 technicians and researchers to almost 4,000. It was now funded almost entirely by the U.S. government, the military, and military subcontractors. In that context, Wiener's refusal seemed self-righteous, self-defeating, or just another product of his infamous eccentricity. Among the very few public endorsements of his position, one came from Albert Einstein, who said, "I greatly admire and approve the attitude of Professor Wiener. I believe that a similar attitude on the part of all the prominent scientists in this country would contribute much toward solving the urgent problem of national security."

Fearful that his anti-militarism could spread, FBI director J. Edgar Hoover ordered the Boston office to open a file on Wiener. It joined a file in Washington that went back to 1940, when he was cleared to be a civilian researcher for the Department of War. The new file, however, was labeled "Security Matter-C" for "persons suspected of subversive activities against the Government of the United States." Neither file contained much evidence of sedition. The worst of it in the Boston file, at least at that point, was a thirdhand report from the chief of Naval Intelligence that someone at a party had overheard Wiener repeating what he had said about military science in *The Atlantic* and complaining that the government was recruiting former Nazi scientists to do the work that he would not. In a visit from FBI agents, MIT president Karl T. Compton assured them that Wiener was "completely harmless" but promised to talk to him. Other sources interviewed by the Bureau reported the common view at MIT that Wiener was simply "erratic . . . a screwball . . . known to be nuts."

Wiener was also MIT's most accomplished mathematician at the time, and, notwithstanding his opinion of military science after World War II, he was a patriot. At the outset of World War I, despite his many defects as a would-be soldier, he was determined "not to be a slacker" and worked every angle to enlist. At one point, Pvt. Wiener actually found himself standing guard at the Aberdeen Proving Ground, but his main job there was working with other mathematicians on improving the accuracy of ballistics tables. Twenty years later, long before Pearl Harbor, he was pleading with Washington for some way to serve the war effort.

"Wiener stories" were passed around at MIT in amusement or pity, not suspicion. Penguin-shaped, goateed, and so myopic he could not be trusted to throw a horseshoe even in the general direction of a stake, he was fluent in a dozen languages, and socially inept in all of them—"a foreigner wherever he was," as one colleague put it. He got lost easily on his frequent meanderings through the MIT labs, where he worked for forty-five years. Some labs posted lookouts to warn of his approach because he was known to cut into ongoing conversations abruptly and wholly out of context. While reading a book or lost in thought, he walked the halls with one finger tracing the wall. When he reached the open door of a classroom or laboratory, he was known to follow his finger inside and around its walls back to the hallway. When he stopped to have a conversation, he sometimes forgot which way he had been going. Once he asked whether he had been walking toward the lunchroom or away from it so he would know if he had had lunch or not. He swam on his back so he could keep smoking his cigar, which helped him think.

To be Norbert Wiener, however, was anything but amusing. His depressive episodes were especially plain and painful to see, and Wiener actually encouraged them. His father's teaching method having taught him to associate achievement with suffering, he forced himself into despair over an unsolved problem as a way of sharpening his focus on it. A close colleague remembered that he would "goad himself by this depression . . . into a higher level or deeper level of probing and examining and a kind of desperation."

At the same time, he lived in fear for his sanity. Beyond the insecurity he learned from his father, he had a younger brother, Fritz, who was diagnosed with schizophrenia as a young man and lived in a mental institution for thirty years, until a new medication allowed him to be discharged and lead a relatively normal life. Until then, Norbert could never be sure he would not share his brother's fate. His daughter Peggy, when young, saw his abruptly changing moods "as a personal flaw. It was not until very much later that I realized . . . how miserable he must have been. I think it's amazing he survived and was at all functional. He must have been incredibly strong."

His adult life was even more beset than his childhood had been. Everything social and physical seemed alien to him. Rejected by a woman he loved, he reluctantly married a woman his parents picked for him: a Radcliffe student named Margaret Engelmann, who had fled Germany with her family when she was 14 years old. She spoke in the High German dialect of her prosperous, Christian family (which actually pleased his mother). But in the 1930s and even during the war, Engelmann also insisted that Hitler was misunderstood, and that Germany deserved the central place in Europe it was denied after World War I. She kept two copies of *Mein Kampf* on the table of their bedroom dresser, one in English, the other in German. She boasted to their children that her family belonged to the Nazi Party and that they were better than German Jews, whom she called "not very nice." Wiener would redden with anger when he heard such remarks, and their children remembered hearing him shouting at her behind closed doors. He did not criticize her in front of the children, however, nor with any but his closest friends. And perhaps it relieved his sense of impotent rage when he became deeply engaged in weapons research for the Allies.

He got his most important assignment in 1940, when waves of German bombers had just begun attacking the cities of England in what came to be known as the Battle of Britain. Developed in secret, Hitler's Luftwaffe had shocked the Allies with its speed, flight ceiling, agility, and evasive maneuvers, which demanded a great deal more than better ballistics tables. The U.S. was still more than a year away from entering the war, but Britain was pleading for help and willing to share its discovery of radar to get it.

Wiener was chosen to work on the problem in part because he was renowned for having managed to use probability theory to comprehend apparently random systems. His best-known early work was on Brownian motion, the thrashing around of microscopically small particles in apparently still water. A few years before Wiener turned to the subject, Einstein had explained that the movement was driven by collisions between molecules in the medium where the particles were suspended, which could be either liquid or gas. His finding came at a time when the very notion of molecules was still a matter of debate. Wiener's task was seemingly even more remote from certainty: He was to comprehend the particles' trajectories, in effect to place their paths in probabilistic envelopes. The popular analogy was to a bunch of drunks leaning against a lamp post: Wiener's formula could not determine exactly where they would end up after they left that spot, but it could define the area where they were most likely to be. What later became known as the "classical Wiener space" and the "Wiener measure" for random processes like Brownian motion was an important advance for probability theory that eventually found its way from mathematics into quantum mechanics, electrical engineering, cosmology, even the pricing of stock options. It also suggested the shape of a conceptual corral for zigzagging German airplanes.

The problem of weapons guidance involved solving for a profusion of fast-changing variables, including wind, weather, noise in the radar signal, the airplane's performance envelope, the pilot's likely choice of evasive maneuvers, and so on. Wiener's insight was to conceive of the ground-based human/mechanical weapons system and the human/mechanical enemy in the air as a single network of information joined by a system of electrical circuits. At a speed beyond the capacity of any human, the system would import and circulate information to and from all points in a continuous loop of "feedback," a term he took from electrical engineering. The process, in Wiener's vision, was free of binary, friend-and-enemy opposition. His "Predictor" looked at aircraft and antiaircraft weapons as an integrated system of all relevant human, mechanical, and other forces and actions directed to a common purpose—in this case to bring down an airplane in flight.

After months of work, Wiener and his engineering partner, Julian Bigelow, could demonstrate their still-theoretical Predictor with two lights streaking across their laboratory walls representing the shell and the target airplane as they approached their calculated position at impact. The Predictor's accuracy was uncanny, so much better than any previous attempt that Warren Weaver, who funded the work as head of applied mathematics at the National Defense Research Committee in Washington, called it "a miracle." He also concluded that it was not a "useful miracle" because engineering a practical weapon based on Wiener's theory could not meet the urgency of the need. Wiener knew the Predictor was a long way from shooting anything, but it led him to insights that would shape his vision of technology, his reputation and legacy as a scientist, and his humane philosophy.

The idea that the powers of people and machines could be spliced together to a given end—that machines as well as people could act with purpose—emerged from years of speculation and research on "thinking machines," at a time when the word "computer" was still the job title for people doing calculations with pencil and paper. Not surprisingly, the early period of computer development built on analogies to the human brain. The way autopilots managed to keep an airplane at altitude and on course, for example, resembled the act of picking up a pencil or drinking from a glass: It was accomplished not by conscious thought but through reflexive responses to continuous feedback, which linked hand and eye to pencil and glass and gyroscope to rudder and ailerons. Likewise, in the same way thermostat and furnace govern each other by exchanging information on temperature, it was communication of the hypothalamus to and from the organs and the environment that kept body temperature at 98.6 degrees. In all such cases, it was communication and feedback that drove purposeful action of every sort, autonomic and intentional; and putting communication at the center of behavior, human and otherwise, led to the identification of a force as fundamental and quantifiable as mass and energy: information.

Wiener was not alone in working his way toward this insight. During the war, he and others met at a series of interdisciplinary meetings, united in the conviction that there was a fundamental breakthrough just beyond their grasp. The anthropologist Margaret Mead remembered these meetings as so stimulating that, during one of them, in 1942, she lost a tooth but did not realize it until the meeting was over. At that meeting, Wiener's longtime friend and collaborator, physician Arturo Rosenblueth, posited a theory of communication emerging from Wiener's antiaircraft work, one that would apply equally to the purposeful behavior of humans and machines. At the same meeting, the neurophysiologist Warren McCulloch and neuroscientist Walter Pitts presented a mathematical proof that computation by neural nets in the human brain was precisely analogous to the method of computation in Alan Turing's "universal" computer. The findings presented at that meeting appeared in journal articles during 1943—in January, "Behavior, Purpose, and Teleology" by Wiener, Bigelow, and Rosenblueth, and in December, "A Logical Calculus of the Ideas Immanent in Nervous Activity" by McCulloch and Pitts. Both papers had key insights for computer development, and when the war was over, such neuro/mechanical/electrical analogies became a priority for more intensive study.

Just before V-J Day, the Josiah Macy Jr. Foundation agreed to sponsor a conference whose promise was reflected in the prominence of the few who were sent an invitation, almost all of whom accepted. Among them were the polymath game theorist and computer architect John von Neumann; the cultural anthropologists Margaret Mead and her then husband, Gregory Bateson; F. S. C. Northrop, chair of the philosophy department at Yale; and G. Evelyn Hutchinson, also of Yale, a leader in several life sciences. The conference opened at New York's Beekman Hotel on March 6, 1946, with a distinctly noncommittal commitment from the Macy Foundation's medical director, Dr. Frank

Fremont-Smith: "Each group, when it comes together, is an experiment. If it excites you all enough to want to meet again, we will plan for further meetings." The conference went on for the next seven years.

No meeting was more ambitiously interdisciplinary than the first. Von Neumann began by describing the latest work in computer development, including his stored-program model, which became the standard for computer architecture into the twenty-first century. Warren McCulloch showed how the sequence of neurons firing in the cerebral cortex could be expressed in logical calculus, which von Neumann said he thought might be applied to computer development.

An example of just how far-ranging their discussion could go came when the neuroscientist Rafael Lorente de Nó spoke on analogies between the human nervous system and computer circuitry. He was interrupted by Wiener, who noted that the computer, given a logical paradox such as "Everything I say is false," responds with endless yes-no oscillations. Arturo Rosenblueth likened those oscillations to cerebellar tremors, which to Bateson suggested an analogy to both psychiatric and social disorders. In the next session that day, Bateson said that the process by which human and machine communication worked toward a desired end reminded him of his work with New Guinea's Iatmul people, who coped with breakouts of aggression by staging a transvestite ceremony, a social corrective resembling communication and feedback.

That first day's discussion went past dinner into the next day and into the years that followed, taking concepts from and applying them to virtually every hard and soft science. Biologists learned from the psychologists' insights on behavior. Epistemologists learned a broader concept of purpose. Neuroscientists and physiologists discovered mechanical analogies to the nervous system. Electrical engineers found new ways to think about signal, noise, and feedback. And all of them, including sociologists and anthropologists, found fresh perspective in the idea of information and communication as the drivers of purposeful behavior, human and otherwise. Bateson, who carried the Macy

Conferences' insights into the 1960s counterculture, described the result of their meetings as "the biggest bite out of the fruit of the Tree of Knowledge that has been taken in the last 2,000 years."

The meetings were also infamously disjointed and argumentative, even hostile at times, but Wiener, who was acknowledged as the group's central figure from the start, managed to give their ideas conceptual shape and a new vocabulary. For an organization of related bits (binary digits) of information, he adopted Euclid's word "data" to define the component parts of information, and he defined communication as the exchange of information useful in the enactment of a purpose—"a difference that makes a difference," as Bateson put it. As a name for this new way of seeing the world, Wiener lit on the Greek word for governor, *Kubernetes*, from which he took the root "cyber." The world of cyberspace and cyborgs (cybernetic organisms) were still in the unforeseen future, but Wiener's Predictor was their direct ancestor, and it helped put its inventor at the frontier of artificial intelligence, machine learning, and the Internet of Things many years before they had names.

Wiener was far from alone in the pursuit of information technology. He spoke frequently with Claude Shannon of Bell Labs, for example—so frequently, in fact, that their talks prompted his habitual fear of losing credit for his ideas. In the end, they shared credit even as their perspectives diverged. Shannon kept his focus on communication and information theory, while Wiener's interest in philosophy led him to consider the moral and social consequences of a world in which the boundary between the human and the mechanized brain paled to indistinction. His hope was that human capabilities would be amplified by their electromechanical counterparts. His fear was that technology would be dehumanizing and that people would eventually be dominated by their increasingly intelligent machines.

In 1948, Wiener managed to make the Macy Conference's work public and roughly comprehensible in a book titled *Cybernetics: Or Control and Communication in the Animal and the Machine*. "The thought of every age is reflected in its technique," he wrote. "If the seventeenth and early eighteenth centuries are the age of clocks, and the later eighteenth and nineteenth centuries constitute the age of steam engines, the present time is the age of communication and control."

Cybernetics was the unlikeliest bestseller of 1948 or perhaps of any year. Its scope of references was vast, ranging from the vision of flatworms and the choreography of bees to the oscillation of organ pipes. He supported his ideas with pages of mathematical expressions that were meaningless to general readers and beyond even some of his Macy Conference colleagues. Yet, without pretending to understand the mathematical reasoning behind it, book reviewers portrayed Wiener as a Promethean figure who had stolen the secrets of human intelligence and brought them to the aborning world of computers. A reviewer for the *New York Times* placed *Cybernetics* among the "seminal books" of Western civilization, in company with works by Galileo and Malthus. A review for fellow researchers by Wiener's friend and colleague, biophysicist Walter Rosenblith, credited the book with introducing the "new trinity of matter, energy, and information." Most reviewers focused on its relevance to the development and potential of computers, including Wiener's fear that automation by purpose-driven machines could cost millions of people their jobs.

In that way and others, *Cybernetics* was politically inflammatory, especially by the standard of J. Edgar Hoover. Most subversive of all, Wiener confessed the fear that cybernetics could and would have military applications. "Those of us who have contributed to the new science of cybernetics thus stand in a moral position which is, to say the least, not very comfortable," he wrote in the introduction.

> We can only hand it over into the world that exists about us, and this is the world of Belsen and Hiroshima. . . . The best we can do is to see that a large public understands the trend and the bearing of the present work, and to confine our personal efforts to those fields . . . most remote from war and exploitation.

Wiener also reported that he had been reaching out to union leaders to warn them of the job losses that would come with automation—this at a time when the Great Strike Wave of 1945–46 had made the labor movement politically toxic. By the time the strikes were over, Congress had Republican majorities in both houses, and they were joined by dozens of Democrats to pass, over Truman's veto, the Taft-Hartley Act, which not only curtailed the right to strike but also inspired an anti-Communist purge of union leadership.

Despite the sharply conservative turn of American politics, Wiener was undaunted, accusing corporations and capitalism itself of calculated inhumanity.

> It cannot be good for [automation] to be assessed in the terms of the market. . . . [A]nd it is precisely the terms of the open market, the "fifth freedom," that have become the shibboleth of the sector of American opinion represented by the National Association of Manufacturers and the *Saturday Evening Post*.

His advocacy for labor and critique of capitalism crossed corporate interests as much as his letter in *The Atlantic* and later assaults on military science challenged the power structure in Washington.

Having offended all sides of the Iron Triangle, he then published an even more plainspoken book, *The Human Use of Human Beings: Cybernetics and Society,* this one clearly meant to be read as the jeremiad it was. First published in late 1950 and again in 1954, when the witch hunt was at its worst, *The Human Use of Human Beings* took direct aim at "Senator McCarthy and his imitators." It also praised what Wiener saw as Communism's signal virtue, "insistence on the rights of the worker." Wiener was no Communist. He proudly advertised *Pravda's* denunciation of him as a "capitalist warmonger" and "cigar-smoking slave of the industrialists." But he saw the flaws in capitalism as well. He called out some of the nation's largest corporations by name—General Electric, Westinghouse, Bell Labs—for making scientists' discoveries into commodities and ignoring the public good in favor of profit. His focus on this issue was sharpened by personal experience: The patent on one of his own inventions had been bought by AT&T, which buried it to protect a similar invention of its own.

The concerns Wiener expressed in *The Human Use of Human Beings* were not caveats. They were the point, and the point was distinctly subversive, as that word was then defined. After the war, Americans found themselves awash in new products and fads, from portable radios and drive-in movies to muscle cars and Hula-Hoops, signs of a growing economy but one in which Wiener saw natural resources being misspent. Such an "increased mastery of nature," he wrote, "may prove in the long run to be an increased slavery to nature. For the more we get out of the world the less we leave." He made his point with the Mad Hatter's tea party in *Alice's Adventures in Wonderland*.

When the tea and cakes were exhausted at one seat, the natural thing for the Mad Hatter and the March Hare was to move on and occupy the next seat. When Alice inquired what would happen when they came around to their original positions again, the March Hare changed the subject.

In another manuscript of 1954, he put social and environmental threats even above the dangers of the Cold War. "Our long-term chief antagonist will not be Russia but . . . the continuing threats of hunger, thirst, ignorance, overpopulation, and perhaps the new dangers of the poisoning of the world . . . by radioactive by-products of an atomic age." That statement and others later reflected his sympathy not only with the nascent antinuclear movement of the 1950s but also his fear of humanity's other impacts on the natural world.

After *The Human Use of Human Beings*, Wiener's career and legacy were marked as much by his humane philosophy and dark prophecies as by his work in math and science. Some of his positions, particularly his renunciation of military-funded research, made for discomfort at the Macy Conferences, where some of the most prominent participants were doing exactly such research. In the early 1950s, Frank Fremont-Smith, the Macy Foundation's chief medical officer and the conferences' director, funded the CIA's first LSD research and its MK-Ultra Project in mind control. The Macy Conference chair, Warren McCulloch, was among the group's most ardent cold warriors, and von Neumann commuted regularly between Princeton and Los Alamos, where he was working on the development of the hydrogen bomb. Von Neumann was outspoken in his advocacy for a preemptive nuclear strike on the Soviet Union: "If you say why not bomb them tomorrow, I say why not today? If you say today at five o'clock, I say why not one o'clock." Wiener's profound unease with that and personal differences with Warren McCulloch help explain why, in 1950, he stopped attending the Macy Conferences, even as he remained by all accounts its central figure.

Because cybernetics had its roots in his antiaircraft research, Wiener was always concerned it would make its way back into defense work, and so it did, as soon as the Soviet Union tested its first nuclear weapon. In 1950, a report to President Truman proposed defending against nuclear attack by building out a global early-warning system, and the inspiration for its description could not have been plainer. It was described as "an organism . . ."

> What then are organisms? They are of three kinds: animate organisms, which comprise animals and groups of animals, including men; partly animate organisms, which involve animals together with inanimate devices such as in the Air Defense System; and inanimate organisms, such as vending machines. . . . It is the function of an organism . . . to achieve some defined purpose.

This particular organism would evolve by 1958 into a worldwide chain of networked computers and radars known as the Semi-Automated Ground Environment air-defense system, or SAGE, one of whose primary developers was the psychologist, computer scientist, and Macy alumnus J. C. R. "Lick" Licklider. SAGE was designed to warn the North American Aerospace Defense Command, or NORAD, of incoming Soviet bombers and, soon enough, long-range, nuclear-tipped missiles.

*   *   *

If Norbert Wiener and Rachel Carson were ever to have met, there was no place more likely than the office of Paul Brooks, an editor at Houghton Mifflin. It was Brooks who had convinced Wiener to write *The Human Use of Human Beings* and, at virtually the same time, commissioned Carson to write a guide to marine life along the shore. In both cases, Brooks's motivation was to make clearly evocative subjects accessible to the general reading public—Wiener's by expressing the social and moral implications of cybernetics in plain language, Carson's by introducing readers to marine life that they could see and experience for themselves along the country's coastlines.

As it happened, she had been considering exactly that for her next book. Not surprisingly, it turned out to be a great deal more than profiles of individual species, as she and Brooks had initially intended. Like *The Sea Around Us*, *The Edge of the Sea* was another reflection of her deep affinity with marine life and the sea itself, a portrait drawn from current research and her own long hours of close study at the shore. As in both her previous books, its underlying theme was the wonder, invincibility, and ineffable dynamics of life, aquatic and otherwise. She was not yet ready to surrender her belief in nature as a holistic, exquisitely balanced system sustained by "a force strong and purposeful, as incapable of being crushed or diverted from its ends as the rising tide."

Even as she wrote that, the rising tide and other forces of the natural world were being drafted into the Cold War. Some scientists proposed using hydrogen bombs to open shipping lanes, excavate harbors, and create earthquakes on demand. Earth scientists proposed methods to control and weaponize local weather, for example by detonating a hydrogen bomb underwater to create clouds of ice that would intercept the heat of the sun and bring on an impromptu winter. Another proposal was to harness lightning as a way of short-circuiting an enemy's brain. The University of Minnesota geophysicist Athelstan Spilhaus suggested rerouting the world's rainfall and global water supply into "artificial canals of the scale of the Nile," which could theoretically turn a friendly nation's deserts into farmland or an enemy's farmland into desert, as desired.

The U.S. Army Chemical Corps embarked on similarly ambitious projects, which were known by the acronym CEBAR, for chemical, biological, and radiological warfare. Entomologists studied the use of insects as delivery systems for toxins into enemy armies and cities. Operation Big Itch (1954) and Operation Big Buzz (1955) tested insects' survival as disease carriers dispersed in low-altitude bombs over Utah and Georgia. In Operation Drop Kick (1956), populated neighborhoods of Savannah, Georgia, and Avon Lake, Florida, were visited by clouds of *Aedes aegypti*, the mosquito known to carry yellow fever and the Zika virus. The point was not to infect anyone but just to see how many people the insects could be counted on to bite. When *Serratia marcescens* was secretly sprayed across San Francisco, however, eleven patients at one of the city's hospitals suffered related infections, and one of them died. To explore how pathogens could best be delivered to enemy positions, a tracer of zinc cadmium sulfide (called FP, for "fluorescent particle") was released from cars and dropped from the air over Minneapolis, and during experiments spanning more than 15 years, it was dropped in long, sustained flights over cities as well as specific schools and housing projects all over the U.S. Considered harmless at first, FP was found to have adverse affects on human kidneys, lungs, and bone, and suspected to be carcinogenic. Still another human pathogen, *Bacillus globigii*, which causes food poisoning, sepsis, and other infections that are especially serious in people whose immune systems are compromised, was released more than 20 times in various places and under various conditions. The preferred agent against humans ultimately proved to be *Yersinia pestis*, the flea that carries bubonic plague, which was cheap to produce and could be spread by several methods, including aerosols. There were more than 200 open-air experiments with insect-borne diseases in population centers beginning in 1949, none of them disclosed until the mid-1970s, some of them still classified.

As far as is known, the most egregious ethical violations came with the attempt to weaponize radiation, which took place throughout the 1950s. At a time when authorities clearly knew the dangers, releases of radiation into the general public were denied and covered up. Various agencies carried out studies meant to determine the effect of radiation in various dosages and delivery systems, whether by injection, ingestion, or direct exposure. Tests were conducted on the best ways to poison water supplies, to kill agriculture and livestock, and to suspend it in aerosols or smoke, which would direct it into the lungs of the enemy. Among the earliest test subjects was Ebb Cade, a Black worker at the Army base in Oak Ridge, Tennessee, who was brought to the base hospital after a car crash. He was kept in the hospital for more than three weeks awaiting treatment for broken bones while, without his consent, he was injected with "large doses" of radioactive plutonium. After his broken bones were set, they were sampled—along with fifteen extracted teeth—for residual plutonium. Sickened and apparently realizing he was only getting worse, Cade wisely disappeared. His principal physician's memo about the case surfaced for the first time many years later: "We were anticipating collecting not just urine and feces but a number of tissues, such as skeleton, liver and other organs. . . . [We've] lost valuable data we were expected to get."

After 1950, both the Public Health Service and the National Institutes of Health were ordered to participate in such experiments and did so. Among the known experiments:

- In St. Louis, public housing projects were sprayed with radioactive mist from ground level and rooftops, and unmarked vehicles sprayed it as they drove slowly through downtown to test building penetration as well as dispersal rates and distances.

- Four neighborhoods in Minneapolis, including an elementary school and private homes, were doused to measure dispersal rates and to determine the extent to which the radioactive particles made it inside.

- Six hospital patients in Rochester, New York, with "good kidney function" were injected with radioactive isotopes to find out the dosage that would cause renal injury, an experiment later found to be an attempt "not only to obtain excretion data but to cause actual physical harm."

- In an experiment supported by MIT, Harvard, the Atomic Energy Commission, and Quaker Oats, more than a hundred boys living at the Wrentham State School for developmentally disabled children in Massachusetts were fed radioactive oatmeal, which was described to their parents as part of a "special, enriched diet."

- In a study at Vanderbilt University between 1945 and 1947, more than 800 poor pregnant women were given drinks laced with radioactive iron to test varying dosages' effects on their unborn babies and themselves.

The subjects in such studies were not asked for their consent. A physician's assistant in the Vanderbilt study testified that they had not decided against getting it: "We simply felt . . . it was unnecessary." In a scientific culture accustomed to wartime and especially nuclear secrecy, misdirection and deception were not new, but such abuse of the U.S. population and environment was unprecedented (so far as is known), and remained unreported until the late twentieth and early twenty-first century.

No complete record of all these experiments survived, in part because the documentation of them was destroyed by fire in a building that seemed to have been built to be burned down. Sprinklers were specifically declined, and there were no fire walls. The evidence that did survive, however, made clear that there were dozens of such studies and experiments, potentially involving hundreds of thousands of U.S. citizens. All the worst were top secret and plainly designed to avoid legal liability if exposed. Disguised variously as "biological," "medical," and "nutritional" research, they were conducted in blatant violation of the postwar Nuremberg Code, which was written to proscribe the kind of experiments done on prisoners in Nazi concentration camps. Under the code, experiments on humans could only be undertaken under two conditions: with the informed consent of volunteers and a compelling health benefit to others, both of which were routinely ignored.

*　　*　　*

Secrecy and deception became especially important after a nuclear disaster in the Marshall Islands in 1954. The Bikini Atoll had been chosen once again as the target for a nuclear test, this time of the hydrogen bomb. The blast, code-named Castle Bravo, was more than twice as powerful as expected, a thousand times more powerful than the bomb dropped on Hiroshima, and the largest thermonuclear device ever detonated by the U.S. The mushroom cloud rose to a height of 25 miles and rained a fine white powder of radioactive coral over more than 7,000 square miles, sickening U.S. soldiers and sailors and the inhabitants of other atolls. To explain the widespread rain of radioactive ash that settled on other atolls after the blast, the AEC insisted that an unforeseen wind-shift was responsible, but documents declassified years later showed that to be a lie. The wind-shift was known the night before, but attempts to cancel the test were waved off. At the Rongelap Atoll, children played with the radioactive ash as if it were snow. Some people tasted it to see what it could be. The crew of a Japanese fishing boat 80 miles away, well outside the "safe zone," returned to port desperately ill, their skin raw with "sunburn." They were hospitalized as soon as they reached the shore, and their tuna catch was destroyed, along with the haul of a hundred other tuna boats at sea that day.

The disaster made headlines for weeks, thanks to loud protest from the Japanese government and reports that Castle Bravo's fallout was being detected around the world. On Rongelap, mothers began giving birth to badly deformed babies, some to dead fetuses they called "grapes." One mother had a baby who was missing the back of his skull and told a researcher that while nursing she had to be careful "that his brain didn't fall into my lap."

By the time the Marshall Islands tests were done, the targeted atolls had been subjected to 67 aboveground blasts and the explosive power of more than 7,000 Hiroshima-sized bombs. After one of them, the targeted island completely disappeared, the only sign of it an enormous gash in the coral reef that had held it up. In the years that followed, an untold number of Marshall Islanders died from thyroid cancer and leukemia and suffered genetic damage that was passed on to later generations.

In *The Edge of the Sea,* Carson portrayed shoreline species with an ecologist's appreciation of how they and their environment sustained each other, but she made no mention of Castle Bravo or other nuclear tests in the book, which was published in the fall of 1955 and became her third bestseller in four years.

*   *   *

For several years after that, family issues made taking on another book all but unthinkable for Carson. Maria was now in her late eighties and

in failing health, and in 1957, Rachel's favorite niece developed a severe
pneumonia and died soon after, leaving a 4-year-old son named Roger
in Rachel's custody. Then facing 50 and having never thought of raising
a child, Carson read a book on parenting that left her feeling even less
equipped for the job. The following year, her mother died, and Roger,
who had now lost both his mother and a grandmother who had always
been at the center of his life, registered his losses by becoming ever
more difficult at home and at school. Only the help of a sympathetic
full-time housekeeper allowed Carson to think about undertaking
another book, and even then she was "miserable most of the time" and
did not recognize her subject when it first presented itself.

In the spring of 1957, her friend Robert Cushman Murphy, a prominent ornithologist, sued the United States Department of Agriculture
(USDA) over its program to eradicate fire ants in the South and gypsy
moths in the North. The plan called for spraying DDT and other toxic
pesticides from crop dusters across millions of acres. Murphy's fellow
plaintiffs were two Long Island neighbors who had planted a large
organic garden on which one of them, afflicted with a chronic gastric
disorder, depended for her diet. Without their consent and despite
their protests, USDA crop dusters swept over their garden and the
fields around them no fewer than 14 times, releasing a DDT-kerosene
mixture that contaminated the soil, ruined their crops, and poisoned
their animals' feed.

Carson was of course disturbed by the USDA's DDT campaign,
but for both personal and professional reasons, she was reluctant
to dive into a book on the subject. In 1958, however, as the trial and
appeals progressed, she was drawn ever more deeply into the subject
by her increasing alarm at the agency's blatant disregard of good
science. Shortly after she agreed to write the book, later titled *Silent
Spring*, she received a letter from the evolutionary biologist Edward O.
Wilson, a newly tenured professor at Harvard, who had heard from
a friend "that you are planning on a book dealing with the effects of
pest control on the environment. I sincerely hope this is so, because

the subject is a vital one and needs to be aired by a writer of your gifts and prestige." Along with the letter, he sent her an article he had written for *Scientific American* on the USDA's fire ant program as well as his recommendation of a just-published book by the eminent zoologist Charles Elton, who had introduced the concept of the "food chain" half a century earlier. Elton's latest work, *The Ecology of Invasions by Animals and Plants*, dealt specifically with the ways in which humans had unwittingly invited species invasions ever since the development of chemical pesticides, which could radically disrupt a beneficial species' food chain while the targeted species developed resistance and remained.

Officials at the Fish and Wildlife Service shared Carson's anger at the neglect of its still-growing library of cautionary research on DDT and other pesticides. Since the agency itself could not protest overtly, Rachel's friend and former FWS superior Clarence Cottam, now a university professor, took up the cause. The coauthor of the agency's first cautionary reports on DDT, Cottam straightforwardly accused the USDA of incompetence, deception, and corruption. After 20 million acres had been covered, he noted, the concentration of DDT in the aerial spray was found to be equally effective when reduced by a factor of 10. "Who was profiting from the excess use of poison?" Cottam asked in a letter to the USDA secretary's office. And why were agency staff "under strict orders to say nothing against the fire ant program" on penalty of being fired? He laid the blame to an "arrogant bureaucracy of federal leadership that, too often, is less concerned with public service than with power, authority, and prestige."

Other controversies lent even greater urgency to Carson's subject. As she was researching the book, the debate over radioactive fallout was joined by concern over the disposal of nuclear waste from reactors, hospitals, and labs. Current practice was to dispose of it at sea, encased in concrete barrels. The fear was that sooner or later they would rupture, and the radiation would then be carried by currents to all the world's oceans and find its way into the food chain. "The truth is that disposal has proceeded far more rapidly than our knowledge justifies," Carson wrote in a new preface to *The Sea Around Us*. "To dispose first and investigate later is an invitation to disaster."

In late 1959, the U.S. cranberry crop was found to have a residue of aminotriazole, a weed killer known to cause thyroid cancer in rats. With Thanksgiving fast approaching, the government acted promptly. Cranberries were pulled from grocery shelves across the country, and their absence from that year's Thanksgiving tables helped to raise awareness of chemical contamination in the nation's food supply.

Nothing more conclusively confirmed Carson's growing concern about a lack of research before the use and release of chemicals than the new "wonder drug" Immunoprin, the trade name for thalidomide. Sold over the counter beginning in 1957 as a treatment for everything from headaches and anxiety to symptoms of the common cold, thalidomide was used most tragically by pregnant women to alleviate morning sickness. Thousands of babies in Germany, where the drug was first produced and sold, were born severely deformed. News and research were slow to catch up, however, and by the time the drug was withdrawn from open shelves, some 10,000 babies around the world were born blind, deaf, and otherwise disabled. At least 2,000 of them were dead when delivered or died in infancy. No human trials had preceded the drug's release, only tests on rodents, which was then standard practice. Dr. Frances Oldham Kelley of the U.S. Food and Drug Administration stood virtually alone in the world when she refused to approve thalidomide for sale in the United States. Even its use in U.S. clinical trials led to the birth of at least 17 deformed babies before researchers were ordered to destroy their remaining supplies.

For the book Carson was writing, radioactive waste, fallout, carcinogenic cranberries, and over-the-counter poisons for expectant mothers were of a piece: ill-conceived responses to dimly understood problems with profitable but potentially lethal consequences for an uninformed public. "When the public protested," she wrote, "it is fed little tranquilizing pills of half truth. We urgently need an end to these false assurances, to the sugar coating of unpalatable facts." To a degree she could not publicly admit, she had experienced that kind of convenient deception in an intimately personal way.

*   *   *

In the spring of 1960, Carson sent Paul Brooks the two chapters she had been promising him for months on synthetic carcinogens being introduced into the environment and the human gene pool. Accompanying the chapters was a letter telling Brooks that she was about to be hospitalized "for surgery that I hope will not be too complicated." She did not tell him of the suspicion she had cancer. In 1957, she had had cysts removed from her breast that proved benign, and she hoped these would be too, but after surgery this time, her surgeon told her he had performed a radical mastectomy. Beyond the cysts, he had removed lymph nodes and some pectoral muscle, which he admitted would slow her recovery, but he assured her that the mastectomy was only precautionary. There was one growth that "bordered on malignancy," he said, but no further treatment would be necessary. Later, she wondered enough about that prognosis to get a second opinion and discovered that she had herself been victimized by the "sugar coating of unpalatable facts." The cysts in her breast had not "bordered on malignancy" but in fact had metastasized, and the surgeon felt he should not frighten her with the truth.

Recovery from that surgery was worse than slow: It was never quite complete, which made finishing *Silent Spring* an often agonizing ordeal. Her new doctor prescribed sterilization and radiation, which was followed by an escalating series of disabilities, including an ulcer, flu-like symptoms, a bladder infection, phlebitis in both legs, and then acute arthritis in her left ankle and right knee that consigned her to a wheelchair. The serial assaults left her feeling "so indescribably weak and ill that I was frightened," she wrote a close friend. "I just had the feeling that at that moment life had burned down to a very tiny flame that might so easily flicker out." When she had gathered sufficient strength, she was hospitalized for a week of physical therapy and more radiation, at the end of which her doctor told her he could not predict when or if she might be able to walk again. After that came a severe case of iritis, an inflammation of the iris that left her almost blind. For a time, she was unable to work at all.

When she could see a bit better, she worked in bed and relied on assistants to take care of routine matters and type up whatever she dictated. She was spent as she finished the first draft of the book, and she still faced the arduous prepublishing process—sending chapters to sources for comments, rewriting, preparing her footnotes and bibliography, correcting galleys, then page proofs—all the while knowing that she was about to face a forceful, well-funded campaign against her by the chemical companies she had accused of deception and greed.

As her book moved toward publication, she felt new and painful lumps on the left side of her chest. A biopsy showed that her cancer had moved throughout the mammary lymph node chain. This time her doctor told her there was no surgical recourse, just a stronger course of radiation. She spoke only to a few close friends about the gravity of her condition. Word that she had cancer, she told one of them, would be "too much comfort to the chemical companies."

"There is no reason even to say I have not been well," she wrote one friend. "If you want or think you need to give any negative report, say I had a bad time with iritis that delayed my work, but it has cleared up nicely. And that you *never saw me look better*. Please say that." The rest of her life was a fight for her reputation, her message, and whatever physical strength and time she had left to defend them.

*   *   *

By the end of her work on *Silent Spring*, Carson's views converged so closely to Wiener's that their writings could be read as a dialogue between two like-minded colleagues speaking over the fence of their respective disciplines. She had expressed some of these concerns in speeches to scientists and naturalists since the early 1950s but never before to the general public, and never with the rigor and spirit of dissent she brought to *Silent Spring*. As she said at the time, she had never wanted to confront what she now knew to be true.

CARSON: "The most alarming of all man's assaults upon the environment is the contamination of air, earth, rivers, and sea with dangerous and even lethal materials. . . . In this now universal contamination of the environment, chemicals are the sinister and little-recognized partners of radiation in changing the very nature of the world—the very nature of its life. . . . Can anyone believe it is possible to lay down such a barrage of poisons on the surface of the earth without making it unfit for all life?"

WIENER: "[We] are living in the shadow of our destructive inventions. . . . For the first time in history, it has become possible for a limited group of a few thousand people to threaten the absolute destruction of millions, and this without any highly specific immediate risk to themselves."

CARSON: "Along with the possibility of the extinction of mankind by nuclear war, the central problem of our age has . . . become the contamination of man's total environment. . . . How could intelligent beings seek to control a few unwanted species by a method that contaminated the entire environment and brought the threat of disease and death even to their own kind?"

WIENER: "[It] is only a humanity which is capable of awe that will also be capable of controlling the new potentials which we are opening for ourselves. We can be humble and live a good life with the aid of the machines, or we can be arrogant and die."

CARSON: "This is an era of specialists, each of whom sees his own problem and is unaware or intolerant of the larger frame into which it fits."

WIENER: "The man who is only allowed to see his own corner of the operation is removed to a large extent from the feeling of responsibility. . . . He can pretend in his own mind that the act he is performing is obviously necessary and is none of his own will. This is true even if it is later clear that his deed is wrong and indefensible. By such a procedure he dilutes his guilt from a voluntary murder . . . to a glorified manslaughter."

CARSON: "It is also an era dominated by industry, in which the right to make a dollar is seldom challenged."

WIENER: "In a profit-bound world, we must exploit [the natural world] as a mine and leave a wasteland behind us for the future. . . . Megabuck science . . . can be expected to end in lowering the intellectual water table and turning vast areas of the soul which need our cultivation into dead and useless deserts."

CARSON: "The very substantial financial investment involved in backing and launching an insecticide may be swept away as the insects prove once more that the effective approach to nature is not through brute force. And however rapidly technology may invent new uses for insecticides and new ways of applying them, it is likely to find the insects keeping a lap ahead."

WIENER: "The penalties for errors of foresight, great as they are now, will be enormously increased as automatization comes into its full use. . . . [If] the rules for victory in a war game do not correspond to what we actually wish for our country, it is more than likely that such a machine may produce a policy which would win a nominal victory on points at the cost of every interest we have at heart, even that of national survival."

CARSON: "It is the public that is being asked to assume the risks. . . . The public must decide whether it wishes to continue on the present road, and it can do so only when in full possession of the facts."

WIENER: "Whatever benefits are awarded for scientific creation should have the good of the community as their purpose, even more than the good of the individual. As such, they should be contingent on a full and free publication of the new ideas of the discoverer. The truth can make us free only when it is a freely obtainable truth."

By the time Carson and *Silent Spring* dramatically entered and spread this conversation, she was near the end of her life, enduring a series of grave medical setbacks and only partial recoveries. At the same time, she was fighting the well-funded, coordinated campaign by the chemical industry that she had predicted, including threats of lawsuits, sexist reviews, deception, and ridicule. *Time* called *Silent Spring* "hysterically emphatic," an "emotional and inaccurate outburst." *Newsweek* said it had "the quality of gossip." *Life* suggested that "Hurricane Rachel" would have to be endured while "[t]he real dangers to public health [are] evaluated, and then controlled, by skilled medical men." *Chemical and Engineering News* called her supporters "freaks" and said that taking *Silent Spring* seriously would spell "the end of all human progress." That review was headlined simply "Silence, Miss Carson!" Stung by her attack on the USDA, its former secretary Ezra Taft Benson wondered "why a spinster with no children was so concerned about genetics."

The Veliscol Chemical Corporation threatened Houghton Mifflin with a lawsuit, charging that it had tried "to create the false impression that all business is grasping and immoral" and that the Audubon

Society, "food faddists," and others were being misled by "sinister parties," presumably Communists, "so that our supply of food will be reduced to [Soviet] parity." The publisher stood firm, and the threat went away.

During attacks by chemical companies and a debilitating recurrence of her cancer, Carson's refuge was the home in Southport, Maine, she shared with her cat, Moppet.

By the time Carson died, she had the satisfaction of seeing her book prompt congressional hearings as well as preemptive action by President John F. Kennedy. Even before the book was published, excerpts in *The New Yorker* so disturbed him that he ordered a commission to investigate. When the report sustained her findings, Kennedy adopted Carson's agenda as his own. In a speech marking the hundredth anniversary of the National Academy of Sciences, he warned against runaway science and technology in language that plainly echoed hers. He vowed "to stop the contamination of water and air by industrial as well as nuclear pollution." He called for "the steady renewal and expansion of the natural bases of life." He called for precautionary steps "to control the effects of our own scientific experimentation" and for a posture of humility toward nature—"[f]or as science investigates the natural environment, it also modifies it, and that modification may have incalculable consequences, for evil as well as for good." He accepted the government's responsibility to "assure expert review before potentially risky experiments are undertaken," and he promised "open examination and discussion of proposed experiments . . . before they are authorized." One month after he gave that speech, Kennedy was assassinated in Dallas, but the Johnson and Nixon administrations honored his environmentalist positions with their own.

Carson lived just long enough to see passage of the first Clean Air Act. She died in the spring of 1964, overtaken by her cancers and attendant health crises, as well as the aggressive treatments that let her live for as long as she did. Three years earlier her doctor had said that, given her cancer's advance, it was somewhat surprising she was still alive, but even after the publication of *Silent Spring*, she forced herself to meet an arduous schedule of speeches, congressional testimony, and media interviews.

The last and most obvious vindication of her views while she still lived came when millions of dead fish floated to the surface of the Mississippi River in Louisiana. Bleeding from the mouth and fins, they threatened to poison the drinking water of more than a million people, and most of them were catfish, a staple of the food supply. In April 1964, just days before Carson's death, Paul Brooks called to tell her that the fish had been killed by minute quantities of endrin, a toxic pesticide discharged by a waste-treatment plant owned by Veliscol. That finding by the U.S. Public Health Service prompted one of *Silent Spring*'s most powerful advocates, Secretary of the Interior Stewart Udall, to call hearings on the subject of chemical pollution and to instruct his staff to enforce a new policy at least for the time being:

It is essential that all pesticides, herbicides, and related chemicals be applied in a manner fully consistent with the protection of the entire environment. . . . The guiding rule for the Department shall be that when there is a reasonable doubt regarding the environmental effects of the use of a given pesticide, no use should be made.

*   *   *

Wiener died that spring as well, stricken by a massive heart attack as he mounted the steps to the Royal Institute of Technology in Stockholm, where he had been invited to lecture. Back at MIT, word of his death made its way quickly through the corridors he walked so often. Even those who had stood watch to warn of his approach felt his loss. His best students remembered him as a teacher entirely unlike his father: a brilliant and sympathetic mentor who opened their minds to the power of mathematical logic and encouraged them in a way he had not been encouraged himself. The acoustical and electrical engineer Amar Bose, who founded the Bose Corporation and taught at MIT for more than 40 years, said he "could never have paid for the education Wiener gave me. More than anything, he gave me the belief in the incredible potential everyone has."

Not long before he died, at a suitably formal White House ceremony, President Lyndon Johnson awarded Wiener the National Medal of Science. Yet even so, he died with the doubts he had always suffered about whether his work was respected or even much noted by his peers. A special issue of the *Bulletin of the American Mathematical Society* devoted to Wiener in 1965 noted that fact in its opening piece about him: "Unwarranted as these doubts were, they were very real and disturbing to him."

Wiener's warning about the perils of technology did not lend itself to legislation as easily as Carson's cause. His practical legacy was rather to generations of scientists, engineers, computer developers, and the tech wizards of Silicon Valley, whom he reminded of the many ways cutting-edge technologies could benefit humanity but also draw its blood. Fifty years after his death, at a conference on Wiener's legacy, every speaker referred to his gift for cautionary prophecy. As one put it, "The concerns he expressed . . . spanned the range from extremely relevant today to merely vital today."

From the time he was seven years old, Wiener was fascinated by "quasi-living automata," electromechanical devices capable of exhibiting human behaviors. In 1949, he revisited one of them in a classroom at MIT.

One of Wiener's early hopes and insights about cybernetics was that it could someday lead to new neuro-mechanical connections that could improve prosthetics for the disabled: manipulable limbs for amputees, for example, and rerouted senses for the blind and deaf. In 1961, that idea began to take practical shape after he fell down a flight of stairs and broke a hip. At Mass General, he was a star patient. The hospital's best orthopedists had only recently returned from the Soviet Union, where they were shown the first prosthetic hand built on cybernetic insights. When the visitors from Boston expressed surprise, they were told the idea had come from Wiener himself, in a lecture he had given in Moscow almost a decade before. When they got home, they asked Wiener to design a similar prosthesis, and Wiener got his student Amar Bose to guide its development. Two years later, the so-called Boston Arm was introduced as the first prosthesis to be directed by the faint impulses of nerves near the site of amputation. As his close MIT colleague Dirk Struik recalled, "I have seldom seen Wiener so happy as when he told how he turned the mishap of his fall into a victory for the handicapped."

Had he lived to see it, Wiener's worst fears would have been fulfilled by the Vietnam War. Defense Secretary Robert McNamara owed his rise to the presidency of Ford Motor Company to his quantitative approach to management. He brought the same approach to the war, including game theory, cost-benefit analysis, computer modeling, and other technical and statistical tools of decision-making. As applied to the Vietnam War, however, such techniques rested on the tragic assumption that inputs and outputs would be more useful than battle-field experience, a mistake that resulted in such misleading measures of success as the number of trucks destroyed on the Ho Chi Minh Trail and after-battle "body counts." General William Westmoreland, however, was a believer. "On the battlefield of the future," he said, "I see an Army built into and around an integrated area control system that exploits the advanced technology of communications, sensors, fire direction, and the required automatic data processing." The fog of war would be lifted, and war would be won at the push of a button.

Wiener would have been appalled at so benign a view of technology in war, which evoked the catastrophic fantasies of Stanley Kubrick's *Dr. Strangelove* and its living model, Herman Kahn, dreamer of Arma-geddon "wargasms" at the RAND Corporation. Wiener's last lectures, papers, and books led him again and again to recount stories in which the arrogant misuse of power was turned back on its misuser. His favor-ite was "The Monkey's Paw," a short story by the turn-of-the-century

British writer W. W. Jacobs. In it, a talisman in the form of a monkey's wizened foot is known to grant three wishes. Its latest owner wishes first for money, which comes to him from supervisors at his son's workplace, as compensation for his son's sudden, accidental death. The owner's second wish is for his son to be brought back to him, but he answers the next knock at his door only to find his son's ghost. Heartbroken, his final wish is for the ghost to go away.

Wiener used this story to greatest effect when the U.S. and Soviet Union began to deploy nuclear-tipped intercontinental ballistic missiles, whose speed left only minutes between detection and impact. Such close timing for such a critical response raised the temptation of automating it, which raised the possibility of finding a ghost at the door. He left this warning to the world in his last book, titled *God & Golem, Inc.* "If you are playing a war game with a certain conventional interpretation of victory," he wrote, "victory will be the goal at any cost, even that of the extermination of your own side."

Wiener left a more complicated prophecy to the young computer developers of the 1970s, whose vision was of one world and one people linked together by a global network of communication enhanced by artificial intelligence, virtual reality, and travel by holography (not Wiener's word but a prediction he made whose name was a very Wienerian concoction from the Greek words for "whole" and "message"). Some early settlers of Silicon Valley especially cherished Wiener's insight that information, to be liberating, had to be "freely obtainable"—later translated into the Internet battle cry "Information wants to be free." Yet Wiener would have been appalled by the result: new channels for hacking and feeding disinformation as weapons of war, and an Internet business model based on the collection of massive amounts of free user data, which could be sold back to its sources and others for use in behavior modification, from product purchases to social uprisings.

The future that Wiener wished for cybernetics was in doubt even before he died. John McCarthy, the computer and cognitive scientist who coined the term "artificial intelligence" in 1955, confessed later that he had intentionally avoided the term cybernetics "to avoid having either to accept . . . Wiener as a guru or having to argue with him." Sadly, Wiener never saw the wave of protests for free speech, civil rights, nuclear disarmament, and peace in Vietnam that spread across college campuses in the middle and late 1960s. He died just before Freedom Summer 1964, when college students traveled to Mississippi to challenge the poll taxes, literacy tests, and bureaucratic fictions that cost Black Americans the right to vote. That fall, back at Berkeley, some of them defied university policy and the Berkeley Police Department to set up tables on campus to collect donations and sign up new recruits. In December, when negotiations with the university had all but broken down, students converged by the thousands on Sproul Hall. There, in a famously eloquent outburst against the "machine" of institutional repression, Mario Savio inaugurated the Free Speech Movement:

> There's a time when the operation of the machine becomes so odious—makes you so sick at heart—that you can't take part. You can't even passively take part. And you've got to put your bodies upon the gears and upon the wheels, upon the levers, upon all the apparatus, and you've got to make it stop. And you've got to indicate to the people who run it, to the people who own it, that unless you're free, the machine will be prevented from working at all.

Norbert Wiener—proto-peacenik in the Cold War, decrier of "mega-buck science" in industry and academia, advocate for labor in a time of union purges, critic of McCarthy at the height of McCarthyism—would have approved.

* * *

Carson's excerpts were about to be published in *The New Yorker* when she braved one last trip to Southern California in order to keep a long-standing promise to speak at Scripps College. The promise was likely to Roger Revelle, a prominent oceanographer, scholar, and science administrator. He and Carson had been friends and colleagues since World War II, when he directed the Navy's funding for oceanographic research and was in charge of the National Academy of Sciences' study of radiation's effect on Bikini Atoll. Years later, as director of the Scripps Institution of Oceanography in La Jolla, California, Revelle coauthored the first paper linking fossil fuel emissions to global warming. He also hired Charles David Keeling to conduct a longitudinal study of atmospheric CO_2. The upward slope of the "Keeling Curve," first reported in a June 1960 paper, has ever since measured the progress and peril of climate change.

Against that backdrop, Carson spoke to the graduating class of 1962 in the voice of the ecological activist she had become. "Man has long talked somewhat arrogantly about the conquest of nature," she said. "It is our misfortune—it may well be our final tragedy—that . . . the price of conquest may be the destruction of man himself."

She articulated that concern at the heart of *Silent Spring* in every speech she gave after its publication, but she ended this one with a special message to her young audience, a challenge by way of apology.

I wish I could stand before you and say that my own generation had brought strength and meaning to man's relation to nature, that we had looked upon the majesty and beauty and terror of the earth we inhabit and learned wisdom and humility. Alas, this cannot be said, for it is we who have brought into being a fateful and destructive power. . . .

Your generation must come to terms with the environment. Your generation must face realities instead of taking refuge in ignorance and evasion of truth. Yours is a grave and a sobering responsibility. . . . You go out into a world where mankind is challenged, as it has never been challenged before, to prove its maturity and its mastery—not of nature, but of itself.

The Best of Us

Rachel Carson had many good reasons not to write her most influential book, including distractions at home and the prospect of mastering mountains of research, much of it grim and outside her field of expertise. Most discouraging, perhaps, was that writing a book about how new substances developed or adopted by industrial scientists were injuring natural species, including human beings, would be a rebuke to all the work for which she was best known: books that portrayed nature as a world apart and above us, as an ineffable realm that held "some universal truth that lies just beyond our grasp . . . the ultimate mystery of life itself." She had made speeches to select groups warning of the damage that chemical toxins posed to the atmosphere, the land, and the seas, but she shrank from writing about it. When Robert Cushman's case against the USDA and its aerial spraying program was coming to trial, she actually wrote to *The New Yorker*'s E. B. White, who had written one of the earliest warnings of DDT, to see if he would be interested in covering the case and its implications. He sent her letter to the magazine's editor, William Shawn, who encouraged Carson to follow the trial herself. After that, she let herself get close enough to the case and the many issues involved to know that she had to go further.

Because her closest friend and Southport neighbor, Dorothy Freeman, had been less than enthusiastic about what she called "Rachel's poison book," Carson explained herself in a letter. She had been wrong to ignore the threat that humans posed to the natural world, she wrote, admitting she should have recognized it the day she heard about Hiroshima.

> Some of the thoughts that came were so unattractive to me that I rejected them completely. . . . It was pleasant to believe . . . that much of Nature was forever beyond the tampering reach of man—he might level the forests and dam the streams, but the clouds and the rain and the wind were God's. . . . These beliefs have been part of me for as long as I have thought about such things. To have them even vaguely threatened was so shocking that . . . I shut my mind, refused to acknowledge what I couldn't help seeing.

She had another reason to avoid the subject, which is reflected in the first chapter of *Silent Spring*. In what she titled "A Fable for Tomorrow," she portrayed a fallen world, a place covered by the "shadow of death. . . ."

> The birds, for example—where had they gone? . . . The few birds seen anywhere were moribund; they trembled violently and could not fly. It was a spring without voices. . . . Even the streams were now lifeless. Anglers no longer visited them, for all the fish had died.

That chapter, which is both the beginning of the book and the part she wrote last, drew on distasteful memories that had always been at odds with her childhood idyll in the fields and forests of Springdale. For all the inspiration and comforting solitude it offered her, Springdale was literally shadowed by Pittsburgh, which had been belching fumes and coal dust since the early years of the nineteenth century—"when even the snow could scarcely be called white," as one visitor wrote. It was a region economically blessed and environmentally cursed by the abundance of coal in the "Pittsburgh seam." Thanks to runoff from the city's coke plants, the Allegheny River that passed by Springdale was murky and fetid, and the various oxides emitted from the city's smokestacks—carbon, sulfur, and nitrogen, mixed in with mercury, benzene, and arsenic emissions—joined the stench from Springdale's own glue factory. She had always found that embarrassing, troubling, even disgraceful. When she went back after college to pack her things for graduate school, the town was defined by two huge power plants within two miles of each other, and it seemed to her that, for all its good jobs and relative prosperity, the place closest to her heart had died.

In that way, *Silent Spring's* eloquent opening chapter was a eulogy for all the nation's Springdales and, as her letter explained, for the quasi-spiritual faith in nature's invulnerability that she had to leave behind. Her elaboration of that subject dominated the many eulogies to her when she died, and it was reechoed in the legislation her work inspired in the years that followed.

In a time as hostile to change as the postwar period, it took such strong-minded people—in Carson's case, someone willing to challenge even her own previous work—to make progress. Carson and others like her worked virtually alone, out on their separate limbs. Myrlie Evers remembered that Medgar often felt that way in his work for the NAACP, and never more so than in the days just before his death.

No limb was quite as shaky as Harry Hay's, but he was sustained by the grit he displayed from childhood as he walked through his "period of terror" to take up a reviled, untimely cause. He and Frank Kameny shared a dictatorial leadership style that cost them close friends even among their disciples, but that mulish tenacity was what it took to assert their rightful place in a country that had cast them out. More than forty years later, looking back at Kameny's failed petition to the Supreme Court, Washington attorney Paul Smith could only wonder at the thought of "Frank Kameny, in 1960, making the same arguments that have now caused the invalidation of sodomy laws, the protection of LGBT civil servants from discrimination, and the repeal of Don't Ask, Don't Tell." Smith is the attorney who used Kameny's arguments at the Supreme Court to win the case of *Lawrence v. Texas* in 2003. The majority opinion, read in court by Justice Anthony Kennedy, declared that all laws that criminalized the private sexual relations of consenting adults were unconstitutional.

Among Pauli Murray's papers is a letter she wrote to her adoptive mother during law school, in the spring of 1943. In it, she explained that she had not come home for a promised visit "because my physical stamina has been so low, I could not get myself together to pack. . . . This little 'boy-girl' personality, as you jokingly call it, sometimes gets me into trouble, Mother." She was worried that people were gossiping about "a young sophomore [who] sort of walked into my life without my realizing what was happening to me, and that caused a great deal of consternation among certain people." She said she had done "nothing of which to be ashamed," but she was concerned that even a casual rumor could ruin her legal career. "[B]ecause the laws of society do not protect me," she wrote, "I'm exposed to any enemy or person who may or may not want to hurt me."

Toward the end of that summer, she finished "Dark Testament," an epic poem she had started in the late 1930s. She worked on it "as one possessed," she wrote in her autobiography, "pouring all my pain and bitterness into [it]. . . . When the poem was completed, I felt as if a demon had been exorcised and a terrible fever inside me had broken."

Yet as she began her last year in law school, the question remained: Why *didn't* the law protect her and others like her? That was the issue she chose to answer in her final thesis, though she addressed only racial discrimination, not yet gender. She tried out her approach for the first time in class, arguing that civil rights could be secured, *Plessy* overturned, and Jim Crow defeated by the Fourteenth Amendment's Equal Protection Clause. To a man (in a class of men), they found her argument and her ambition for it absurd. Some literally laughed at the idea.

Years later, Ruth Bader Ginsburg would describe Murray as "independent, intelligent, poetic, feisty, determined, confident in her counsel": the kind of person, in other words, who stuck to her law-school thesis despite what her classmates and even a favorite teacher thought.

It was because of her determination or perhaps her desperation that the Equal Protection argument against *Plessy* helped Thurgood Marshall as he developed his argument in *Brown* and that prevailed years later in *White v. Crook* and *Reed v. Reed*. Long after Murray was gone, those two gender-discrimination cases were cited as precedent in many others, including *Obergefell v. Hodges*, which legalized same-sex marriage in 2015. Perhaps it is inevitable that such decisions would have been reached eventually, but progress is always a figment until it is not, and those who make it happen, especially in times as averse to change as the postwar years, make history.

Thanks to the people in this book and others like them, the 1960s take their place in a continuum of social progress rather than as some sudden generational cleavage. In a rare convergence of history and calendar, the transition could reasonably be dated to 1960, when both SNCC and SDS were founded. That spring too, hearings of the House Un-American Activities Committee held at San Francisco's city hall drew hundreds of Berkeley students and other protestors, who found their way into the rotunda and sat there and on the marble staircase singing protest songs. On day two of the hearings, at HUAC's request, San Francisco police turned fire hoses on them, washing them out of the rotunda, down the stairs, and out of the building. The plainest result was that some 5,000 protestors turned out for the last day of the hearings. The committee later made a movie about the San Francisco "riot" called *Operation Abolition*, which became a camp-film-festival favorite at colleges across the nation and made HUAC a victim of the ultimate subversion: It was laughable. Around that time, a board member of SDS, allegedly in all seriousness, suggested convening a discussion group, one of whose topics would be "Has the older generation anything left to say?"

Ah, youth. My generation had our victories too, but looking back, I cannot help feeling that people like those in this book were the more authentic rebels, in part because they did not think of themselves that way. In a decade and a nation perhaps readier with opprobrium than ever before, they defied the most powerful forces and conventions of their time just to be the people they were, in the country it had always promised to be. Thanks to that, they lit a path for the rest of us to a somewhat less imperfect union, which is about the best thing any citizen can do.

Acknowledgments

Every author listed in the bibliographies and source notes has my gratitude for their scholarship in the fields implicated here, but I must acknowledge a special debt to those whose ideas were especially important and who were not called out by name in the text: Allan Bérubé, Antoine Bousquet, Dorothy Sue Cobble, Stephanie Coontz, John D'Emilio, Sara Evans, Peter Galison, Steve J. Heims, Kevin Kelly, Linda Kerber, Susan Lynn, Manning Marable, Lisa Martino-Taylor, Serena Mayeri, J. R. McNeill, Joanne Meyerowitz, Kay Mills, Edmund Russell, James Gustave Speth, Amy Swerdlow, Jeanne Theoharis, Fred Turner, Timothy Tyson, Kate Weigand, Jonathan Weisgall, Simon Wendt, Michael Vinson Williams, and Donald Worster.

I am doubly grateful to those authors whose work influenced this one and who also read part or all of the prepublication manuscript for errors of fact and interpretation. Those kind enough to do so include Taylor Branch, Winifred Breines, Lillian Faderman, Todd Gitlin, James Gleick, Jacob Hamblin, Ronald Kline, Linda Lear, and Bill McKibben. As it never goes without saying, neither they nor other scholars are responsible for any errors I may have made.

I am once again indebted to many libraries and librarians, including Rebecca Aldi and her colleagues in the Beinecke Library at Yale; Myles Crowley and his colleagues at the libraries of MIT; Laurie S. Ellis, Jennifer Fauxsmith, and their colleagues in the Schlesinger Library at

Radcliffe; Stephanie Krauss in the Center for the History of Medicine at Harvard's Countway Library; the staff of the Sophia Smith Collection of Women's History at Smith College; the staff at the Tamiment Library and Robert F. Wagner Labor Archives at New York University; and, as always, the professional staff at the inestimable New York Public Library.

I could never have written this book without the support and sometimes professional help of good friends, including Amy and Cliff Aronson, Gigi and Harry Benson, Donna and Peter Bonventre, Nicole and Gay Dillingham, Lisa Grunwald and Steve Adler, Deena Holliday, Lisa Kasteler and Jim Calio, Becky and Dan Okrent, Jackie and Joe Poirot, and Jayme Sheiber.

For her patience through the usual doubts and crises, I am again deeply indebted to Liz Darhansoff, my literary agent and friend of many years. At Simon & Schuster, I benefited from the close editing of Jim Fallon and Jamie Selzer, the supervision of Morgan Hart, the elegant design of Kyle Kabel, and the diligent attention of Hana Park, who, among other gifts, steered me to the wonderful picture researcher Crary Pullen.

Most of all, I thank Priscilla Painton, whose critical intelligence and careful readings of this book are reflected on every page. No author could ask for a more supportive or incisive editor.

Finally, for a great deal more than help with this book, I give thanks for Allison Gaines Pell, Ben Pell, Nick Gaines, Carra Pope, Will Gaines, Lillian Gaines, Patricia and Dr. Robert W. Gaines, Bonnie and Rob Lochner, Nancy and Morton Lipton, and their daughter Karen Lipton Gaines, mother to several of the above, and for three decades my most challenging and encouraging partner.

Bibliographies

INTRODUCTION

Belgrad, Daniel. *The Culture of Spontaneity: Improvisation and the Arts in Postwar America*, new edition. Chicago: University of Chicago Press, 1998.

Boyer, Paul. *By the Bomb's Early Light: American Thought and Culture at the Dawn of the Atomic Age*. Chapel Hill: University of North Carolina Press, 1994.

Friedrich, Otto. *The End of the World: A History*. New York: Penguin, 1982.

Lhamon, W. T., Jr. *Deliberate Speed: The Origins of a Cultural Style in the American 1950s*. Cambridge, MA, and London: Harvard University Press, 1990.

Lott, Eric. "Double V, Double-Time: Bebop's Politics of Style." In *Jazz Among the Discourses*, Krin Gabbard, ed. Durham, NC: Duke University Press, 1995.

Mee, Charles L., Jr. *The Deal: Churchill, Truman, and Stalin Remake the World*. Boston: New Word City, 2014.

Morgan, Bill. *I Celebrate Myself: The Somewhat Private Life of Allen Ginsberg*. New York: Viking, 2006.

Smyth, H. D. *Atomic Energy for Military Purposes*. York, PA: Maple Press, 1945.

GAY RIGHTS

Baim, Tracy. *Barbara Gittings: Gay Pioneer*. Chicago: Prairie Avenue Productions, 2015.

Bayley, Edwin R. *Joe McCarthy and the Press*. Madison: University of Wisconsin Press, 1981.

Bérubé, Allan. *Coming Out Under Fire: The History of Gay Men and Women in World War II*. Chapel Hill: University of North Carolina Press, 1990.

Bronski, Michael. *A Queer History of the United States*. Boston: Beacon Press, 2011.

Cervini, Eric. *The Deviant's War: The Homosexual vs. the United States of America*. New York: Farrar, Straus and Giroux, 2020.

Corber, Robert J. *Homosexuality in Cold War America: Resistance and the Crisis of Masculinity*. Durham, NC: Duke University Press, 1997.

Cory, Donald Webster [Edward Sagarin]. *The Homosexual in America: A Subjective Approach*. New York: Greenberg, 1951.

Cybernetics: The Macy Conferences, 1946–1953: The Complete Transactions, revised edition. Claus Pias, ed. Zurich: Diaphanes, 2016.

D'Emilio, John. *Making Trouble: Essays on Gay History, Politics, and the University*. New York: Routledge, 1992.

———. *Sexual Politics, Sexual Communities: The Making of a Homosexual Minority in the United States 1940–1970*. Chicago: University of Chicago Press, 1983.

Faderman, Lillian. *The Gay Revolution: The Story of the Struggle*. New York: Simon & Schuster, 2015.

———. *Odd Girls and Twilight Lovers: A History of Lesbian Life in 20th Century America*. New York: Columbia University Press, 1991.

Gay and Lesbian Rights in the United States: A Documentary History. Walter L. Williams and Yolanda Retter, eds. Westport, CT, and London: Greenwood Press, 2003.

Gay Is Good: The Life and Letters of Gay Rights Pioneer Frank Kameny. Michael G. Long, ed. Syracuse, NY: Syracuse University Press, 2014.

Hansen, Joseph. *A Few Doors West of Hope: The Life and Times of Dauntless Don Slater*. Homosexual Information Center, 1998.

Homophile Studies in Theory and Practice. W. Dorr Legg, ed. San Francisco: One Institute Press & GLB Publishers, 1994.

Hurewitz, Daniel. *Bohemian Los Angeles and the Making of Modern Politics*. Berkeley: University of California Press, 2007.

Johnson, David K. *The Lavender Scare: The Cold War Persecution of Gays and Lesbians in the Federal Government*. Chicago: University of Chicago Press, 2004.

Kaiser, Charles. *The Gay Metropolis: The Landmark History of Gay Life in America*. New York: Grove Press, 1997.

Katz, Jonathan Ned. *Gay American History: Lesbians and Gay Men in the U.S.A.*, revised edition. New York: Meridian, 1992.

Kinsey, Alfred, et al. *Sexual Behavior in the Human Male*. Philadelphia: W. B. Saunders, 1948.

Lait, Jack, and Lee Mortimer. *Washington Confidential*. New York: Crown Publishers, 1951.

Loughery, John. *The Other Side of Silence: Men's Lives and Gay Identities: A Twentieth-Century History*. New York: Henry Holt and Company, 1998.

Marcus, Eric. *Making Gay History: The Half-Century Fight for Lesbian and Gay Equal Rights.* New York: Harper Perennial, 2002.

Meeker, Martin. *Contacts Desired: Gay and Lesbian Communications and Community, 1940s–1970s.* Chicago: University of Chicago Press, 2006.

Murdoch, Joyce, and Deb Price. *Courting Justice: Gay Men and Lesbians v. The Supreme Court.* New York: Basic Books, 2002.

Patterson, James T. *Grand Expectations: The United States, 1945–1974.* New York and Oxford, UK: Oxford University Press, 1996.

Radically Gay: Gay Liberation in the Words of Its Founder, Harry Hay. Will Roscoe, ed. Boston: Beacon Press, 1996.

Sears, James T. *Behind the Mask of the Mattachine: The Hall Call Chronicles and the Early Movement for Homosexual Emancipation.* New York and London: Harrington Park Press, 2006.

Setterington, Ken. *Branded by the Pink Triangle.* Toronto: Second Story Press, 2013.

Stein, Marc. *City of Sisterly and Brotherly Loves: Lesbian and Gay Philadelphia, 1945–1972.* Philadelphia: Temple University Press, 2004.

Teal, Donn. *The Gay Militants.* New York: Stein and Day, 1971.

Timmons, Stuart. *The Trouble with Harry Hay: Founder of the Modern Gay Movement.* Boston: Alyson Publications, 1990.

We Are Everywhere: A Historical Sourcebook of Gay and Lesbian Politics. Mark Blasius and Shane Phelan, eds. New York: Routledge, 1997.

White, C. Todd. *Pre-Gay L.A.: A Social History of the Movement for Homosexual Rights.* Urbana and Chicago: University of Illinois Press, 2009.

Papers and Articles

"The American Gay Rights Movement and Patriotic Protest," Simon Hall. *Journal of the History of Sexuality*, vol. 19, no. 3 (September 2010), pp. 536–562.

"Behind the Mask of Respectability: Reconsidering the Mattachine Society and Male Homophile Practice, 1950s and 1960s," Martin Meeker. *Journal of the History of Sexuality*, vol. 10, no. 1 (January 2001), pp. 78–116.

"Birth of a Consciousness," Harry Hay. *Gay & Lesbian Review*, November–December 2016, pp. 1–10.

"Children of a Lesser Holocaust," Alistair Newton. *Gay & Lesbian Review*, January–February 2012, https://glreview.org/article/children-of-a-lesser-holocaust/.

"Communist and Homosexual: The FBI, Harry Hay, and the Secret Side of the Lavender Scare, 1943–1961," Douglas M. Charles. *American Communist History*, vol. 11, no. 1 (2012), pp. 101–124.

"The Founding of the Mattachine Society: An Interview with Harry Hay,"

Jonathan Katz. *Radical America*, vol. 11, no. 4 (July–August 1977), pp. 27–40. Reprinted in Katz, *Gay American History*, pp. 406–420.

"From Subversion to Obscenity: The FBI's Investigations of the Early Homophile Movement in the United States, 1953–1958," Douglas M. Charles. *Journal of the History of Sexuality*, vol. 19, no. 2 (May 2010), pp. 262–287.

"Gay Life in Stalin's Gulag," Kirill Guskov. openDemocracy, December 11, 2018. Interview with Dan Healy, author of *Russian Homophobia from Stalin to Sochi*. https://www.opendemocracy.net/en/odr/gay-life-in-stalins-gulag/.

"'Homo-Hunting' in the Early Cold War: Senator Kenneth Wherry and the Homophobic Side of McCarthyism," Randolph W. Baxter. *Nebraska History*, vol. 84 (2003), pp. 119–132.

"Homophobia and the Trajectory of Postwar American Radicalism: The Career of Bayard Rustin," John D'Emilio. *Radical History Review*, vol. 1995, no. 62 (Spring 1995), pp. 80–103.

"'Homosexual Citizens': Washington's Gay Community Confronts the Civil Service," David K. Johnson. *Washington History*, vol. 6, no. 2 (Fall–Winter 1994/1995), pp. 44–63.

"Lifting the Ban on Gays in the Civil Service: Federal Policy Toward Gay and Lesbian Employees Since the Cold War," Gregory B. Lewis. *Public Administration Review*, vol. 57, no. 5 (September–October 1997), pp, 387–395.

"National Security and Personal Isolation: Sex, Gender, and Disease in the Cold-War United States," Geoffrey S. Smith. *International History Review*, vol. 14, no. 2 (May 1992), pp. 307–337.

"The Pink Triangle and Political Consciousness: Gays, Lesbians, and the Memory of Nazi Persecution," Erik N. Jenson. *Journal of the History of Sexuality*, vol. 11, no. 1/2 (January–April 2002), pp. 319–349.

"'Politics in an Age of Anxiety': Cold War Political Culture and the Crisis in American Masculinity, 1949–1960," K. A. Cuordileone. *Journal of American History*, vol. 87, no. 2 (September 2000), pp. 515–545.

"Queer Hoover: Sex, Lies, and Political History," Claire Bond Potter. *Journal of the History of Sexuality*, vol. 15, no. 3 (July 2006), pp. 355–381.

Transcript, State Department Employee Loyalty Investigation, Subcommittee of the Foreign Relations Committee, U.S. Senate, 81st Congress, May 8–June 21, 1950.

"Unacceptable Mannerisms: Gender Anxieties, Homosexual Activism, and Swish in the United States, 1945–1965," Craig M. Loftin. *Journal of Social History*, vol. 40, no. 3 (Spring 2007), pp. 577–596.

"'Unceasing Pressure for Penetration': Gender, Pathology, and Emotion in George Kennan's Formation of the Cold War," Frank Costigliola. *Journal of American History*, vol. 83, no. 4 (March 1997), pp. 1309–1339.

"We Are a Separate People." Interviews of Harry Hay by Mitchell Tuchman, October 1981–January 1982. Center for Oral History Research, University of California, Los Angeles.

FEMINISM

Archives

Communism, Socialism, and Left-Wing Politics Collection. Sophia Smith Collection of Women's History, Smith College, Northampton, MA.

Federated Press Records, 1918–1955. Butler Library, Columbia University, New York, NY. (BF/FP)

Papers of Betty Millard. Sophia Smith Collection of Women's History, Smith College Special Collections, Smith College, Northampton, MA.

Papers of Eleanor Flexner. Schlesinger Library, Harvard Radcliffe Institute, Harvard University, Cambridge, MA

Papers of Gerda Lerner. Schlesinger Library, Harvard Radcliffe Institute, Harvard University, Cambridge, MA. (GL/SL)

Papers of Pauli Murray. Schlesinger Library, Harvard Radcliffe Institute, Harvard University, Cambridge, MA. (PM/SL)

Records of the Communist Party of the United States. Tamiment Library and Robert F. Wagner Labor Archives, New York University, New York, NY.

Records of the United Electrical, Radio, and Machine Workers of America, 1936–2006.

Archives & Special Collections, University of Pittsburgh Library System, Pittsburgh, PA. (BF/UE)

Records of the Women's International Democratic Federation. Sophia Smith Collection of Women's History, Smith College, Northampton, MA.

Books

Azaransky, Sarah. *The Dream Is Freedom: Pauli Murray and American Democratic Faith*. New York and Oxford, UK: Oxford University Press, 2011.

Breines, Wini. *The Trouble Between Us: An Uneasy History of White and Black Women in the Feminist Movement*. New York and Oxford, UK: Oxford University Press, 2006.

Brooks, Maegan Parker. *Fannie Lou Hamer: America's Freedom Fighting Woman*. Lanham, MD: Rowman & Littlefield, 2020.

Carson, Clayborne. *In Struggle: SNCC and the Black Awakening of the 1960s*. Cambridge, MA, and London: Harvard University Press, 1995.

Cobble, Dorothy Sue. *The Other Women's Movement: Workplace Justice and*

Social Rights in Modern America. Princeton, NJ, and Oxford, UK: Princeton University Press, 2004.

Coontz, Stephanie. *A Strange Stirring:* The Feminine Mystique *and American Women at the Dawn of the New Left*. New York: Basic Books, 2011.

Evans, Sara. *Personal Politics: The Roots of Women's Liberation in the Civil Rights Movement*. New York: Vintage Books, 1979.

Feminist Coalitions: Historical Perspectives on Second-Wave Feminism in the United States. Stephanie Gilmore, ed. Urbana and Chicago: University of Illinois Press, 2008.

Fleming, Cynthia Griggs. *Soon We Will Not Cry: The Liberation of Ruby Doris Smith Robinson*. Lanham, MD: Rowman & Littlefield Publishers, 1998.

Flexner, Eleanor, and Ellen Fitzpatrick. *Century of Struggle: The Women's Rights Movement in the United States*. Cambridge, MA, and London: Harvard University Press, 1959.

Friedan, Betty. *The Feminine Mystique*, 50th anniversary edition. New York: W. W. Norton, 2013.

Giardina, Carol. *Freedom for Women: Forging the Women's Liberation Movement, 1953–1970*. Gainesville: University Press of Florida, 2010.

Giddings, Paula. *When and Where I Enter: The Impact of Black Women on Race and Sex in America*. New York: William Morrow, 1984.

Gilmore, Stephanie. *Groundswell: Grassroots Feminist Activism in Postwar America*. New York: Routledge, 2013.

Gore, Dayo F. *Radicalism at the Crossroads: African American Women Activists in the Cold War*. New York and London: New York University Press, 2011.

Hamer, Fannie Lou. *To Praise Our Bridges: An Autobiography*. Pamphlet available at https://snccdigital.org/wp-content/themes/sncc/flipbooks/mev _hamer_updated_2018/index.html.

Hands on the Freedom Plow: Personal Accounts by Women in SNCC. Faith S. Holsaert, et al., eds. Urbana and Chicago: University of Illinois Press, 2012.

Harrison, Cynthia. *On Account of Sex: The Politics of Women's Issues, 1945–1968*. Berkeley and London: University of California Press, 1988.

Hartmann, Susan M. *The Other Feminists: Activists in the Liberal Establishment*. New Haven, CT: Yale University Press, 1998.

Horowitz, Daniel. *Betty Friedan and the Making of* The Feminine Mystique: *The American Left, the Cold War, and Modern Feminism*. Amherst: University of Massachusetts Press, 1998.

Kerber, Linda. *No Constitutional Right to be Ladies: Women and the Obligations of Citizenship*. New York: Hill and Wang, 1998.

Komarovsky, Mirra. *Women in the Modern World*. New York: Little, Brown, 1953.

Lee, Chana Kai. *For Freedom's Sake: The Life of Fannie Lou Hamer*. Chicago: University of Chicago Press, 1999.

Lerner, Gerda, ed. *Black Women in White America: A Documentary History*. New York: Pantheon, 1972.

———. *Fireweed: A Political Autobiography*. Philadelphia: Temple University Press, 2002.

———. *The Grimké Sisters from South Carolina: Pioneers for Women's Rights and Abolition*, revised edition. Chapel Hill: University of North Carolina Press, 2004.

———. *The Majority Finds Its Past: Placing Women in History*. Chapel Hill: University of North Carolina Press, 1979.

Lynn, Susan. *Progressive Women in Conservative Times: Racial Justice, Peace, and Feminism, 1945 to the 1960s*. New Brunswick, NJ: Rutgers University Press, 1992.

Mayeri, Serena. *Reasoning from Race: Feminism, Law, and the Civil Rights Movement*. Cambridge, MA, and London: Harvard University Press, 2014.

McDuffie, Erik S. *Sojourning for Freedom: Black Women, American Communism, and the Making of Black Left Feminism*. Durham, NC: Duke University Press, 2011.

Mills, Kay. *This Little Light of Mine: The Life of Fannie Lou Hamer*. New York: Dutton, 1993.

Murray, Pauli. *Dark Testament and Other Poems*. New York and London: Liveright Publishing, 1970.

———. *Proud Shoes: The Story of an American Family*. New York: Harper & Brothers, 1956.

———. *Song in a Weary Throat: Memoir of an American Pilgrimage*. New York: Harper & Row, 1987. (Later republished as *Pauli Murray: The Autobiography of a Black Activist, Feminist, Lawyer, Priest, and Poet*.)

Nembhard, Jessica Gordon. *Collective Courage: A History of African American Cooperative Economic Thought and Practice*. University Park: Pennsylvania State University Press, 2014.

Olson, Lynne. *Freedom's Daughters: The Unsung Heroines of the Civil Rights Movement from 1830 to 1970*. New York: Scribner, 2001.

Ransby, Barbara. *Ella Baker and the Black Freedom Movement: A Radical Democratic Vision*. Chapel Hill: University of North Carolina Press, 2003.

Robnett, Belinda. *How Long? How Long? African-American Women in the Struggle for Civil Rights*. New York and Oxford, UK: Oxford University Press, 1997.

Rosenberg, Rosalind. *Divided Lives: American Women in the Twentieth Century*, revised edition. New York: Hill and Wang, 2008.

———. *Jane Crow: The Life of Pauli Murray.* New York and Oxford, UK: Oxford University Press, 2017.

Rupp, Leila J., and Vera Taylor. *Survival in the Doldrums: The American Women's Rights Movement, 1945 to the 1960s.* New York and Oxford, UK: Oxford University Press, 1987.

Saxby, Troy R. *Pauli Murray: A Personal and Political Life.* Chapel Hill: University of North Carolina Press, 2020.

Sisters in the Struggle: African American Women in the Civil Rights–Black Power Movement. Bettye Collier-Thomas and V. P. Franklin, eds. New York and London: New York University Press, 2001.

The Speeches of Fannie Lou Hamer: To Tell It Like It Is. Maegan Parker Brooks and Davis W. Houck, eds. Jackson, MS: University Press of Mississippi, 2011.

Swerdlow, Amy. *Women Strike for Peace: Traditional Motherhood and Radical Politics in the 1960s.* Chicago: University of Chicago Press, 1993.

U.S. History as Women's History: New Feminist Essays. Linda K. Kerber, et al., eds. Chapel Hill: University of North Carolina Press, 1995.

Walker, Alice. *In Search of Our Mothers' Gardens.* New York: Open Road, Integrated Media, 2011.

Watters, Pat, and Reese Cleghorn. *Climbing Jacob's Ladder: The Arrival of Negroes in Southern Politics.* New York: Harcourt, Brace and World, 1967.

Weigand, Kate. *Red Feminism: American Communism and the Making of Women's Liberation.* Baltimore, MD: Johns Hopkins University Press, 2001.

Words of Fire: An Anthology of African-American Feminist Thought. Beverly Guy-Sheftall, ed. New York: The New Press, 1995.

Papers and Articles

"The 1950s: Gender and Some Social Science." Wini Breines. *Sociological Inquiry*, vol. 56, no. 1, pp. 69–92.

"An American Credo," Pauli Murray. *Common Ground,* vol.5, no. 2 (Winter 1945), pp. 22–24.

"Attacking the Washington 'Femmocracy': Antifeminism in the Cold War Campaign against 'Communists in Government,' " Landon R. Y. Storrs. *Feminist Studies*, vol. 33, no. 1 (Spring 2007).

"Becoming the Third Wave," Rebecca Walker. *Ms.*, January 1992, pp. 39–41.

"Before the Second Wave: College Women, Cultural Literacy, Sexuality, and Identicy, 1940–1965," Babette Faehnel. PhD dissertation, University of Massachusetts, Amherst (May 2009).

"Betty Friedan and the Radical Past of Liberal Feminism," Joanne Boucher. *New Politics*, vol. 9, no. 3 (Summer 2003).

"Beyond the Feminine Mystique: A Reassessment of Postwar Mass Culture, 1946–1958," Joanne Meyerowitz. *Journal of American History*, vol. 79, no. 4 (March 1993), pp. 1455–1482.

"Boy-Girl, Imp, Priest: Pauli Murray and the Limits of Identity," Doreen M. Drury. *Journal of Feminist Studies in Religion*, vol. 29, no. 1 (Spring 2013), pp. 142-147.

"The Congress of American Women: Left-Feminist Peace Politics in the Cold War," Amy Swerdlow. In *U.S. History as Women's History: New Feminist Essays*, Linda Kerber et al., eds. Chapel Hill: University of North Carolina Press, 1995, pp. 296–312.

"Demarginalizing the Intersection of Race and Sex: A Black Feminist Critique of Antidiscrimination Doctrine, Feminist Theory, and Antiracist Politics," Kimberlé Crenshaw. *University of Chicago Legal Forum*, vol. 1989, no. 1, pp. 139–167.

"Eleanor Flexner and the History of American Feminism," Ellen C. Dubois. *Gender & History*, vol. 3, no. 1 (March 1991), pp. 81–90.

"Fannie Lou Hamer: Mississippi Grassroots Organizer," Susan Johnson. *National Black Law Journal*, vol. 2, no. 2 (1972), pp. 155–162.

"The Female Generation Gap: Daughters of the Fifties and the Origins of Contemporary American Feminism," Ruth Rosen. In *U. S. History as Women's History*, 313–334.

"Gerda Lerner (1920–2013). Pioneering Historian and Feminist," Linda Gordon et al. *Clio: Women, Gender, History*, no. 38 (2013), pp. 254–263.

"Howard University Students Demonstrate New Technique in Securing Equal Rights." Pauli Murray manuscript dated April 25, 1944. PM/SL

" 'It's Good to Blow Your Top': Women's Magazines and a Discourse of Discontent, 1945–1965," Eva Moskowitz. *Journal of Women's History*, vol. 8, no. 3 (Fall 1996), pp. 66–98.

"Jane Crow and the Law: Sex Discrimination and Title VII," Pauli Murray and Mary O. Eastwood. *George Washington Law Review*, vol. 43, no. 2 (December 1965), pp. 232–256.

"The Making of a Modern Feminist Vanguard, 1964–1973: Southern Women Whose Leadership Shaped the Movement and the Nation—A Synthetic Analysis," Carol Giardina. *Journal of Southern History*, vol. 85, no. 3 (August 2019), pp. 611–652.

"Memorandum: The Role of the Negro Women in the Civil Rights Revolution," Pauli Murray. Manuscript, August 27, 1963. PM/SL

"MOW to NOW: Black Feminism Resets the Chronology of the Founding of Modern Feminism," Carol Giardina. *Feminist Studies*, vol. 44, no. 3 (2018), pp. 736–765.

Murray, Pauli. "The Negro Woman in the Quest for Equality," *Acorn*. Official Publication of Lamba Kappa Mu Sorority, Inc., June 1964. Reprinted as "Jim Crow and Jane Crow" in Lerner, *Black Women in White America: A Documentary History*.

———. "Three Thousand Miles on a Dime in Ten Days" and "Song of the Highway." In *Negro Anthology 1931–1933*, Nancy Cunard, ed. London: Wishart & Co, 1934.

"NAACP Sponsored Sit-ins by Howard University Students in Washington, D.C., 1943–1944," Flora Bryant Brown. *Journal of Negro History*, vol. 85, no. 4 (Autumn 2000), pp. 274–286.

"Pauli Murray and the 'Juncture of Women's Liberation and Black Liberation,' " Susan M. Hartmann. *Journal of Women's History*, vol. 14, no. 2 (Summer 2002), pp. 74–77.

"Pauli Murray's Campaign Against Harvard Law School's 'Jane Crow' Admissions Policy," Mary Elizabeth Basile. *Journal of Legal Education*, vol. 57, no. 1 (March 2007), pp. 77–101.

"Poetry, Ethics, and the Legacy of Pauli Murray," Christiana Z. Peppard. *Journal of the Society of Christian Ethics*. Spring/Summer 2010, vol. 340, no. 1, pp. 21–43.

"The Question Seldom Asked: Women and the CPUSA," Rosalyn Baxandall. In *New Studies in the Politics and Culture of U.S. Communism*, Michael E. Brown et al., eds. New York: Monthly Review Press, 1993.

"Race to the Bottom: How the Post-Racial Revolution Became a Whitewash," Kimberlé Crenshaw. *The Baffler*, no. 35 (June 2017), pp. 40–57.

"Recapturing Working-Class Feminism: Union Women in the Postwar Era," Dorothy Sue Cobble. In *Not June Cleaver: Women and Gender in Postwar America, 1945–1960*, Joanne Meyerowitz, ed. Philadelphia: Temple University Press, 1994, pp. 57–83.

"Red Feminism and Left History," Paul Mishler. *Science & Society*, vol. 67, no. 4 (Winter 2003/2004), pp. 485–488.

"Rethinking the Second Wave," Nancy MacLean. *Nation*, September 25, 2002, https://www.thenation.com/article/archive/rethinking-second-wave/.

"Re-Visioning the Women's Liberation Movement's Narrative: Early Second Wave African American Feminists," Rosalyn Baxandall. *Feminist Studies*, vol. 27, no. 1 (Spring 2001), pp. 225–245.

"Running with the Reds: African American Women and the Communist Party during the Great Depression," Lashawn Harris. *Journal of African American History*, vol. 94, no. 1 (Winter 2009), pp. 21–43.

"Should the Civil Rights Cases and *Plessy v. Ferguson* Be Overruled? An Examination of Constitutional Principles Applied to Civil Rights in Light of Recent American History," Pauli Murray. Unpublished thesis, Howard University School of Law, May 1944. PM/SL

"Sixties Stories' Silences: White Feminism, Black Feminism, Black Power," Wini Breines. *NWSA Journal*, vol. 8, no. 3 (Autumn 1996), pp. 101–121.

"The Unread Red Feminists: Silenced Precursors of the U.S. Second Wave," Susan Archer Mann. *At the Center: Feminism, Social Science and Knowledge*, vol. 20 (2015), pp. 291–310.

" 'To Organize in Every Neighborhood, in Every Home': The Gender Politics of American Communists between the Wars," Van Gosse. *Radical History Review*, vol. 1991, no. 50 (Spring 1991), pp. 109–141.

"Toward a Field of Intersectionary Studies: Theory, Applications, and Praxis," Sumi Cho, et al. *Signs*, vol. 38, no. 4 (Summer 2013), pp. 785–810.

"Women in the Old and New Left: The Evolution of a Politics of Personal Life," Ellen Kay Trimberger. *Feminist Studies*, vol. 5, no. 3 (Autumn 1979), pp. 431–450.

"Women's Employment and the Domestic Ideal in the Early Cold War Years," Susan M. Hartmann. In *Not June Cleaver*, 1994, pp. 84–100.

CIVIL RIGHTS

Alexander, Michelle. *The New Jim Crow: Mass Incarceration in the Age of Colorblindness*, revised edition. New York: The New Press, 2012.

Arsenault, Raymond. *Freedom Riders: 1961 and the Struggle for Racial Justice*. New York and Oxford, UK: Oxford University Press, 2006.

The Black Power Movement: Rethinking the Civil Rights–Black Power Era. Joseph E. Peniel, ed. New York: Routledge, 2006.

Blacks in the Military: Essential Documents. Bernard C. Nalty and Morris J. MacGregor, eds. Wilmington, DE: Scholarly Resources, Inc., 1981.

Bloom, Joshua, and Waldo E. Martin, Jr. *Black Against Empire: The History and Politics of the Black Panther Party*. Oakland: University of California Press, 2013.

Branch, Taylor. *At Canaan's Edge: America in the King Years, 1965–68*. New York: Simon & Schuster, 2006.

———. *Parting the Waters: America in the King Years, 1954–63*. New York: Simon & Schuster, 1989.

———. *Pillar of Fire: America in the King Years, 1963–65*. New York: Simon & Schuster, 1998.

Brandt, Nat. *Harlem at War: The Black Experience of World War II*. Syracuse, NY: Syracuse University Press, 1996.

Brooks, Jennifer E. *Defining the Peace: World War II Veterans, Race, and the Remaking of Southern Political Tradition*. Chapel Hill: University of North Carolina Press, 2004.

Chafe, William H. *Civilities and Civil Rights: Greensboro, North Carolina, and the Black Struggle for Freedom.* New York and Oxford, UK: Oxford University Press, 1980.

Cobb, Charles E., Jr. *This Nonviolent Stuff'll Get You Killed: How Guns Made the Civil Rights Movement Possible.* New York: Basic Books, 2014.

Colley, David P. *Blood for Dignity: The Story of the First Integrated Combat Unit in the U. S. Army.* New York: St. Martin's Press, 2003.

Cone, James H. *Martin & Malcolm & America: A Dream or a Nightmare.* New York: Orbis Books, 1991.

Davenport, Christian. *How Social Movements Die: Repression and Demobilization of the Republic of New Africa.* Cambridge, UK: Cambridge University Press, 2015.

D'Emilio, John. *Lost Prophet: The Life and Times of Bayard Rustin.* New York: Simon & Schuster, 2003.

Dittmer, John. *Local People: The Struggle for Civil Rights in Mississippi.* Urbana and Chicago: University of Illinois Press, 1995.

Dray, Philip. *At the Hands of Persons Unknown: The Lynching of Black America.* New York: Modern Library, 2003.

Dudziak, Mary L. *Cold War Civil Rights.* Princeton, NJ, and Oxford, UK: Princeton University Press, 2000.

Egerton, John. *Speak Now Against the Day: The Generation Before the Civil Rights Movement in the South.* New York: Knopf, 1994.

Estes, Steve. *I Am a Man! Race, Manhood, and the Civil Rights Movement.* Chapel Hill: University of North Carolina Press, 2005.

Euchner, Charles. *Nobody Turn Me Around: A People's History of the 1963 March on Washington.* Boston: Beacon Press, 2010.

Evers-Williams, Myrlie, and Manning Marable. *The Autobiography of Medgar Evers: A Hero's Life and Legacy Revealed Through His Writings, Letters, and Speeches.* New York: Basic Books, 2005.

Evers-Williams, Myrlie, with William Peters. *For Us, the Living.* Garden City, NY: Doubleday, 1967.

Farmer, James. *Lay Bare the Heart: An Autobiography of the Civil Rights Movement.* Gettysburg, PA: Arbor House, 1985.

Forman, James. *The Making of Black Revolutionaries.* Seattle: University of Washington Press, 1985.

Freedom North: Black Freedom Struggles Outside the South, 1940–1980. Jeanne Theoharis and Komozi Woodard, eds. New York: Palgrave Macmillan, 2003.

Gardner, Michael R. *Harry Truman and Civil Rights: Moral Courage and Political Risks.* Carbondale: Southern Illinois University Press, 2002.

Garrow, David J. *Bearing the Cross: Martin Luther King, Jr., and the Southern Christian Leadership Conference.* New York: Open Road, 1986.

Gergel, Richard. *Unexampled Courage: The Blinding of Sgt. Isaac Woodard and the Awakening of President Harry S. Truman and Judge J. Waties Waring.* New York: Sarah Crichton Books/Farrar, Straus and Giroux, 2019.

Gerstle, Gary. *American Crucible: Race and Nation in the Twentieth Century.* Princeton, NJ, and Oxford, UK: Princeton University Press, 2001.

Gilmore, Glenda Elizabeth. *Defying Dixie: The Radical Roots of Civil Rights, 1919–1950.* New York: W. W. Norton, 2008.

Goluboff, Risa L. *The Lost Promise of Civil Rights.* Cambridge, MA, and London: Harvard University Press, 2007.

Hamlin, Françoise N. *Crossroads at Clarksdale: The Black Freedom Struggle in the Mississippi Delta after World War II.* Chapel Hill: University of North Carolina Press, 2012.

Henry, Aaron, and Constance Curry. *Aaron Henry: The Fire Ever Burning.* Jackson: University Press of Mississippi, 2000.

Hill, Lance. *The Deacons for Defense: Armed Resistance and the Civil Rights Movement.* Chapel Hill: University of North Carolina Press, 2004.

Höhn, Maria, and Martin Klimke. *A Breath of Freedom: The Civil Rights Struggle, African American GIs, and Germany.* New York: Palgrave Macmillan, 2010.

The Invisible Soldier: The Experience of the Black Soldier, World War II. Mary Penick Motley, ed. Detroit, MI: Wayne State University Press, 1975.

James, Rawn, Jr. *The Double V: How Wars, Protest, and Harry Truman Desegregated America's Military.* New York: Bloomsbury Press, 2013.

Joseph, Peniel E. *Stokely: A Life.* New York: Civitas Books, 2014.

———. *Waiting 'Til the Midnight Hour: A Narrative History of Black Power in America.* New York: Henry Holt and Company, 2006.

Kluger, Richard. *Simple Justice: The History of* Brown v. Board of Education *and Black America's Struggle for Equality.* London: André Deutsch Limited, 1975.

Knauer, Christine. *Let Us Fight as Free Men: Black Soldiers and Civil Rights.* Philadelphia: University of Pennsylvania Press. 2014.

Kruse, Kevin M., and Stephen Tuck. *Fog of War: The Second World War and the Civil Rights Movement.* New York and Oxford, UK: Oxford University Press, 2012.

Lewis, David Levering. *W. E. B. DuBois: The Fight for Equality and the American Century, 1919–1963.* New York: Henry Holt and Company, 2000.

MacGregor, Morris J., Jr. *Integration of the Armed Forces, 1940–1965.* Washington, D.C.: Center of Military History, United States Army.

Marable, Manning. *Malcolm X: A Life of Reinvention.* New York: Viking, 2011.

——. *Race, Reform and Rebellion: The Second Reconstruction and Beyond in Black America, 1945–2006,* 3rd edition. Jackson: University of Mississippi Press, 2007.

McWhirter, Cameron. *Red Summer: The Summer of 1919 and the Awakening of Black America.* New York: St. Martin's Press, 2011.

Morehouse, Maggie M. *Fighting in the Jim Crow Army: Black Men and Women Remember World War II.* Lanham, MD: Rowman & Littlefield, 2000.

Morris, Aldon D. *The Origins of the Civil Rights Movement: Black Communities Organizing for Change.* New York: Simon & Schuster, 1984.

Morris, Willie. *The Ghosts of Medgar Evers: A Tale of Race, Murder, Mississippi, and Hollywood.* New York: Random House, 1998.

Negro Anthology, 1931–1933. Nancy Cunard, ed. London: Wishart & Co., 1934.

Nossiter, Adam. *Of Long Memory: Mississippi and the Murder of Medgar Evers.* New York: Da Capo Press, 2009.

Parker, Christopher S. *Fighting for Democracy: Black Veterans and the Struggle Against White Supremacy in the Postwar South.* Princeton, NJ, and Oxford, UK: Princeton University Press, 2009.

Payne, Charles M. *I've Got the Light of Freedom: The Organizing Tradition and the Mississippi Freedom Struggle.* Berkeley: University of California Press, 2007.

Phillips, Kimberley L. *War! What Is It Good For? Black Freedom Struggles and the U.S. Military from World War II to Iraq.* Chapel Hill: University of North Carolina Press, 2012.

Raines, Howell. *My Soul Is Rested: Movement Days in the Deep South Remembered.* New York: Penguin Books, 1977.

Ransby, Barbara. *Ella Baker and the Black Freedom Movement: A Radical Democratic Vision.* Chapel Hill: University of North Carolina Press, 2003.

Records of Military Agencies Relating to African Americans from the Post–World War I Period to the Korean War. Compiled by Lisha B. Penn. Washington, D.C.: National Archives and Records Administration, 2006.

Shapiro, Herbert. *White Violence and Black Response: From Reconstruction to Montgomery.* Amherst: University of Massachusetts Press, 1988.

Singh, Nikhil Pal. *Black Is a Country: Race and the Unfinished Struggle for Democracy.* Cambridge, MA, and London: Harvard University Press, 2004.

Strain, Christopher B. *Pure Fire: Self-Defense as Activism in the Civil Rights Era.* Athens: University of Georgia Press, 2005.

Theoharis, Jeanne. *A More Beautiful and Terrible History: The Uses and Misuses of Civil Rights History.* Boston: Beacon Press, 2018.

——. *The Rebellious Life of Mrs. Rosa Parks.* Boston: Beacon Press, 2013.

Time on Two Crosses: The Collected Writings of Bayard Rustin. Devon W. Carbado and Donald Weise, eds. New York: Cleis Press, 2014.

Ture, Kwame, and Charles V. Hamilton. *Black Power: The Politics of Liberation.* New York: Vintage, 1992.

Tyson, Timothy B. *The Blood of Emmett Till.* New York: Simon & Schuster, 2017.

———. *Radio Free Dixie: Robert F. Williams and the Roots of Black Power.* Chapel Hill: University of North Carolina Press, 1999.

Umoja, Akinyele Omowale. *We Will Shoot Back: Armed Resistance in the Mississippi Freedom Movement.* New York and London: New York University Press, 2013.

Van Deburg, William L. *New Day in Babylon: The Black Power Movement and American Culture, 1965–1975.* Chicago: University of Chicago Press, 1992.

Wendt, Simon. *The Spirit and the Shotgun: Armed Resistance and the Struggle for Civil Rights.* Gainesville: University Press of Florida, 2007.

White, Walter. *A Rising Wind.* Garden City, NY: Doubleday, Doran and Company, 1945.

Williams, Michael Vinson. *Medgar Evers: Mississippi Martyr.* Fayetteville: University of Arkansas Press, 2011.

Williams, Robert F. *Negroes with Guns.* Mansfield Center, CT: Martino Publishing, 2013.

Wynn, Neil A. *The Afro-American and the Second World War,* revised edition. New York: Holmes & Meier, 1993.

X, Malcolm. *The Autobiography of Malcolm X.* New York: Random House, 1965.

Papers and Articles

"African Americans and World War II," Andrew E. Kersten. *OAH Magazine of History,* vol. 16, no. 3 (Spring 2002), pp. 13–15.

"Beyond Jim Crow Liberalism: Judge Waring's Fight Against Segregation in South Carolina, 1942–52," David W. Southern. *Journal of Negro History,* vol. 66, no. 3 (Fall 1981), pp. 202–227.

"The Blinding of Isaac Woodard," Andrew Myers. In *Proceedings of the South Carolina Historical Association,* 2004, pp. 63–73.

"The Columbians, Inc.: A Chapter of Racial Hatred from the Post–World War II South," Steven Weisenburger. *Journal of Southern History,* vol. 69, no. 4 (November 2003), pp. 821–860.

"Coming Home from Battle to Face a War: The Lynching of Black Soldiers in the World War I Era," Vincent Mikkelsen. PhD dissertation, Florida State University (2007), https://fsu.digital.flvc.org/islandora/object/fsu:180643/datastream/PDF/view.

"Ex-GI Buddies Backing Isaac Woodard in Damage Suit." *Chicago Defender*, Nov. 22, 1947, p. 3.

"The 'Forgotten Years' of the Negro Revolution," Richard M. Dalfiume. *Journal of American History*, vol. 55, no. 1 (June 1968), pp. 90–106.

"The Harlem and Detroit Riots of 1943: A Comparative Analysis," L. Alex Swan. *Berkeley Journal of Sociology*, vol. 16 (1971–1972), pp. 75–93.

"Harry Truman and the NAACP: A Case Study in Presidential Persuasion on Civil Rights," Garth E. Pauley. *Rhetoric and Public Affairs*, vol. 2, no. 2 (Summer 1999), pp. 211–241.

"J. Edgar Hoover and the 'Red Summer' of 1919," Mark Ellis. *Journal of American Studies*, vol. 28, no. 1 (April 1994), pp. 39–59.

" 'Let Economic Equality Take Care of Itself': The NAACP, Labor Litigation, and the Making of Civil Rights in the 1940s," Risa Lauren Goluboff. *UCLA Law Review* 52 (2005), pp. 1393–1486.

"The Long Civil Rights Movement and the Political Uses of the Past," Jacquelyn Dowd Hall. *Journal of American History*, vol. 91, no. 4 (March 2005), pp. 1233–1263.

"The Lost Decade of Civil Rights," David L. Chappell. *Historically Speaking*, vol. 10, no. 2 (April 2009), pp. 37–41.

"Race, Rape, and Radicalism: The Case of the Martinsville Seven, 1949–1951," Eric W. Rise. *The Journal of Southern History*, vol. 58, no. 3 (August 1992), pp. 461–490.

"Racial Militancy and Interracial Violence in the Second World War," Harvard Sitkoff. *Journal of American History*, vol. 58, no. 3 (December 1971), pp. 661–681.

"Reconsidering the 'Long Civil Rights Movement,' " Eric Arnesen. *Historically Speaking* vol. 10, no. 2 (April 2009), pp. 31–34.

"Resonant Ripples in a Global Pond: The Blinding of Isaac Woodard," Andrew Myers. Paper prepared for the 2002 American Studies Association Conference, https://faculty.uscupstate.edu/amyers/conference.html.

"Restoring Justice to Civil Rights Movement Activists?: New Historiography and the 'Long Civil Rights Era,' " Athena Mutua. Buffalo Legal Studies Research Paper Series No. 2008–12 (2008), https://digitalcommons.law.buffalo.edu /working_papers/8.

"Robert F. Williams and the Indigenous Civil Rights Movement in Monroe, North Carolina, 1961," Marcellus C. Barksdale. *Journal of Negro History*, vol. 69, no. 2 (Spring 1984), pp. 73–89.

"Robert F. Williams, 'Black Power,' and the Roots of the African American Freedom Struggle," Timothy B. Tyson. *Journal of American History*, vol. 85, no. 2 (September 1998), pp. 540–570.

" 'The Saddest Story of the Whole Movement': The Clyde Kennard Case and the Search for Racial Reconciliation in Mississippi, 1955–2007," Timothy J. Minchin and John A. Salmond. *Journal of Mississippi History*, vol. 71 (Fall 2009), pp. 191–234.

" 'The Slowest State' and 'Most Backward Community': Racial Violence in South Carolina and Federal Civil-Rights Legislation, 1946–1948," Karl Frederickson. *South Carolina Historical Magazine*, vol. 98, no. 2 (April 1997), pp. 177–202.

"Targeting Black Veterans: Lynching in America," Equal Justice Initiative, Montgomery, Alabama, 2017, https://eji.org/reports/targeting-black-veterans/.

"White Supremacy and the Disfranchisement of Blacks in Georgia, 1946," Joseph L. Bernd. *Georgia Historical Quarterly*, vol. 66, no. 4 (Winter 1982), pp. 492–513.

ECOLOGY

Archives

Papers of Frank Fremont-Smith, Center for the History of Medicine, Countway Library, Harvard Medical School.

Papers of Norbert Wiener, MIT Libraries, Department of Distinctive Collections. NW/MIT

Papers of Rachel Carson, Beinecke Rare Book and Manuscript Library, Yale University, New Haven, CT. RC/BL

Books

Advisory Committee on Human Radiation Experiments, Final Report. Washington, D.C.: U.S. Government Printing Office, 1995. (ACHRE).

Always, Rachel: The Letters of Rachel Carson and Dorothy Freeman 1952–1964. Martha Freeman, ed. Boston: Beacon Press, 1995.

Bateson, Gregory. *Mind and Nature: A Necessary Unity*. New York: Dutton, 1979.

———. *Steps to an Ecology of Mind*. New York: Ballantine Books, 1972.

Bousquet, Antoine. *The Scientific Way of Warfare: Order and Chaos on the Battlefields of Modernity*. New York: Columbia University Press, 2009.

Brooks, Paul. *The House of Life: Rachel Carson at Work*. Boston: Houghton Mifflin, 1972.

———. *Two Park Street: A Publishing Memoir*. Boston: Houghton Mifflin, 1986.

Carson, Rachel. *The Edge of the Sea*. Boston: Houghton Mifflin, 1950, 1979, 2011.

———. *Lost Woods: The Discovered Writing of Rachel Carson*. Linda Lear, ed. Boston: Beacon Press, 1998.

———. *The Sea Around Us*. Boston: Houghton Mifflin, 1955, 1983.

———. *Silent Spring.* Boston: Houghton Mifflin, 2002. (Originally published in 1962.)

———. *Under the Sea-Wind.* New York: Penguin Classics, 2007. (Originally published in 1941.)

Chaney, Anthony. *Runaway: Gregory Bateson, the Double Bind, and the Rise of Ecological Consciousness.* Chapel Hill: University of North Carolina Press, 2017.

Comstock, Anna Botsford. *Handbook of Nature Study,* 2nd edition. Ithaca, NY: Comstock Publishing Company/Cornell University Press, 1939.

Conway, Flo, and Jim Siegelman. *Dark Hero of the Information Age: In Search of Norbert Wiener, the Father of Cybernetics.* New York: Basic Books, 2005.

Cybernetics: The Macy Conferences 1946–1953: The Complete Transactions. Claus Pias, ed. Zurich: Diaphanes, 2016.

Divine, Robert A. *Blowing on the Wind: The Nuclear Test Ban Debate 1954–1960.* New York and Oxford, UK: Oxford University Press, 1978.

Dupuy, Jean-Pierre. *On the Origins of Cognitive Science: The Mechanization of Mind.* M. B. DeBevoise, trans. Cambridge, MA, and London: MIT Press, 2009.

The Effects of Atomic Radiation on Oceanography and Fisheries, Publication 551. Washington, D.C.: National Academy of Sciences, National Research Council, 1957.

Environmental Histories of the Cold War. J. R. McNeill and Corinna R. Unger, eds. German Historical Institute, Cambridge, UK: Cambridge University Press, 2010.

Foer, Franklin. *World Without Mind: The Existential Threat of Big Tech.* New York: Penguin Press, 2017.

Gibson, James William. *The Perfect War: Technowar in Vietnam.* New York: Atlantic Monthly Press, 1986.

Gleick, James. *The Information: A History, a Theory, a Flood.* New York: Pantheon Books, 2011.

Gottlieb, Robert. *Forcing the Spring: The Transformation of the American Environmental Movement.* Washington, D.C., and London: Island Press, 2005.

Graham, Frank, Jr. *Since Silent Spring.* Boston: Houghton Mifflin, 1970.

Hagen, Joel B. *An Entangled Bank: The Origins of Ecosystem Ecology.* New Brunswick, NJ: Rutgers University Press. 1992.

Hamblin, Jacob Darwin. *Arming Mother Nature: The Birth of Catastrophic Environmentalism.* New York and Oxford, UK: Oxford University Press, 2013.

Haraway, Donna. *Simians, Cyborgs, and Women: The Reinvention of Nature.* New York: Routledge, 1991.

Hayles, N. Katherine. *How We Became Posthuman: Virtual Bodies in Cybernetics, Literature, and Informatics.* Chicago: University of Chicago Press, 1999.

Heims, Steve J. *The Cybernetics Group*. Cambridge, MA, and London: MIT Press, 1991.

———. *John von Neumann and Norbert Wiener: From Mathematics to the Technologies of Life and Death*. Cambridge, MA, and London: MIT Press, 1980.

Hines, Neal O. *Proving Ground: An Account of Radiobiological Studies in the Pacific, 1946–1961*. Seattle: University of Washington Press, 1962.

Johnston, Barbara Rose, and Holly M. Barker. *Consequential Damages of Nuclear War: The Rongelap Report*. Walnut Creek, CA: Left Coast Press, 2008.

Kelly, Kevin. *Out of Control: The New Biology of Machines, Social Systems, and the Economic World*. New York: Basic Books, 1994.

Kinkela, David. *DDT and the American Century: Global Health, Environmental Politics, and the Pesticide That Changed the World*. Chapel Hill: University of North Carolina Press, 2011.

Klein, Naomi. *On Fire: The (Burning) Case for a Green New Deal*. New York: Simon & Schuster, 2019.

Kline, Ronald R. *The Cybernetics Moment: Or Why We Call Our Age the Information Age*. Baltimore, MD: Johns Hopkins University Press, 2015.

Kolbert, Elizabeth. *The Sixth Extinction: An Unnatural History*. New York: Henry Holt and Company, 2014.

Lapp, Ralph E. *The Voyage of the Lucky Dragon*. New York: Penguin Books, 1958.

Lear, Linda. *Rachel Carson: Witness for Nature*. Boston and New York: Houghton Mifflin Harcourt, 2009.

Lytle, Mark Hamilton. *The Gentle Subversive: Rachel Carson, Silent Spring, and the Rise of the Environmental Movement*. New York and Oxford, UK: Oxford University Press, 2007.

Marsden, George M. *The Twilight of the American Enlightenment: The 1950s and the Crisis of Liberal Belief*. New York: Basic Books, 2014.

Martino-Taylor, Lisa. *Behind the Fog: How the U.S. Cold War Radiological Weapons Program Exposed Innocent Americans*. New York: Routledge, 2018.

———. *The End of Nature*, New York: Random House, 2006.

McKibben, Bill. *Falter: Has the Human Game Begun to Play Itself Out?* New York: Henry Holt and Company, 2019.

McNeill, J. R. *Something New Under the Sun: An Environmental History of the Twentieth-Century World*. New York: W. W. Norton, 2000.

McNeill, J. R., and Peter Engelke. *The Great Acceleration: An Environmental History of the Anthropocene Since 1945*. Cambridge, MA, and London: Belknap Press of Harvard University Press, 2014.

Montagnini, Leone. *Harmonies of Disorder: Norbert Wiener: A Mathematician-Philosopher of Our Time*. New York: Springer International Publishing, 2017.

Moore, Kelly. *Disrupting Science: Social Movements, American Scientists, and the Politics of the Military, 1945–1975.* Princeton, NJ, and Oxford, UK: Princeton University Press, 2008.

Oreskes, Naomi, and Erik M. Conway. *Merchants of Doubt: How a Handful of Scientists Obscured the Truth on Issues from Tobacco Smoke to Global Warming.* New York: Bloomsbury, 2010.

Possible Minds: 25 Ways of Looking at AI. John Brockman, ed. New York: Penguin Press, 2019.

Purdy, Jedediah. *After Nature: A Politics for the Anthropocene.* Cambridge, MA, and London: Harvard University Press, 2015.

———. *This Land Is Our Land: The Struggle for a New Commonwealth.* Oxford, UK, and Princeton, NJ: Princeton University Press, 2019.

Rachel Carson: Legacy and Challenge. Lisa H. Sideris and Kathleen Dean Moore, eds. Albany: State University of New York Press, 2008.

Rich, Nathaniel. *Losing Earth: A Recent History.* New York: Farrar, Straus and Giroux, 2019.

Rid, Thomas. *Rise of the Machines: A Cybernetic History.* New York: W. W. Norton, 2016.

Rorty, Richard. *Achieving Our Country: Leftist Thought in Twentieth-Century America.* Cambridge, MA, and London: Harvard University Press, 1999.

Russell, Edmund. *War and Nature: Fighting Humans and Insects with Chemicals from World War I to* Silent Spring. Cambridge, UK: Cambridge University Press, 2011.

Shurcliff, W. A. *Bombs at Bikini: The Official Report of Operation Crossroads.* New York: Wm. H. Wise & Co. Inc., 1947.

Souder, William. *On a Farther Shore: The Life and Legacy of Rachel Carson.* New York: Crown Publishers, 2012.

Speth, James Gustave. *The Bridge at the End of the World: Capitalism, the Environment, and Crossing from Crisis to Sustainability.* New Haven, CT: Yale University Press, 2008.

Subversive Science: Essays Toward an Ecology of Man. Paul Shepard and Daniel McKinley, eds. Boston: Houghton Mifflin, 1969.

Turner, Fred. *From Counterculture to Cyberculture: Stewart Brand, the Whole Earth Network, and the Rise of Digital Utopianism.* Chicago: University of Chicago Press, 2006.

Uncommon Ground: Rethinking the Human Place in Nature. William Cronon, ed. New York: W. W. Norton, 1996.

Wallace-Wells, David. *The Uninhabitable Earth: Life After Warming.* New York: Tim Duggan Books, 2019.

Weisgall, Jonathan M. *Operation Crossroads: The Atomic Tests at Bikini Atoll.* Annapolis, MD: Naval Institute Press, 1994.

Wiener, Norbert. *Cybernetics, or Control and Communication in the Animal and the Machine,* 2nd edition. Cambridge, MA, and London: MIT Press, 1961.

———. *Ex-Prodigy: My Childhood and Youth.* Cambridge, MA, and London: MIT Press, 1964. (First published in 1953 by Simon & Schuster.)

———. *God & Golem, Inc.: A Comment on Certain Points Where Cybernetics Impinges on Religion.* Cambridge, MA, and London: MIT Press, 1964.

———. *The Human Use of Human Beings: Cybernetics and Society.* Boston: Houghton Mifflin, 1954.

———. *I Am a Mathematician: The Later Life of a Prodigy.* Cambridge, MA, and London: MIT Press, 1964. (Originally published by Simon & Schuster in 1956.)

———. *Invention: The Care and Feeding of Ideas.* Cambridge, MA, and London: The MIT Press, 1993. (Published posthumously.)

Winner, L. *Autonomous Technology: Technics-out-of-Control as a Theme in Political Thought.* Cambridge, MA, and London: MIT Press, 1977.

The World the Sixties Made: Politics and Culture in Recent America. Van Gosse and Richard Moser, eds. Philadelphia: Temple University Press, 2003.

Worster, Donald. *Nature's Economy: A History of Ecological Ideas,* 2nd edition. Cambridge, UK: Cambridge University Press, 2011.

Papers and Articles by Rachel Carson and Norbert Wiener

Carson, Rachel. "The Little Brown House." Manuscript. RC/BL

———. "My Favorite Recreation." *St. Nicholas: A Monthly Magazine for Boys and Girls,* July 1922. RC/BL

———. "Of Man and the Stream of Time." Pamphlet, Scripps College, Claremont, California, 1962. Also collected in *Lost Woods: The Discovered Writing of Rachel Carson.* Linda Lear, ed. Boston: Beacon Press, 1998.

———. "The Real World Around Us." Speech to Theta Sigma Phi, 1954. Collected in *Lost Woods.*

———. "Undersea." *Atlantic Monthly,* vol. 78 (September 1937), pp. 55–67.

Wiener, Norbert. "My Connection with Cybernetics. Its Origin and Its Future." *Cybernetica* (1958), pp. 1–14.

———. "Prolegomena to Theology." The Terry Lectures at Yale University, typescript, 1962. NW/MIT

———. "A Rebellious Scientist After Two Years." *Bulletin of the Atomic Scientists,* vol. 4, no. 11 (1948), pp. 338–339.

———. "A Scientist's Dilemma in a Materialistic World." Typescript, 1957. NW/MIT

———. "A Scientist Rebels." *Atlantic Monthly*, vol. 179 (1947), pp. 46.

———. "Some Moral and Technical Consequences of Automation." *Science*, vol. 131, no. 3410 (May 6, 1960), pp. 1355–1358.

———. "The Theory of Ignorance: Graduating Essay." Typescript, 1906. NW/MIT

———. "Time, Communication and the Nervous System." *Annals of the New York Academy of Sciences*, vol. 50, no. 4 (October 1948), pp. 197–220.

Wiener, Norbert, and Arturo Rosenblueth. "The Role of Models in Science." *Philosophy of Science*, vol. 12, no. 4 (October 1945), pp. 316–321.

Wiener, Norbert, Arturo Rosenblueth, and Julian Bigelow. "Behavior, Purpose, and Teleology." *Philosophy of Science*, vol. 10, no. 1 (January 1943), pp. 18–24.

———. "Teleological Mechanisms." *Annals of the New York Academy of Sciences*, vol. 50, no. 4 (1948), pp. 187–278.

Papers and Articles by Others

"The Biology of the Bikini Atoll, with Special Reference to the Fishes," Leonard P. Schultz. Annual Report of the Smithsonian Institution for 1947.

"Bombshell in Beltsville: The USDA and the Challenge of *Silent Spring*," Linda J. Lear. *Agricultural History*, vol. 66, no. 2 (Spring 1992), pp. 151–170.

"Chemical Fallout: Rachel Carson's *Silent Spring*, Radioactive Fallout, and the Environmental Movement," Ralph H. Lutts. *Environmental Review*, vol. 9, no. 3 (Autumn 1985), pp. 210–225.

"Cyberneticizing the American War Machine: Science and Computers in the Cold War," Antoine Bousquet. *Cold War History*, vol. 8, no. 1 (February 2008), pp. 77–102.

"The Cybernetics of Competition: A Biologist's View of Society," Garrett Hardin. Perspectives in Biology and Medicine, vol. 7, no. 1 (Autumn 1963): 58–64. Reprinted in Subversive Science: Essays Toward an Ecology of Man. Paul Shepard and Daniel McKinley, eds. Boston: Houghton Mifflin, 1969, pp. 275–296.

"Cybernetics of Cybernetics," Margaret Mead. In *Purposive Systems: Proceedings of the First Annual Symposium of the American Society for Cybernetics*. Heinz von Foerster et al., eds. New York and Washington, D.C.: Spartan Books, 1968, pp. 1–14.

"DDT and Its Effect on Fish and Wildlife," Clarence Cottam and Elmer Higgins. U.S. Department of the Interior, Fish and Wildlife Service, Circular 11. Washington, D.C.: U.S. Government Printing Office (1946).

"DDT: An Issue of Property Rights," Roger E. Meiners and Andrew P. Morriss. *PERC Reports*, vol. 19, no. 3 (Fall 2001).

"Environmental Awareness in the Atomic Age: Radioecologists and Nuclear Technology," Rachel Rothschild. *Historical Studies in the Natural Sciences*, vol. 43, no. 4, pp. 492–530.

"Existential Risks: Analyzing Human Extinction Scenarios and Related Hazards," Nick Bostrom. *Journal of Evolution and Technology*, vol. 9, no. 1 (2002).

"Gregory Bateson and the Mathematicians: From Interdisciplinary Interaction to Societal Functions," Steve J. Heims. *Journal of the History of the Behavioral Sciences*, vol. 13, no. 2 (1977), pp. 141–159.

"How to Be Universal: Some Cybernetic Strategies, 1943–1970," Geof Bowker. *Social Studies of Science*, vol. 23, no. 1 (February 1993), pp. 107–127.

"Human Ecology: The Subversive, Conservative Science," Garrett Hardin. *American Zoologist*, vol. 25, no. 2 (1985), pp. 469–476.

"Information Ecology—A Viewpoint," Alexei L. Eryomin. *International Journal of Environmental Studies*, vol. 54 (1998), pp. 241–253.

"The Legacy of Norbert Wiener: A Centennial Symposium," David Jerison et al. *Proceedings of Symposia in Pure Mathematics*, vol. 60 (1997).

" 'Like a Keen North Wind': How Charles Elton Influenced *Silent Spring*," Frederick R. Davis. *Endeavour*, vol. 36, no. 4 (December 2012), pp. 143–148.

"Living in the Anthropocene: Toward a New Global Ethos," Paul J. Crutzen and Christian Schwägerl. *Yale Environment 360*, January 24, 2011.

"Man and Machine in the 1960s," Sungook Hong. *Techné*, vol. 7, no. 3 (Spring 2004), pp. 50–78.

"Norbert Wiener and the Counter-Tradition to the Dream of Mastery," D. Hill. *IEEE Technology and Society Magazine*, vol. 34, no. 3 (September 2015), pp. 60–72, doi: 10.1109/MTS.2015.2461171.

"Norbert Wiener on Technology and Society," Greg Adamson. *2014 IEEE Conference on Norbert Wiener in the 21st Century (21CW)*, 2014, pp. 1–7, doi: 10.1109/NORBERT.2014.6893930.

"Norbert Wiener's Place in the History of Science and Philosophy," P. R. Masani. *Current Science*, vol. 67, no. 12 (December 1994), pp. 920–930.

"The Ontology of the Enemy: Norbert Wiener and the Cybernetic Vision," Peter Galison. *Critical Inquiry*, vol. 21, no. 1 (Autumn 1994), pp. 228–266.

" 'Our First Line of Defense': Two University Laboratories in the Postwar American State," Michael Aaron Dennis. *Isis*, vol. 85, no. 3 (September 1994), pp. 427–455.

"The Rachel Carson Letters and the Making of *Silent Spring*," John Paull. *SAGE Open*, vol. 3 (July–September 2013), doi: 10.1177/2158244013494861.

"Reshaping Technology in Wartime: The Effect of Military Goals on Entomological Research and Insect-Control Practices," John H. Perkins. *Technology and Culture*, vol. 19, no. 2 (April 1978), pp. 169–186.

"A Rogue Bureaucracy: The USDA Fire Ant Campaign of the Late 1950s," Pete Daniel. *Agricultural History*, vol. 64, no. 2 (Spring 1990), pp. 99–114.

" 'The Science-Spirit in a Democracy': Liberty Hyde Bailey, Nature Study, and the Democratic Impulse of Progressive Conservation," Kevin C. Armitage. In *Natural Protest: Essays on the History of American Environmentalism*, Michael Egan and Jeff Crane, eds. New York: Routledge, 2009, pp. 89–116.

" 'Silence, Miss Carson!' Silence, Gender, and the Reception of *Silent Spring*," Michael B. Smith. *Feminist Studies*, vol. 27, no. 3 (Autumn 2001), pp. 733–752.

"Sixty Years of Cybernetics: From Youthful to Useful," George J. Klir. *Kybernetika*, vol. 44, no. 3 (2008), pp. 307–313.

"Wiener on the Logics of Russell and Schröder: An Account of His Doctoral Thesis, and of His Discussion of It with Russell." I. Grattan-Guinness. *Annals of Science*, vol. 32, no. 2 (1975), pp. 103–132.

" 'Woman vs. Man vs. Bugs': Gender and Popular Ecology in Early Reactions to *Silent Spring*," Maril Hazlett. *Environmental History*, vol. 9, no. 4 (October 2004), pp. 701–729.

EPILOGUE

Books

Always, Rachel: The Letters of Rachel Carson and Dorothy Freeman 1952–1964. Martha Freeman, ed. Boston: Beacon Press, 1995.

Evers-Williams, Myrlie, with William Peters. *For Us, the Living*. Garden City, NY: Doubleday, 1967.

Murray, Pauli. *Song in a Weary Throat: Memoir of an American Pilgrimage*. New York: Harper & Row, 1987.

Papers and Articles

"Kameny's Storybook Ending," Charles Francis. *Washington Blade*, October 20, 2011.

"Poetry, Ethics, and the Legacy of Pauli Murray," Christiana Z. Peppard. *Journal of the Society of Christian Ethics*, vol. 30, no. 1 (Spring/Summer 2010), pp. 21–43.

"Smoky Ol' Town: The Significance of Pittsburgh in U.S. Air Pollution History," James Longhurst. *EM magazine*, June 2007, pp. 13–16.

Notes on Sources

A place reference in books to "loc" instead of a page number denotes an e-book edition.

Introduction

xiii *On April 16, 1945 . . . best of Americans*: Morgan, *I Celebrate Myself: The Somewhat Private Life of Allen Ginsberg*, pp. 66ff.

xiii *"with the intensity . . . cannot be described"*: General Thomas Farrell, in *Atomic Energy for Military Purposes* (the "Smyth Report"), H. D. Smyth, Appendix 6, War Department Release, July 16, 1945, p. 254.

xiv *the second bomb hit Nagasaki*: Mee, Jr., *The Deal*, loc. 4018ff.

xiv *"For all we know"*: Boyer, *By the Bomb's Early Light*, p. 7.

xiv *"[S]eldom, if ever"*: *By the Bomb's Early Light*, p. 7; *In Search of Light: The Broadcasts of Edward R. Murrow, 1938–1961* (New York: Alfred A. Knopf, 1967), p. 102.

xv *"grimly Pyrrhic" . . . "things were split"*: James Agee, "The Peace: The Bomb," *Time*, August 20, 1945, p. 19.

xv *"put into the hands of common man"*: Ibid.

xv *That confidence was shattered*: Otto Friedrich, *The End of the World: A History*. New York: Penguin, 1982, pp. 179ff.

xv *Enlightenment itself was among the casualties*: See, for example, Theodore Besterman, *Voltaire* (New York: Harcourt, Brace & World, 1969), pp. 357ff, and Isaiah Berlin, *The Roots of Romanticism* (Princeton, NJ, and Oxford, UK: Princeton University Press, 1999).

xvi *As the Enlightenment gave way to Romanticism*: See, for example, Morse Peckham, *Beyond the Tragic Vision: The Quest for Identity in the Nineteenth Century* (New York: George Braziller, 1962).

xvii *"get on with it . . . as fast as you can, citizen":* Charles Olson, "Projective Verse," first published in the third issue of *Poetry New York* in 1950, archived at https://www.poetryfoundation.org/articles/69406/projective-verse.

xviii *"dark ages":* Marty Jezer, *The Dark Ages: Life in the United States 1945–1960* (Boston: South End Press, 1982).

xviii *"Eisenhower siesta":* William Manchester, *The Glory and the Dream: A Narrative History of America, 1932–1972,* vol. 2. (New York: Little, Brown, 1974), p. 772.

xviii *"A stench of fear . . . the courage of isolated people":* Norman Mailer, "The White Negro: Superficial Reflections on the Hipster," in *Advertisements for Myself* (New York: G. P. Putnam's Sons, 1959), loc. 5979.

Gay Rights

3 *he was tortured by nightmares:* Timmons, *The Trouble with Harry Hay,* loc. 2266ff.

3 *they did not set free . . . time served in the camps:* Alistair Newton, "Children of a Lesser Holocaust": Ken Setterington, *Branded by the Pink Triangle,* p. 91.

5 *"Harry snuggles up to interviewers":* Joseph Hanson, *A Few Doors West of Hope: The Life and Times of Dauntless Don Slater,* p. 23.

5 *striking clue . . . resistance to authority:* Timmons, *Trouble,* loc. 226ff.

6 *As a preteenager . . . never said he was sorry:* Tuchman, *Oral History,* tape 2, side 1, October 28, 1981.

6 *"Your father knew Cecil Rhodes":* Timmons, loc. 323.

6 *the family seemed somehow "wounded . . . :* Ibid., loc. 273.

6 *what it is he has spawned":* Tuchman, *Oral History,* tape 3, side 2, November 3, 1981.

7 *During the summer . . . Wobblies:* Tuchman, *Oral History,* tape 5, side 1, November 17, 1981.

7 *"You couldn't have been part of that":* author's interview in D'Emilio, *Sexual Politics, Sexual Communities,* loc. 1206.

8 *law enforcement sweeps . . . lobotomy to castration:* Baxter, " 'Homo-Hunting' in the Early Cold War," pp. 119–132.

8 *"Maybe instead of a girlish boy":* Timmons, *Trouble,* loc. 2085.

8 *"All you do is simply make up your mind":* Tuchman, *Oral History,* tape 7, side 2, December 18, 1981.

9 *"falling uncontrollably back":* Ibid., loc. 2508.

9 *nobody, with one exception" . . . " 'seduction station' ":* Charles Kaiser, *The Gay Metropolis,* loc. 686.

10 *"No one asked me"*: Bérubé, *Coming Out Under Fire,* loc. 4146.

10 *"He was holding onto the edge of a cliff"*: Timmons, *Trouble,* loc. 2618.

10 *"Other married men I knew . . . getting through every day"*: Tuchman, *Oral History,* tape 8, side 1, December 29, 1981.

10 *"the theoretician of People's Songs"*: Timmons, loc. 2715ff.

11 *One day at the factory . . . for any reason at all:* Johnson, *The Lavender Scare,* pp. 15ff; see also Timmons, loc. 2821ff.

12 *The danger of being fired . . . attacks on gay men:* K. A. Cuordileone, "Politics in an Age of Anxiety," *Journal of American History,* vol. 87, no. 2 (September 2000), p. 515.

12 *"links in a chain" . . . security armor:* State Department order, quoted in Johnson, *Lavender Scare,* pp. 15ff.

12 *Eventually some one million:* Eric Cervini, *The Deviant's War,* p. 4; William N. Eskridge, Jr., *Gaylaw: Challenging the Apartheid of the Closet* (Cambridge, MA, and London: Harvard University Press, 1999), p. 60.

12 *"sexual psychopaths"*: Johnson, *Lavender Scare,* p. 56.

13 *as John Cheever wrote: The Journals of John Cheever* (New York: Knopf, 1991), p. 157.

15 *"10,000 faggots"*: Lait and Mortimer, *Washington Confidential,* quoted in D'Emilio, *Sexual Politics,* loc. 994.

15 *"cookie pushers"*: Baxter, "Homo-Hunting," p. 122.

15 *"flagrantly homosexual" . . . "bad security risk" . . . "unusual mental twists"*: Congressional Record, vol. 96, part 2, 81st Congress, February 20, 1950, pp. 1952–1981; State Department Employee Loyalty Investigation: Hearings Before a Subcommittee of the Committee on Foreign Relations, Pursuant to S. Res. 231, 81st Congress, 2nd Session, Part 1, pp. 2–175 and pp. 277–292.

16 *"In this shady class"*: Statement by Deputy Undersecretary Peurifoy, February 13, 1950, Department of State Bulletin 22: 327; Senate Subcommittee of the Committee on Appropriations, Departments of State, Justice, Commerce, and the Judiciary Appropriations for 1951, 81st Congress, 2nd sess., February 28, 1950, 581–603.

16 *"PANSY PANIC"*: Max Lerner, *New York Post,* July 10, 1950 (headline by the editor).

17 *The* Times' *headline read . . . "correspondents corps"*: New York Times, April 19, 1950.

17 *On the floor of the House . . . "unfortunate people"*: Congressional Record, vol. 96, Part 4, 81st Congress, 2nd Session, March 29–April 24, 1950.

18 *"If you want to be against McCarthy"*: quoted in Curodileone, "Politics," p. 515.

19 *"With full realization . . . progress of society"*: Eann MacDonald [pseud],

"Preliminary Concepts, International Bachelors Fraternal Orders for Peace and Social Dignity," July 7, 1950, in *Gay and Lesbian Rights in the United States*, Williams and Retter, eds., p. 72. Details of the group's original mission are in *Radically Gay: Gay Liberation in the Words of Its Founder Harry Hay*, Roscoe, ed., pp. 60ff.

19 *"Because the media . . . Wrong"*: Hay, "Birth of a Consciousness," *Harvard Gay and Lesbian Review*, Winter 1995. https://glreview.org/article/birth -of-a-consciousness/.

20 *"by the end of the summer . . . blackmail"*: Ibid.

20 *Harry found the name . . . "vicious retaliation"*: Harry Hay interview in Katz, *Gay American History*, pp. 412–413.

21 *"all about the stars . . . tormenting gay chauvinism"*: Author's interview in Timmons, *Trouble*, loc. 2653ff.

21 *There was little he could say . . . "sixteen to eighteen hours"*: Tuchman, *Oral History*, tape 3, side 1, November 3, 1981.

22 *"missions and purposes"*: Hay, "Birth of a Consciousness."

22 *a quiet side conversation . . . "That's how they grew"*: Timmons, *Trouble*, loc. 3273ff.

23 *"We were talking about . . . perhaps for the first time in our lives"*: Author's interview, Timmons, *Trouble*, loc. 3106.

23 *That spring, Dale Jennings*: Katz, *Gay American History*, pp. 406–420.

24 *Jennings himself wrote about the case*: "To Be Accused," *ONE Magazine*, January 1953, in Williams and Retter, *Gay and Lesbian Rights*, pp. 74–75.

25 *After the Jennings case . . . "interesting to see"*: "Well, Medium, and RARE," *Los Angeles Mirror*, March 12, 1953; Meeker, "Behind the Mask of Respectability," pp. 84–85; Hurewitz, *Bohemian Los Angeles*, p. 263.

25 *"We all thought . . . a bad name"*: "The Founding of the Mattachine Society: An Interview with Harry Hay," in Katz, *Gay American History*, p. 417.

26 *"Five hundred people" . . . "never seen so many people"*: ibid.

26 *In his speech . . . "an outrageous thought"*: Author's interview, Marcus, *Making Gay History*, p. 34.

26 *Undaunted, Harry followed Rowland . . . "minorities must come first"*: Katz, "The Founding," p. 42.

27 *"We don't seat Communists"*: Marcus, *Making Gay History*, loc. 910.

28 *"It all turned to shit"*: Katz, "The Founding," p. 43.

28 *"we thought he hated us"*: Ibid.

28 *"He simply cut them off"*: Tuchman, *Oral History*, tape 9, side 1, December 29, 1981.

28 *"It broke my heart"*: Ibid.

28 *"I wish to state"* . . . *any questions at all:* "Testimony of Harry Hay, Accompanied by Counsel Frank Pestana," in Investigation of Communist Activities in the Los Angeles, California Area, Part 1, Hearings Before the Committee on Un-American Activities, House of Representatives, 84th Congress, 1st Session, June 27–July 2, 1955.

29 *"Discretion here"* . . . *"part of valor":* Cervini, *Deviant's War,* loc. 1229.

29 *Harry read about that* . . . *"There is no other choice":* Jeff Winters, "A Frank Look at the Mattachine: Can Homosexuals Organize," *ONE Magazine,* 1954, reprinted in *We Are Everywhere,* Blasius and Phelan, eds., pp. 316–319.

29 *"would be willing to cooperate"* Cervini, *Deviant's War,* loc. 1367; "Homosexual Activities in San Francisco," FBI File #100–37394, July 28, 1961.

30 *Three months before Pearl Harbor* . . . *"in those days":* Sources differ on whether he was drafted or enlisted. See Faderman, *The Gay Revolution,* p. 129; Long, *Gay Is Good,* loc. 98; Cervini, *The Deviant's War,* loc. 148.

30 *as a mortar crewman* . . . *Combat Infantryman Badge:* Murdoch and Price, *Courting Justice,* loc 785ff.

31 *Just before school started* . . . *"complaint dismissed"* Long, *Gay Is Good,* loc. 134ff.

31 *"Information has come to the attention* . . . *'immoral conduct' ":* Cervini, *The Deviant's War,* pp. 26ff.

31 *He borrowed $600* . . . *newly activist Mattachine Society:* Faderman, *Gay Revolution,* pp. 128ff.

32 *His 60-page petition* . . . *"a disgrace to any civilized society":* Petition Denied, Revolution Begun: Petition for a Writ of Certiorari by Franklin Edward Kameny, Pro Se, Kameny Papers Project, Charles Francis, ed. Kameny Papers Project, Kindle edition, 2011, loc. 474ff.

32 *"requirement of brevity":* Murdoch and Price, *Courting Justice,* loc. 758.

33 *"Petitioner asserts, flatly":* Kameny, *Petition Denied,* loc. 158.

33 *Markham Ball* . . . *take on the issue:* Murdoch and Price, *Courting Justice,* loc. 765.

34 *"Things are too hot right now":* D'Emilio, *Sexual Politics,* loc. 2388.

34 *He found it first* . . . *with the predictable result:* Details of the Kameny-Nichols meeting and Nichols's background are from Johnson, *The Lavender Scare,* pp. 184ff.

35 *By the time he met Kameny* . . . *"centered our lives":* Ibid., p. 185.

35 *The new group* . . . *"tooth-and-nail politics":* D'Emilio, *Sexual Politics,* loc. 2875.

36 *"by any lawful means* . . . *Constitution of the United States":* Long, *Gay Is Good,* loc. 284.

36 *Kameny had found the perfect case . . . "then we'll fight them"*: Faderman, *Gay Revolution*, pp. 146–147.

37 *Dowdy noticed a story*: "Group Aiding Deviates Issued Charity License," *Washington Star*, September 16, 1962.

37 *Kameny answered every question . . . "You forgot animals"*: "The Mattachine Society of Washington: Extension of Remarks of Hon. John Dowdy of Texas, in the House of Representatives," Congressional Record, July 5, 1963; Faderman, *Gay Revolution*, 135-136.

38 *At the time, Ellis was writing . . . "would have to be a psychopath"*: Jody Shotwell, "ECHO Convention '63," *Ladder*, December 1963; Faderman, *Gay Revolution*, p. 144.

39 *"There was absolutely nothing . . . dirty words in those days"*: Marcus, *Making Gay History*, loc. 1729.

39 *"There was a fantastic man" . . . "We were not going to help them"*: Marcus, *Making Gay History*, loc. 2008.

40 *"fairy project"*: Faderman, *Gay Revolution*, p. 99.

40 *Hooker's method*: Ibid., pp. 98–102.

40 *"arrant nonsense"*: Ibid., p. 89.

41 *" 'defensive, neurotic, disturbed denial' of science"*: "A Preface to the Second Edition: One Decade Later," in Cory, *The Homosexual in America*; D'Emilio, *Sexual Politics*, loc. 3209.

41 *"He was even more explicit"*: Edward Sagarin, "Structure and Ideology in an Association of Deviants," Ph.D. dissertation, New York University, 1966; Sagarin, "Homosexuals: The Many Masks of Mattachine," in *Odd Man In: Societies of Deviants in America* (Chicago: Quadrangle Press, 1969); D'Emilio, *Sexual Politics*, loc. 3250.

41 *"[Y]ou have left the mainstream"*: Kameny to Sagarin, April 7, 1965, in D'Emilio, *Sexual Politics*, loc. 3230.

41 *"Giving all views a fair hearing"*: Marcus, *Making Gay History*, loc. 1734.

44 *Clark struggled unsuccessfully*: "Kameny Heir Says No Ashes for Public Memorial," *Washington Blade*, February 23, 2012.

44 *Kameny's wry reaction*: "Former Astronomer Thanks His Lucky Stars He Turned to a Life of Activism," *Detroit News*, October 8, 1993; Murdoch and Price, *Courting Justice*, p. 805.

44 *"I am proud of my military service"*: Charles Francis, "Kameny's Storybook Ending," *Washington Blade*, October 20, 2011.

45 *director John Berry apologized . . . "Apology accepted"*: "Eye Opener: Apology for Frank Kameny," *Washington Post*, June 29, 2009; Faderman, *Gay Revolution* pp. 167–168.

45 *"a very good feeling to have"*: authors' interview, Murdoch & Price, *Courting Justice*, loc. 817.

46 *"Frank, this is where the pickets fit"*: Francis, "Kameny's Storybook Ending."

Feminism

51 *she died after a cerebral hemmorhage*: Agnes Murray's death certificate cited in Saxby, *Pauli Murray: A Personal and Political Life*, loc. 295.

51 *"I could not wait to see him"*: Murray, *Song in a Weary Throat*, loc. 972.

52 *"confused world of uncertain boundaries"*: Murray, *Song in a Weary Throat*, loc. 587.

52 *"a tug of war"* . . . *"I had no place"*: Murray, *Proud Shoes*, pp. 266ff.

52 *she left pictures of herself*: Photograph album, Papers of Pauli Murray, 1827–1985. PM/SL

54 *"fight its way out of a thicket"*: Coontz, *A Strange Stirring*, p. 144.

54 *"dead history"*: Friedan, *The Feminine Mystique*, p. 107.

54 *"Men there's a revolution . . . a very short time"*: " 'Wench with Wrench' on Trail of Male, Worker-Writer Says," Betty Goldstein [Friedan], Federated Press, November 24, 1943. BF/FP

55 *In 1952 . . . chauvinist husbands*: Moskowitz, "It's Good to Blow Your Top."

55 *"Until I started writing it"*: New York Times, "Up from the Kitchen Floor," March 4, 1973.

55 *"Any short list"*: As Daniel Horowitz was discovering another Betty Friedan, Susan Hartmann was researching her book *The Other Feminists*; Dorothy Sue Cobble was finding labor feminists in *The Other Women's Movement*; Kate Weigand was unearthing "red feminism" in the U.S. Communist Party; Joanne Meyerowitz was finding 1950s feminism in "Beyond the Feminine Mystique"; Amy Swerdlow was recovering the history of *Women Strike for Peace*; and the list goes on.

55 *point out what she considered . . . "something we simply cannot afford to do"*: Lerner to Betty Friedan, March 7, 1963. GL/SL

56 *"I was so angry that day"*: Author's interview of Utica Blackwell in Mills, *This Little Light of Mine*, p. 17.

57 *Gerda would remember . . . "How could they do that?"*: Lerner, *Fireweed*, p. 48.

58 *"a misfit, a freak, an outcast"*: Ibid., p. 23.

59 *"allowed me to find a territory . . . character and being"*: Ibid., pp. 64–65.

61 *In 1943, in a special issue on Russia:* "Lenin the Father of Modern Russia," *Life*, January 1, 1943.

62 *"Mrs. New York—And She Can Cook Too!":* Weigand, *Red Feminism*, p. 87.

62 *"a specialized arm . . . drive for world conquest":* "Report on the Congress of American Women," October 23, 1949, Committee on Un-American Activities, U.S. House of Representatives, p. 1.

63 *advice of a good friend:* Lerner, *Fireweed*, p. 242.

63 *"It is then that you take . . . more than it can":* Ibid., p. 346.

64 *the first such college-level course:* "Rethinking the Second Wave," Nancy MacLean.

64 *"What I wanted to do . . . Gerda would have none of it":* Why Women Need to Climb Mountains, a documentary film on Lerner's life and career.

65 *The picture taken . . . fearless confidence:* Murray, "Three Thousand Miles on a Dime in Ten Days," pp. 90–92.

66 *She spent days and weeks . . . did little to help:* Rosenberg, *Jane Crow*, pp. 50–51.

66 *the appeal of a Virginia sharecropper:* "John Dewey and the Question of Race: The Fight for Odell Waller," Sam F. Stack, Jr., *Education & Culture* no. 25, vol. 1 (2009): pp. 17–35.

67 *"I kept saying to myself":* Southern Oral History Program interview with Pauli Murray, February 13, 1976.

67 *"I get out two words":* Ibid.

68 *"too humiliated to respond":* Murray, *Song in a Weary Throat*, loc. 3715.

68 *As she put it in her autobiography:* Ibid., loc. 3733ff.

69 *looking for a case:* Azaransky, *The Dream Is Freedom*, pp. 21–22.

70 *He bought a copy . . . "bible" for civil-rights litigation:* Rosenberg, *Jane Crow*, loc. 5784.

74 *"The time has come . . . which is not inclusive":* Murray to Randolph, August 21, 1963. PM/SL

75 *"The Role of the Negro Women in the Civil Rights Revolution" . . . "militance, dedication, and ability":* Murray to Randolph, August 27, 1963. PM/SL

75 *"In 1963, no civil rights campaign":* Ibid.

76 *Three months later, when the group met again:* Giardina, "MOW to NOW," pp. 736ff.

76 *"the Negro woman can no longer postpone . . .":* Pauli Murray, "The Negro Woman in the Quest for Equality," speech at the NCNW Leadership Conference, New York, NY, November 14, 1963. PM/SL

76 *"sex" was added to the criteria:* Jo Freeman, "How Sex Got into Title VII: Persistent Opportunism as a Maker of Public Policy," *Law & Inequality*, vol. 9, no. 2 (1991), pp. 163–184.

76 *"terribly complicated" . . . "conceived out of wedlock"*: Murray, *Song in a Weary Throat*, loc. 7227ff.

77 *"What will it take"*: Ibid., loc. 7243.

77 *Decades later, it was clear:* See Giardina, "From MOW to NOW," which reframes the role of Black women in the rise of postwar feminism.

78 *One of her strongest childhood memories . . . "going to beat her kids"*: "Fannie Lou Hamer Speaks Out," *Essence*, October 1971, in *The Speeches of Fannie Lou Hamer: To Tell It Like It Is*, Brooks and Houck, eds., p. 54.

78 *"There weren't many weeks" . . . "I have a right to be angry"*: Giddings, *When and Where I Enter*, loc. 4872; Fannie Lou Hamer interview, The Civil Rights Documentation Project (Moorland-Spingarn Collection, Howard University, Washington, D.C.), pp. 3, 28.

78 *"I was rebelling" . . . "what was going on in Mississippi"*: The Speeches of Fannie Lou Hamer, p. 124.

79 *"as high as I could get it . . . since I could remember"*: SNCC pamphlet by Hamer, "To Praise Our Bridges," p. 12.

79 *"as a horse knows about Christmas"*: Mills, *This Little Light*, p. 37; Fannie Lou Hamer interview, Oral History Department, Moorland-Spingarn Research Center, Howard University.

80 *Hamer began to sing:* Mills, *This Little Light*, p. 37.

80 *her voice "as a voice" . . . "I don't think there was a wasted hum when she sang"*: Harry Belafonte quoted in Mills, *This Little Light*, p. 19.

82 *during a long layover in Winona . . . put them all under arrest:* Mills, *This Little Light*, pp. 56ff. The word "n-----s" is spelled out in the original.

84 *"All night we could hear her crying"*: "Fannie Lou Hamer, Civil Rights Leader, Dies," *Washington Post*, March 17, 1977.

85 *"I have been thinking about this" . . . "knows that she is good"*: Stembridge, "Some Notes on Education," in Giddings, *When and Where*, p. 300; also see Carson, *In Struggle*, p. 155; and Olson, *Freedom's Daughters*, p. 167.

88 *"lost the truth"*: Olson, *Freedom's Daughters*, p. 392.

88 *"nobody's free unless everybody's free"*: The Speeches of Fannie Lou Hamer, pp. 134ff.

89 *"this kind of angel feeling . . . fighting all this time"*: "It's in Your Hands," speech to the NAACP Legal Defense Fund, 1971.

89 *the story of a wise old man:* Ibid.

90 *"stunning, even thrilling"*: Linda Gordon, "Gerda Lerner: Leftist and Feminist," *Journal of Women's History*, vol. 26, no. 1 (Spring 2014), pp. 31–36.

90 *She sat with it for hours:* Darlene Hine Clark, in *Why Women Need to Climb Mountains*.

91 *"The first things I can think of"*: Lerner, *Fireweed*, p. 7.

91   *"Whatever contributions . . . my life as a Communist":* Ibid., pp. 146–147.

91   *"never been a normal kind of mother . . . on my own terms":* Ibid., p. 146.

92   *"Like the good fairy . . . strength in the face of danger":* Ibid., p. 59.

93   *"ferociousness and bloodletting":* Murray to Kathryn Clarenbach, November 21, 1967. PM/SL

93   *"I saw no Catholic sisters . . . my name to its policies":* Ibid.

94   *"the* Brown v. Board of Education *for women":* Rosenberg, *Jane Crow,* p. 296.

94   *"the most important thing to happen":* Ibid.

94   *"We knew we were standing on their shoulders" . . . "he had granddaughters":* Quotes from Justice Ginsburg are in the transcript of a conference, "*Reed v. Reed* at 40: Equal Protection and Women's Rights," in *American University Journal of Gender, Social Policy & the Law,* vol. 20, no. 2 (2012), pp. 315–344.

95   *Chief Justice Warren Burger read the decision: Reed v. Reed,* 404 U.S. 71, online at Justia, https://supreme.justia.com/cases/federal/us/404/71/#tab-opinion-1949534.

95   *"What makes me optimistic":* Ginsburg, "*Reed v. Reed* at 40."

95   *"Chief Justice Rehnquist explained":* Ibid.

95   *He himself wrote the opinion:* Riva B. Siegel, " 'You've Come a Long Way, Baby': Rehnquist's New Approach to Pregnancy Discrimination in Hibbs," *Stanford Law Review,* vol. 58, no. 6 (April 2006), pp. 1871–1898.

96   *"Ruth, did you write that?":* Ginsberg, "*Reed v. Reed* at 40."

97   *"While some may laud the whole spectacle . . . I am the Third Wave":* Walker, "Becoming the Third Wave."

97   *"I am discouraged . . . when a faculty member":* Alice Walker, "A Talk: Convocation 1972," *In Search of Our Mother's Gardens,* 1983, pp. 231–243.

98   *"I must love the questions . . .":* Alice Walker, "Reassurance," *In Search of Our Mothers' Gardens,* Harcourt Brace Jovanovich, 1983.

Civil Rights

102   *"Hell no, God damn it" . . . "or I will drop you":* Gergel, *Unexampled Courage,* pp. 15ff.

102   *ophthalmology report . . . "hopeless":* Ibid., pp. 22–23; report of Chester W. Chinn, M.D., May 7, 1946.

102   *Before taking him from his cell . . . their father's house in the Bronx:* Gergel, *Unexampled Courage,* pp. 18–23.

103   *Frederick Douglass heartily approved: Black History: A Reappraisal,* Melvin Drimmer, ed. (New York: Doubleday, 1968), p. 259; Williams, *Medgar Evers: Mississippi Martyr,* p. 34.

103   *"close our ranks":* W. E. B. DuBois, "Close Ranks," *Crisis,* July 1918, p. 111.

104 *one every five days:* Dray, *At the Hands of Persons Unknown*, 2003, p. 256.

104 *Among the first to return:* Mikkelsen, "Coming from Battle to Face a War," p. 139; Dray, *Persons Unknown*, p. 247.

104 *"the Negro's particular decoration":* Hot Springs Echo quoted in Robert Thomas Kerlin, *The Voice of the Negro* (New York: E.P. Dutton, 1920), p. 73.

105 *Rosa Parks was six years old . . . "I wanted to see him shoot that gun":* Rosa Parks with Jim Haskins, *Rosa Parks: My Story* (New York: Penguin, 1992), pp. 30–31.

105 *"Self-defense is so deeply ingrained":* in Mary King, *Freedom Song: A Personal Story of the 1960s Civil Rights Movement* (New York: William Morrow, 1987), p. 318.

107 *That night, a white mob . . . drive away with him:* Marjorie Smith, "Racial Confrontation in Columbia, Tennessee: 1946," MA thesis, Atlanta University, 1971, online at http://digitalcommons.auctr.edu/dissertations; Egerton, *Speak Now Against the Day,* loc. 748–755.

107 *he was saved from lynching:* Mikkelsen, "Coming Home from Battle," pp. 229–230; Egerton, *Speak Now Against the Day,* loc. 7410-7461.

107 *George Dorsey, a veteran . . . no one was ever convicted:* Egerton, *Speak Now,* loc. 7416–7550. The word "n----r" is spelled out in the original.

108 *Truman was facing . . . a memo around that time:* Gardner, *Harry Truman and Civil Rights,* p. 15.

108 *"very much alarmed":* Truman letter to Clark, September 6, 1946. *The Civil Rights Legacy of Harry S. Truman,* Raymond H. Geselbracht, ed. (Kirksville, MO: Truman State University Press, 2007), p. 56.

109 *"I am not asking for social equality":* Letter from Truman to Ernest W. Roberts, August 18, 1948. The word "N-----s" is spelled out in Roberts' letter to Truman.

109 *By the day of Georgia's primary . . . no Black votes counted at all:* Bernd, "White Supremacy and the Disfranchisement of Blacks in Georgia, 1946," pp. 492–513.

110 *On his way home:* Elizabeth Evers-Jordan interview in Evers-Williams, *Medgar Evers,* p. 33.

111 *began amassing an arsenal:* Evers-Williams, *Medgar Evers,* p. 31.

111 *"I call for every red-blooded white man" . . . "DON'T TRY IT":* Dittmer, *Local People,* p. 2. The word "n----r" is spelled out in the original.

111 *"Dr. Jack, I'm surprised at you":* Author's interview with Charles Evers in Williams, *Medgar Evers,* p. 41. The word "n-----s" is spelled out in the original.

112 *"Around town, Negroes said":* Evers-Williams and Marable, *The Autobiography of Medgar Evers,* loc. 1955.

112 *The outcome of the hearings . . . "opening salvo":* Payne, *I've Got the Light of Freedom*, p. 67; Dittmer, *Local People*, p. 9.

113 *"I do not believe" . . . broke down in tears:* Tinsley E. Yarbrough, *A Passion for Justice: J. Waties Waring and Civil Rights* (New York and Oxford, UK: Oxford University Press, 1987), p. 50ff.

113 *After Waring gave his instructions:* Ibid.

115 *Before he asked her . . . married shortly after:* Evers-Williams with Peters, *For Us, the Living*, pp. 56–58.

115 *"I don't want you to get upset":* author's interview with Myrlie Evers-Williams in Williams, *Medgar Evers*, p. 21.

118 *After that he carried a .45 . . . a shotgun . . . a small armory:* Williams, *Medgar Evers*, p. 106.

119 *Klan mounted ever more determined attacks:* Staff of the Equal Justice Initiative, "Targeting Black Veterans: Lynching in America."

119 *the Rev. George Lee and . . . Gus Courts . . . Lamar Smith:* Payne, *I've Got the Light of Freedom*, loc. 853ff; Dittmer, *Local People*, pp. 53–54; Evers-Williams, *For Us, the Living*, p. 154ff.

120 *she confessed that she was lying:* Tyson, *The Blood of Emmett Till*, New York, pp. 164–165.

120 *his greatest challenge to date:* Williams, *Medgar Evers*, pp. 123–126; also see Tyson, *Radio Free Dixie*, p. 85.

121 *sold their vividly appalling account of the crime:* William Bradford Huie, "Shocking Story of Approved Killing in Mississippi," *Look*, January 24, 1956.

121 *Howard's tour reached Montgomery:* "MIA Mass Meeting at Holt Street Baptist Church," Martin Luther King, Jr. Research and Education Institute, online at https://kinginstitute.stanford.edu/king-papers/documents/mia-mass-meeting-holt-street-baptist-church; Theoharis, *The Rebellious Life of Mrs. Rosa Parks*, loc. 2428ff.

123 *"That was one of the first incidents":* Tyson, *Radio Free Dixie*, p. 50.

123 *"laborers, farmers, domestic workers" . . . people "who didn't scare easy":* Williams, *Negroes with Guns*, loc. 590ff.

124 *white citizens drew up a petition:* Tyson, *Radio Free Dixie*, p. 85.

124 *just to keep order:* Tyson, *Radio Free Dixie*, p. 86.

124 *"He is looking for a funeral":* Ibid., loc. 1767. The word "n----r" is spelled out in the original.

124 *A telephoned bomb threat:* Barksdale, "Robert F. Williams and the Indigenous Civil Rights Movement in Monroe, North Carolina, 1961"; Tyson, *Radio Free Dixie*, p. 87–88.

125 *"We shot it out with the Klan":* Williams, *Negroes with Guns*, p. 57.

125 *Decades later, B. J. Winfield:* Tyson, *Radio Free Dixie*, p. 89.

127 *"Kennard's car could be hit by a train":* Minchin and Salmond, "The Saddest Story of the Whole Movement."

127 *Instead, he was framed:* Ibid.

127 *"I could tell he was choked with emotion":* Evers-Williams, *For Us, the Living*, p. 244.

128 *"Our brother is here":* Tyson, *Radio Free Dixie*, p. 205.

128 *"as bad as the white people":* Tyson, *Radio Free Dixie*, p. 147.

128 *as Williams swore in testimony years later:* Statements of Robert F. Williams, Internal Security Subcommittee, Committee on the Judiciary, Second Session, March 24, 1970 (Washington, D.C.: U.S. Government Printing Office, 1971), p. 89.

129 *"NAACP Leader Urges 'Violence' ":* New York Times, May 7, 1959, p. 22.

129 *Williams was questioned:* Statements of Robert F. Williams, Internal Security Subcommittee, p. 90.

130 *Evers disagreed diplomatically:* Dittmer, *Local People*, p. 86; Medgar Evers, "Monthly Report," April 19, 1960, NAACP Papers.

131 *"Nobody dared move a peg":* Raines, *My Soul Is Rested*, p. 234.

131 *The impact of the library sit-in:* Dittmer, *Local People*, pp. 88–90; Evers-Williams, *For Us, the Living*, pp. 235ff.

131 *And then, in May 1961:* Dittmer, *Local People*, pp. 91ff.

133 *That summer, SNCC's James Forman:* Tyson, *Radio Free Dixie*, p. 263ff.

133 *"Robert, you have caused a lot of race trouble":* Ibid., p. 280.

134 *"Rob never stopped being Rob":* Mabel Williams interview with Stephanie Banchero in Tyson, *Radio Free Dixie*, p. 292.

136 *"Can you believe that white man":* Jonathan Rieder, "The Day President Kennedy Embraced Civil Rights—and the Story Behind It," *Atlantic*, June 11, 2013.

137 *An enormous crowd gathered . . . "I stand for what's right:* Branch, *Parting the Waters*, loc. 16735ff.

139 *In late August . . . a documentary of the event:* Euchner, *Nobody Turn Me Around*, loc. 1710ff.

139 *SNCC's Michael Thelwell was sickened:* Euchner, *Nobody Turn Me Around*, loc. 1734.

140 *He was named in absentia to honorific posts:* Tyson, *Radio Free Dixie*, pp. 297ff.

140 *"gentle exception":* Tyson, *Radio Free Dixie*, p. 303; Andrew Myers, "When Violence Met Violence: Facts and Images of Robert F. Williams and the Black Freedom Struggle in Monroe, North Carolina," MA thesis, University of Virginia, 1993, pp. 75–76.

141 *"I had always considered myself"*: Robert F. Williams interview with Banchero, in Tyson, *Radio Free Dixie*, loc. 5739ff.

141 *"They have a lot of young teenagers"*: Robert F. Williams interview with Thomas Mosby, Ralph Bunche Oral History Collection, Moorland-Spingarn Research Center, Howard University; Tyson, *Radio Free Dixie*, loc. 5744ff.

141 *"The Black leaders our youth know"*: Tyson, *Radio Free Dixie*, loc. 5762; James Bock, "A New Debate over Nonviolence," *Baltimore Sun-Journal*, March 2, 1977.

141 *"his courage and commitment to freedom"*: from Williams family videotape, cited in Tyson, *Radio Free Dixie*, loc. 5762.

142 *Because he was blinded . . . "I just can't see"*: Gergel, *Unexampled Courage*, pp. 259–261.

142 *In 1964, he was evaluated*: Ibid., pp. 259–261.

143 *never knowing all that followed*: Ibid., pp. 258ff.

143 *a unit known as the "Black Panthers"*: Major Craig A. Trice, "The Men That Served with Distinction: The 761st Tank Battalion," MA thesis presented to the U.S. Army Command and General Staff College, Fort Leavenworth, KS, 1997, pp. 7ff.

144 *"One day, like a storm"*: Malcolm X, *The Autobiography of Malcolm X*, p. 9.

Ecology

147 *"unusually pretty"*: Handwritten account by Maria Carson, Papers of Rachel Carson, Beinecke Library, Yale University.

147 *her mother came to visit so frequently*: Lear, *Rachel Carson: Witness for Nature*, loc. 678ff.

148 *"Nature study cultivates the child's imagination"*: Comstock, *Handbook of Nature Study* (Ithaca, NY: Cornell University Press, 1911), p. 1.

148 *Her first surviving work*: Rachel Carson, "The Little Brown House." RC/BL

149 *"Near at hand we heard"*: St. Nicholas, July 1922, vol. 49, part 2, p. 999.

149 *"seeing the things one looks at"*: Report of the Michigan Academy of Science, Wynkoop Hallenbeck, Croford Co. of Lansing, Michigan, State Printers, 1902, p. 39, online at https://archive.org/details/reportofmichigan1902mich.

150 *He told the* World *reporter*: New York World Sunday magazine, Oct. 7, 1906; Conway and Siegelman, *Dark Hero of the Information Age*, pp. 3, 17.

151 *Norbert did not even know his father was Jewish*: Ibid., p. 23.

151 *"an easy, conversational tone . . . morally raw all over"*: Ibid., pp. 67ff.

151 *"my taskmaster was at the same time my hero"*: Ibid., p. 101.

152 *it was then that he "relearned the world . . . totally astonishing"*: Authors' interview, Conway and Siegelman, *Dark Hero*, p. 14.

152 *"The Theory of Ignorance"*: Manuscript. NW/MIT

152 *His dissertation focused*: Grattan-Guinness, "Wiener on the Logics of Russell and Schroder," pp. 103–132.

153 *"Nevertheless he turned out well"*: The Autobiography of Bertrand Russell *1872–1914* (London: George Allen & Unwin, 1967), pp. 41–42, quoted in Grattan-Guinness, "Wiener on the Logics," p. 103.

153 *Wiener called Russell "an iceberg"*: Grattan-Guinness, "Wiener on the Logics," p. 104.

155 *a technocracy movement . . . "beneath and above"*: Peter J. Taylor, "Technocratic Optimism, H. T. Odum, and the Partial Transformation of Ecological Metaphor after World War II," *Journal of the History of Biology,* vol. 21, no. 2 (Summer 1988), pp. 213–244; Howard Scott, "History and Purpose of Technocracy," Technocracy Incorporated, 1964, online at https://archive .org/details/HistoryAndPurposeOfTechnocracy.howardScott.

155 *The more persistent legacy of the bomb . . . take other life forms with them*: Hamblin, *Arming Mother Nature*; Boyer, *By the Bomb's Early Light*; *Advisory Committee on Human Radiation Experiments, Final Report* [hereafter ACHRE], online at https://bioethicsarchive.georgetown.edu /achre.

157 *"Smoke and Fumes Committee"*: Oreskes and Conway, *Merchants of Doubt*; Center for International Environmental Law, https://www.smokeand fumes.org/documents.

157 *some fabulous grotesques*: Alexis C. Madrigal, "Old, Weird Tech: The Bat Bombs of World War II," *Atlantic,* April 14, 2011.

157 *saturating an enemy's water supply with LSD*: "Testing and Use of Chemical and Biological Agents by the Intelligence Community: MKULTRA," 94th Congress, 2nd Session Senate Report No. 94-755, pp. 390–392, online at https://web.archive.org/web/20050421233209/http://www.mindcon trolforums.com/church-committee-drugtesting-report.htm#mkultra.

157 *destroyed by fire . . . classified even in 2021*: During the design stage for a new National Personnel Records Center in St. Louis, the Department of Defense balked at the architect's plan to install a sprinkler system and fire walls. The architect objected but later discovered that they had been omitted without his consent. Martino-Taylor, *Behind the Fog*, pp. 61ff and 93.

159 *"I love all the beautiful things"*: "Who I Am and Why I Came to P.C.W.," 1925, RC/BLYU.

159 *she wrote more about Skinker:* Lear, *Witness,* loc. 940.

159 *On one such night:* Ibid., loc. 837

160 *"spoke to something":* Undated page on her letterhead. RC/BL

161 *she watched him as he read it:* Carson, "Undersea," *Atlantic Monthly* 78 (September 1937), pp. 55–67.

162 *"Everything else followed . . . something to write about":* Carson, "The Real World Around Us," in *Lost Woods,* Lear, ed., loc. 1620.

162 *a biological survey of Bikini Atoll:* Schultz, "The Biology of the Bikini Atoll, With Special Reference to the Fishes," pp. 301–316.

163 *military science at its most oxymoronic:* Descriptions of the test planning and results are in Weisgall, *Operation Crossroads*; also Elizabeth M. DeLoughrey, "The Myth of Isolates: Ecosystem Ecologies in the Nuclear Pacific," *Cultural Geographies,* vol. 20, no. 2 (April 2013, 167–184, doi: 10.1177/1474474012463664); and Shurcliff, *Bombs at Bikini.*

164 *DDT was a war hero . . . Battle of Stalingrad:* Kinkela, *DDT and the American Century,* loc. 329–460.

164 *Exactly one week after V-J Day . . . "Gimbels Works Fast!":* Ibid., loc. 248.

164 *The FWS's earliest DDT studies:* Cottam and Higgins, "DDT and Its Effect on Fish and Wildlife."

164 *a story proposal to* Reader's Digest *. . . "whole balance of nature":* RC to Harold Lynch, July 14, 1945, RC/BLYU; Lear, *Rachel Carson,* loc. 2341ff.

166 *a message to his fellow scientists . . . "irresponsible militarists":* "A Scientist Rebels," *Bulletin of the Atomic Scientists* vol. 3, no. 1, p. 31 (January 1947); reprinted from *The Atlantic Monthly,* vol. 178, no. 6 (December 1946).

167 *Albert Einstein, who said . . . "national security":* Conway and Siegelman, *Dark Hero,* p. 242.

167 *"erratic . . . known to be nuts":* NW FBI files, Conway and Siegelman, *Dark Hero,* pp. 255ff.

168 *"Wiener stories" were passed around:* Heims, *John Von Neumann and Norbert Wiener,* p. 343; Bruce Jackson, " 'The Greatest Mathematician in the World': Norbert Wiener Stories," in *Western Folklore,* vol. 31, no. 1 (January 1972), pp. 1–21.

168 *helped him think:* Jackson, ''The Greatest Mathematician"; D. K. Wilgus, "More Norbert Wiener Stories," *Western Folklore,* vol. 31, no. 1, January 1972, pp. 22ff.

168 *"goad himself . . . desperation":* Heims, *John von Neumann and Norbert Wiener,* pp. 123–124.

168 *a younger brother, Fritz:* Conway and Siegelman, *Dark Hero,* p. 97.

169 *"a personal flaw . . . incredibly strong":* Authors' interview with Peggy Wiener Kennedy, Conway and Siegelman, *Dark Hero,* p. 98.

169 *Hitler was misunderstood . . . "not very nice"*: Authors' interview with Barbara Wiener Raisbeck, Conway and Siegelman, *Dark Hero*, pp. 100ff.

171 *it was not a "useful miracle"*: Diary of Warren Weaver, November 10, 1942, in Montagnini, *Harmonies of Disorder*, p. 129; Conway and Siegelman, *Dark Hero*, p. 120.

173 *"Each group, when it comes together"*: Heims, *The Cybernetics Group*, p. 25.

173 *No meeting was more ambitiously interdisciplinary*: Cybernetics: The Macy Conferences, 1946–1953; Heims, *The Cybernetics Group*, pp. 18ff.

174 *"the biggest bite"*: Bateson's lecture at Sacramento State College's Two Worlds Symposium, April 12, 1966; reprinted as "From Versailles to Cybernetics" in his *Steps to an Ecology of Mind*.

174 *"a difference that makes a difference"*: Bateson, "Form, Substance, and Difference," in *Steps to an Ecology of Mind*.

174 *"The thought of every age . . . communication and control"*: Wiener, *Cybernetics, or Control and Communication in the Animal and the Machine*, p. 39.

175 *"new trinity of matter, energy, and information"*: Annals of the American Academy of Political and Social Science, vol. 264 (July 1949), pp. 187–188.

175 *"Those of us who have contributed"*: Wiener, *Cybernetics*, p. 28. For a bracing assessment of Wiener's war work, see Galison, "The Ontology of the Enemy: Norbert Wiener and the Cybernetic Vision."

176 *"It cannot be good for [automation]"*: Wiener, *Cybernetics*, p. 27.

177 *"increased mastery of nature"*: Wiener, *Human Use of Human Beings*, p. 46.

177 *"When the tea and cakes were exhausted"*: Ibid., p. 46.

177 *"Our long-term chief antagonist"*: Wiener, *Invention: The Care and Feeding*, p. 143.

178 *funded the CIA's first LSD research*: Kline, *The Cybernetics Moment*, p. 186.

178 *"If you say why not bomb them"*: Quoted in Clay Blair, Jr., "Passing of a Great Mind," *Life*, February 25, 1957, pp. 89–104.

178 *"What then are organisms?"*: Turner, *From Counterculture to Cyberculture*, loc. 441ff; "Air Defense System: ADSEC Final Report," Air Defense Systems Engineering Committee, October 24, 1950, MITRE Corporation Archives, Bedford, MA.

179 *It was Brooks who had convinced*: Brooks, *Two Park Street*, pp. 149–156.

179 *"a force strong and purposeful"*: Carson, *The Edge of the Sea*, p. 250.

179 *forces of the natural world were being drafted into the Cold War*: See Hamblin, *Arming Mother Nature*; *Environmental Histories of the Cold War*, McNeill, ed.; and articles by Athelstan F. Spilhaus: "Man in the Sea," *Science*, vol. 145, no. 3636 (September 4, 1964), p. 993; "Sea and Air

Resources," *Geographical Review*, vol. 44, no. 3 (July 1954), pp. 346–351; "Control of the World Environment," *Geographical Review*, vol. 46, no. 4 (October 1956), pp. 451–459.

180 *similarly ambitious projects . . . known by the acronym CEBAR:* Jacob Hamblin, *Arming Mother Nature*; Leonard A. Cole, "Open-Air Biowarfare Testing and the Evolution of Values," *Health Security*, vol. 14, no. 5 (October 2016), 315–322, doi: 10.1089/hs.2016.0040; Ronald E. Doel, "Constituting the Postwar Earth Sciences: The Military's Influence on the Environmental Sciences in the USA after 1945," *Social Studies of Science* vol. 33, no. 5 (October 2003), pp. 635–666.

180 *FP was found to have adverse affects:* Martino-Taylor, *Behind the Fog*, pp. 66–102; Cole, "Open-Air Biowarfare Testing."

181 *Ebb Cade . . . "data we were expected to get":* ACHRE, pp. 239ff; Martino-Taylor, *Behind the Fog*, pp. 26–28.

181 *Among the known experiments:* ACHRE, pp. 320ff; Martino-Taylor, *Behind the Fog*, pp. 24–32, 103–146.

183 *Castle Bravo:* "60th Anniversary of Castle BRAVO Nuclear Test, the Worst Nuclear Test in U.S. History," National Security Archive, George Washington University, February 28, 2014, https://nsarchive2.gwu.edu /nukevault/ebb459/.

184 *an unforeseen wind-shift:* Jonathan M. Weisgall, "Time to End the 40-Year Lie," *Bulletin of the Atomic Scientists*, vol. 50, no. 3 (May–June 1994), p. 3, doi: 10.1080/00963402.1994.11456513.

184 *The crew of a Japanese fishing boat:* Lapp, *The Voyage of the Lucky Dragon*.

184 *the disaster made headlines for weeks:* Weisgall, "Time to End the 40-Year Lie."

184 *giving birth to badly deformed babies:* Johnston and Barker, *The Rongelap Report*; DeLoughrey, "The Myth of Isolates," p. 177.

185 *"miserable most of the time":* Lytle, *The Gentle Subversive*, pp. 115ff.

185 *In the spring of 1957, her friend Robert Cushman Murphy . . . sued the United States Department of Agriculture:* Paull, "The Rachel Carson Letters and the Making of *Silent Spring*," pp. 1–12; Lear, *Rachel Carson*, loc 5898ff.

185 *a letter from the evolutionary biologist Edward O. Wilson:* Details of Elton's influence are in Davis, "Like a Keen North Wind."

186 *"Who was profiting from the excess use of poison?":* Daniel, "A Rogue Bureaucracy: The USDA Fire Ant Campaign of the Late 1950s."

187 *Nothing more conclusively confirmed Carson's growing concern . . . thalidomide:* Lear, *Rachel Carson*, loc. 8004ff.

188 *"little tranquilizing pills of half truth":* Carson, *Silent Spring*, loc. 156.

188 *"for surgery that I hope will not be too complicated"*: Carson to Paul Brooks, March 21, 1960. RC/BL

188 *"bordered on malignancy"*: Lear, *Rachel Carson*, loc. 7135.

189 *"so indescribably weak"*: RC to Dorothy Freeman, February 2, 1961, in Freeman, *Always, Rachel*, p. 337.

189 *"too much comfort"*: RC to Marjorie Spock and Polly Richards, April 12, 1960, in Lear, *Rachel Carson*, loc. 7141.

189 *"There is no reason"*: RC to Dorothy Freeman, May 20, 1962, in Freeman, *Always, Rachel*, p. 405.

190 *She had expressed some of these concerns*: See, for example, "Design for Nature Writing," remarks on accepting the John Burroughs Medal, April 7, 1952, in *Atlantic Naturalist,* vol. 7, no. 5 (August 1952), pp. 232–234.

190 *"The most alarming"*: Carson, *Silent Spring*, pp. 5, 7.

190 *"[W]e are living in the shadow"*: Wiener, *I Am a Mathematician*, p. 300.

190 *"Along with the possibility"*: Carson, *Silent Spring*, p. 8

190 *"[I]t is only a humanity"*: Wiener, unpublished manuscript discovered at the *New York Times* and published May 20, 2013, section D, p. 8.

191 *"This is an era of specialists"*: Carson, *Silent Spring*, p. 14.

191 *"The man who is only allowed"*: Wiener, *Prolegomena to Theology*, the Terry Lectures, 1962, notes and draft copy. NW/MIT

191 *"It is also an era dominated by industry"*: Carson, *Silent Spring*, p. 14.

191 *"In a profit-bound world"*: Wiener, *I Am a Mathematician*, p. 362.

191 *"Megabuck science"*: Wiener, *Invention: The Care and Feeding*, p. 33.

191 *"The very substantial financial investment"*: Carson, *Silent Spring*, p. 272.

191 *"The penalties for errors"*: Wiener, *God and Golem, Inc.*, pp. 82–83.

191 *"[If] the rules for victory"*: Wiener, "Some Moral and Technical Consequences of Automation."

192 *"It is the public"*: Carson, *Silent Spring*, p. 14

192 *"Whatever benefits are awarded"*: Wiener, *Invention: The Care and Feeding*, p. 154.

192 *"hysterically emphatic"*: "The Price for Progress," *Time*, September 28, 1962, pp. 45–48.

192 *"the quality of gossip"*: "Hiss of Doom?" *Newsweek*, August 6, 1962, p. 55.

192 *"Hurricane Rachel"*: "The Gentle Storm Center," *Life*, October 12, 1962, p. 248.

192 *"freaks . . . the end of all human progress"*: William Darby, "Silence, Miss Carson!" *Chemical and Engineering News*, vol. 40, no. 40 (October 1, 1962), pp. 60–63.

192 *"why a spinster"*: Lear, *Rachel Carson*, loc. 8340.

192 *The Veliscol Chemical Corporation threatened*: Robert Gottlieb, *Forcing*

the Spring: The Transformation of the American Environmental Movement (Washington, DC, and London: Island Press), 2005, loc. 1459.

193 *Kennedy adopted Carson's agenda as his own . . . "before they are authorized"*: Text of JFK speech, *New York Times*, October 23, 1963, p. 24.

194 *the fish had been killed . . . by Veliscol*: Frank Graham Jr. *Since Silent Spring* (Boston: Houghton Mifflin, 1970), pp. 96ff.; Lear, *Rachel Carson*, loc. 9113ff.

194 *"It is essential that all pesticides"*: quoted in Graham, *Since Silent Spring*, pp. 106–107.

195 *a teacher entirely unlike his father*: Jerison, "The Legacy of Norbert Wiener," p. 19ff.

195 *"Unwarranted as these doubts were"*: N. Levinson, "Wiener's Life," *Bulletin of the American Mathematical Society*, vol. 27, no. 1, pp. 1–32.

196 *"The concerns he expressed"*: "CPSR's Norbert Wiener Award: A Fitting Legacy for the First Cyber-Activist," Daniel Borenstein presentation at the 2014 IEEE Conference, Norbert Wiener in the 21st Century.

196 *One of Wiener's early hopes*: Conway and Siegelman, *Dark Hero*, pp. 322–324.

197 *"I have seldom seen Wiener so happy"*: Ibid., p. 324.

197 *"On the battlefield of the future"*: William Westmoreland, "Address to the Association of the U.S. Army, October 14, 1969," in Bousquet, *The Scientific Way of Warfare: Order and Chaos on the Battlefields of Modernity*, p. 125.

198 *"If you are playing a war game"*: Wiener, *God & Golem, Inc.*, p. 60.

198 *"freely obtainable"*: Wiener, *Invention: The Care and Feeding*, p. 154.

199 *avoided the term cybernetics*: John McCarthy, "[Review of] Bloomfield, Brian, ed., *The Question of Artificial Intelligence*," in *Annals of the History of Computing*, vol. 10, no. 3 (July–September 1988), p. 227; Kline, *The Cybernetics Moment*, p. 18.

199 *"There's a time when the operation"*: "An End to History," Mario Savio, December 2, 1964, transcript at https://voicesofdemocracy.umd.edu.

200 *Against that backdrop, Carson spoke*: Carson, "Of Man and the Stream of Time," booklet, Scripps College, Claremont, California, 1962.

Epilogue

201 *"some universal truth . . . the ultimate mystery of life itself"*: Carson, *The Edge of the Sea*, loc. 3164–3165.

201 *"Rachel's poison book"*: Lear, *Rachel Carson*, loc. 11025.

202 *"Some of the thoughts that came"*: Rachel Carson letter to Dorothy Freeman, February 1, 1958, Freeman, *Always, Rachel*, pp. 248–249.

202 *"even the snow could scarcely be called white"*: Longhurst, "Smoky Ol' Town," p. 13.

202 *the various oxides:* Ibid.

203 *"Frank Kameny, in 1960"*: Francis, "Kameny's Storybook Ending."

204 *A letter she wrote to her adoptive mother:* Murray to Pauline Dame, June 2, 1943. PM/SL

204 *"as one possessed"*: Murray, *Song in a Weary Throat*, loc. 4313.

204 *"independent, intelligent, poetic, feisty"*: Peppard, "Poetry, Ethics, and the Legacy of Pauli Murray," p. 22; *Pauli Murray and Caroline Ware: Forty Years of Letters in Black and White*, Anne Firor Scott, ed. (Chapel Hill: University of North Carolina Press, 2006), pp. 138–139.

Index

About the Author

A native of Dayton, Ohio, **James R. Gaines** is the former managing editor of *Time*, *Life*, and *People* magazines and the author of several books, including *Wit's End: Days and Nights of the Algonquin Round Table*; *Evening in the Palace of Reason: Bach, Frederick the Great, and the Age of Enlightenment*; and *For Liberty and Glory: Washington, Lafayette, and Their Revolutions*. He lives in Santa Fe, New Mexico.